LIVING LOST

WHY WE'RE ALL STUCK ON THE ISLAND

J. WOOD

GARRETT COUNTY PRESS

Garrett County Press First Edition 2007

For more information address:

GARRETT COUNTY PRESS

www.gcpress.com

Printed in the U.S.A.

GARRETT COUNTY PRESS BOOKS ARE PRINTED ON RECYCLED, ACID FREE PAPER.
INTERIOR DESIGN & ILLUSTRATION BY KEVIN STONE
COVER DESIGN BY SUSAN SCHULTZ

Library of Congress Cataloging-in-Publication Data

Wood, J., 1972-
Living Lost : why we're all stuck on the island / by J. Wood. --
Garrett County Press 1st ed.
p. cm.
ISBN 1-891053-02-7 (alk. paper)
1. Lost (Television program) I. Title.
PN1992.77.L67W66 2006
791.45'72--dc22

Special thanks to Colleen McHugh.

LIVING LOST

WHY WE'RE ALL STUCK ON THE ISLAND

INTRODUCTION

How does smoke stomp?

If you watch the television show *Lost*, and if you're reading this you most likely do, figuring out how smoke stomps is just one of the puzzles within the puzzle that keeps you Krazy-glued to your couch Wednesday nights and frustrates you when the episode is a repeat (which you watch anyway to see if there's something you missed the first time around). From its ground-breaking pilot episode onward, *Lost* has become something of a television and pop culture phenomenon on the level of *Twin Peaks, Northern Exposure* or *The X-Files*. It's an oddly-structured series that taps directly into your imagination – it hooks you even before you have a chance to decompress during the commercials. This is a strange new show that ruptures presumptions and expectations. It's a show about strangers stuck on a strange island dealing with strange events, people, creatures, and conditions. At its core, this is a show about *estrangement*.

This short book looks at how and why *Lost* manages so thoroughly to mesmerize its audience. It digs into the show's creators' unusual and innovative storytelling methods, suggests some new ways for you to "read" the show, and offers discussions and arguments that will enrich your viewing experience, whether you're watching the new episodes as they're broadcast, or binging later on DVD. It deals with both the show and *The Lost Experience*, the alternate reality game that feeds the show's mythology. These suggestions may not solve all of the show's puzzles, but hopefully they'll provide some new ways to get lost in *Lost*.

The real place to begin is before the show ever aired. In 2004, Lloyd Braun, the then-chairman of the ABC Entertainment Group, had an idea for a show that might help spike ABC's flagging ratings. He wanted to produce a drama that was a hybrid of two of the big hits of 2000: the reality TV show *Survivor* and the Tom Hanks film *Cast Away*. Braun was not happy with the initial scripts he received, and turned to J.J. Abrams, the creator of ABC's then-hit *Alias*. Abrams wasn't on board until he confirmed he could write the show in a near-science fiction manner reminiscent of *The Twilight Zone*.* (In fact, the blurry title that twists into the screen from a distance is a homage to *Twilight Zone*.●) Abrams then met writer-producer Damon Lindelof, who had worked on television projects like *Crossing Jordan*, *Wasteland* and *Nash Bridges*. Abrams and Lindelof got to work on a Monday and soon discovered they shared a love of 1970s/80s pop-culture, comic books, and science fiction that gave them instant cre-

---

*Olga Craig, "The Man Who Discovered 'Lost' -- and Found Himself Out of a Job," *The SundayTelegraph (London)*, Aug. 14, 2005: 16.

●Bill Keveny, "J.J. Abrams," *USA Today*, Jan. 5, 2005: 1D.

ative shorthand. Within a week they had churned out the outline of what became the pilot episode. "By that Friday we had written a 20-page outline. And they green-lit the pilot on Saturday. At that point, we didn't even have a script, but in less than 12 weeks we had to start shooting."❂ Score one for deadlines wringing creativity out of a couple of guys.

Braun declared the pilot the best piece of writing for television he'd ever seen, and approved a $12 million budget – the largest budget ever for a pilot. This did not please parent company Disney's CEO Michael Eisner or its president Robert Iger: Not only were they unhappy about the budget, but they thought it simply wouldn't succeed. Eisner called the idea a "crazy project that's never going to work." Iger said, "This [show] is a waste of time." They were especially unhappy that whatever the island's mysterious "thing" was had been left unexplained to the audience (and unknown by the writers) at the end of the pilot. The pilot was shot for around $10 million, nearly $2 million under budget, but Braun was fired before it even aired. When *Lost* premiered on September 22, 2004, it brought in nearly 18 million viewers, three times the expected audience, and with the help of Braun's pre-planned ad campaign, became wildly and immediately successful. One year later, the show's first season was nominated for 12 Emmy Awards, including "Best Drama Series," which it won (along with five others, including one for J.J. Abrams's direction of the two-part pilot episode). By the end of September 2005, Eisner, who was already on the outs with Disney, stepped down – a year before his contract was up. Braun went to work for Yahoo!, Eisner ended up with a cable TV talk show, *Conversations*

❂Joe Rhodes, "How 'Lost' Careered Into Being A Hit Show," *New York Times*, Nov. 10, 2004: E1.

with Michael Eisner, and Iger took over at the helm of ABC, dismantling much of what Eisner had established.*

The writing of the show has involved its own behind-the-scenes drama. After directing the pilot, J.J. Abrams continued writing until the second season, when he had too many other projects already scheduled (including the feature films *Mission: Impossible III* and *Star Trek XI)* to keep up with the hit show's demands. Lindelof, along with fellow creator Jeffrey Lieber and producer Carlton Cuse, wrote and continued to produce the show through Abrams's company, Bad Robot Productions. It's fair to say the writers never quite anticipated what they had gotten themselves into; this was, after all, just supposed to be a pilot, and the initial disapproval of Eisner and Iger suggested it wouldn't go much beyond that. They had originally planned to have surgeon Jack Shephard (Matthew Fox) die in the pilot, then made the last-minute change to keep him alive, and even considered replacing Fox with Michael Keaton. When the pilot proved to be much more successful than Eisner & Co. ever expected, the writers had to scramble to build on this strange pilot that had bent so many rules of television.

The show (and the island) itself works like a video game, with a back-story that the players have to enter and deal with. Some time in its narrative history (in the 1970s), the Dharma Initiative set up the hardware on the island with some instructions, and the people who would eventually populate the island functioned both as the software used in that machine (without necessarily knowing it), and the users of that software. This is rather appro-

*Due to the success of *Lost,* Braun reportedly had the chance to return to television, so he asked his daughter if she'd rather give up the TV or the computer; when she said the TV, Braun decided to stay with the Internet company. (Craig 16.)

priate, since much of the feel of the puzzles in *Lost* is inspired by the computer game *Myst,* and some shots echo visuals from the game. Furthermore, the generation stuck with the tag "Generation X" was the first big video gaming generation. Those of us who cut our teeth on Pac Man and Donkey Kong (and Oregon Trail, if you had an old Apple computer around) grew into more complex individuals who demanded more complex games – up-up-down-down-left-right-left-right-B-A-start eventually wasn't enough of a challenge – and by the late 1980s new games demanding strategy and the ability to closely follow a narrative emerged. These games required the intellectual faculties of a literary critic with the finger reflexes of a court stenographer. Teenagers who could barely follow the thread of a square root could sustain a logical thought process for weeks on end in order to make it to the Mother Brain in Metroid. And it's this generation that makes up the median age group of the survivors on the island, as well as the show's writers and directors. At a deep level, in terms of references, language, presentation, and narrative strategy employing mystery, this is a series that speaks to Generation X as few others have.

Lost's creators were hardly the first TV writers to use strategic mystery to keep their audience watching. Joss Whedon, the creator of *Buffy the Vampire Slayer, Angel,* and *Firefly,* famously withheld information from his audience at the commercial breaks, at the ends of episodes, and even within characterizations and storylines to generate a sense of narrative lack that the story (hopefully) would later fulfill. For Whedon, this was more or less to satisfy his own sense of story, rather than what producers felt audiences wanted, and it worked: Whedon's shows developed cult followings well into syndication. Abrams, Lieber and Lindelof similarly tease their audience, and go further by populating their own series with a web of characters, methodically revealing each character's back-story in ways that inform their interactions with the other survivors on the island. The writers constantly repeat and add information, most of which took place before the characters ever boarded Oceanic flight 815. So initially, the audience doesn't necessarily understand a character's real motives as they witness their actions, and this guessing game is part of what is so engaging.

Another level of the indirect character revelation happens as a result of the way the writers structure individual shows. Each episode is basically one-to-two days on that island. Over the course of a season, there are 24 episodes; the first season covered just under two months' time on the island (48 days, about two days per episode) and the second season covered just under a month (23 days). In most episodes, the main story is inter-cut with a side story, usually a particular character's back-story. The back-stories and the main stories are paced both to interrupt and to inform each other, creating an internal tension that satisfies fans by keeping them unsatisfied.*

This use of narrative lack goes on at many levels, particularly when it comes to the dangers that torment the survivors. It takes a month and a half on the island (meaning a year and a half on television) to see what is stomping through the jungle – Is it a dinosaur? A polar bear? A monster? When viewers finally got an answer, it raised even more questions – it was literally a thing that couldn't be grasped: smoke. And other island dangers are just as puzzling. Why are there polar bears on this tropical island? How does one person's "hallucination" become visible to others (like Sawyer seeing Kate's horse)? What happened to Rose's cancer? How was Locke able to walk after the crash? Where the hell is

*Take that, Ross and Rachel.

Danielle? Who operates the Dharma Initiative, and what have they been doing on the island for decades? What about Hanso? What makes Walt so special? And just how did these people survive the crash in the first place?

And what's up with those numbers?

The show succeeds, in part, through radical twists on classic story-telling – it goes to the root of what makes for solid narrative, and invents elements to adapt those means to a televised episodic format. Fans get it all: Frame stories. Pastiche. Stream-of-consciousness. Metanarratives stretching from the main stories to the back-stories and back again. An omniscient narrator in the back-stories who competes with a limited third-person narrator back on the island. The narrative time structure goes straight back to Homer, dropping the audience *in medias res,* into the action right after the plane crash. And most of all, conflicts. Conflicts exist within a character him or herself (Charlie, Eko, Ana-Lucia), between two characters (Locke and Charlie, Sawyer and Jack, Jin and Michael), and between a character and the group (Sawyer, Jin, Charlie). There are conflicts with nature (the polar bears), with the supernatural (the smoke monster), with technology (the hatch's computer), existential conflicts (Locke exclaims in the first season that "each one of us was brought here for a reason," whatever that reason may be), and finally intellectual conflicts (faith vs. science, the social contract vs. the state of nature, and the conditions of justice). Many of these questions are further alluded to by consistent name and literary references.

In short, this is one literary and literate television show.

But these literary qualities alone aren't enough to sustain such an obsessive interest in the show. Arguably, this show wouldn't have had the same appeal in the 1990s U.S. or earlier. *Lost* draws on a specific sense of 21st century isolation and distress; it taps into some very here-and-now concerns, and speaks to the audience's deeper lizard-brain psyche as it weaves its sophisticated tales. The pilot begins with a close-up of Jack's eye as it opens and the pupil contracts, drawing the audience in, and drawing our attention to the importance of perception; from the outset, scenes are framed through detailed, personal lenses. As Jack's eye opens, the plane has just gone down, leaving a number of survivors stuck on an isolated island unable to communicate with the wider world. Something unseen on the island seems to be hunting them, and they don't know when the next attack may come, in what way, or by whom. At first this "ghost fear" of an impending attack seems to come from something monstrous, then becomes more tangible with the arrival of the Others, characters a lot more pirate-ish than dinosaur-ish. By the second season, new threats emerged from within their own group, and the specter of an unknown disease requiring quarantine loomed in the background. These story elements, which continue to be written on a week-by-week basis,○ are phantom parallels to our real concerns since September 11, 2001. What *Lost* does so successfully is take these very real concerns straight off the front pages, abstract them into their psychological impression, and then crystallize that sense back into the framework of the narrative. These characters aren't being threatened by otherworldly aliens or vampires, creatures normally only seen on the screen or in pulp fiction; this situation involves the psychodynamics of terrorism

○ In a *New York Times* interview, Carlton Cuse mentioned that they were writing episodically like Charles Dickens: "We often think: 'How much did Dickens know when he was writing his stories? How much of it was planned out, and how much was flying by the seat of his pants because he had to get another chapter in?'" Kate Arthur, "Dickens, Challah and That Mysterious Island," *The New York Times*, May 25, 2006.

that the contemporary audience experiences in the everyday world and plays it out on television 24 times a year. As such, *Lost* performs a very necessary function: It gives a narrative (and a safely-distant context) to a real-felt sense of trauma. By giving these abstract ideas a tangible narrative with a beginning and ending each week, that sense of terror is contained by the show, and thus becomes something that might actually be manageable.

Arguably, the reason *Lost* "works," the reason it developed such an obsessive now-global audience searching for clues everywhere they can find them (including outside of the show itself), the reason it is able to sustain its hazy and demanding storyline is because the show is framed on these specific psychodynamics. Viewers are already experiencing this tension en masse (almost no matter where they live). In North America, most haven't yet had the space to develop the language needed to understand those psychodynamics, but *Lost* arguably helps the audience to do just that.

This book considers how the show tells its story, and how those unique methods help make the show work so well. The first section introduces a number of concepts that the narrative returns to on a regular basis; it also examines how the writers develop each concept in relation to other concepts as a way of mapping out the narrative structure. The second section builds on the first section, discussing how the overall narrative of the show abstracts and co-opts our very real concerns over the War on Terror(ism), and looks at how *Lost* became a repository for the sense of distress that has been generated, rightly or wrongly, through our media, government, and the collective cultural response to such voices. The last section is an appendix covering the major characters; each entry gets into what drives each character, and develops some larger points on how that character works into the overall narrative, and is meant to be as much reference as analysis.

If you're already caught in *Lost*'s web, this book can function as a kind of manual, with in-depth discussions of the characters, examinations of the themes the narrative returns to, and an explanation of the show's larger meaning. It will hopefully broaden your understanding of the mythology of the show and the way the narrative functions, and may just be a handy reference to grab when you want to find some quick information on a point you already understood (or at least thought you understood). If you're a casual viewer who isn't yet sure what has made *Lost*'s narrative such a phenomenon, or wants to get a better grip on the story so far, this book should help you get up to speed and on what's going on in the narrative. Ideas herein are not intended to be any sort of final analysis, but rather to identify entry points into more areas of this increasingly complex narrative. Few primetime television shows have received so much *theorizing* by their audience (and most of this theorizing has already proven inaccurate, which speaks to the show's power to engage the viewers' imagination).

From the outset, though, here's what *won't* be seriously entertained or proved:

> The survivors are dead and in hell or Purgatory;
> They're caught in some space-time warp;
> Their fates are being controlled by aliens, demons,
> god, or mad scientists;
> They're the unwitting participants in some big

Truman Show rip off;
They're all part of someone's dream;
They are the subjects of some conniving
government test;
Finally, that this is all a patchwork of Michael
Crichton and Stephen King stories.

There are scads of websites and forums dedicated to disclosing the inner secrets of *Lost* like it's *The Bible Code*. One site, Lostpedia,⧠ utilizes the open source MediaWiki software developed for Wikipedia, and is invaluable as a repository of information from the various websites, forums and other media concerning the show.▲ Lostpedia is a great resource for anyone who really wants to dive into *Lost*. There are also podcasts debating these issues for your MP3 listening pleasure, including an official one from the creators of the show where they continually drop bait for their rabid fans.

And the creative team openly admits that is what they are doing – dropping bait. They know their audience (demographics are a wonderful thing). They have recognized the fans' obsession, and are incorporating it into the framework of the story. They may in fact be changing previously-laid plans in order to maintain engagement and suspense. The hardcore jacked-in fan base

⧠ www.lostpedia.com

▲ Quick bit of info on Lostpedia, Wikipedia, and wikis in general: They're open to regular update by registered members. Since a wiki page is in a near-constant state of update/ flux, it's very difficult to accurately cite any single page in a wiki - for instance, a theory might eventually be proved false, and the theory's wiki pages would then be changed by members. The open nature of wikis like Wikipedia has led to a state where yes, misinformation is possible, but so is immediate correction of misinformation by registered members who regularly use and have a staked interest in the site. Think of such sites more as coffee house discussions with lots of evidence rather than the equivalent of an encyclopedia made of paper.

is privy to revelations and distractions that at once acknowledge their chatter and interest, and use their willingness to follow certain lines of thought to distraction; it keeps them in the hunt, but not necessarily on the right trail.

Of course finding the answer isn't the point, it's the process of searching – *Lost* wouldn't be nearly as interesting if we were given quick and easy answers as to what's going on; it's the supense that keeps our eyeballs pinned to the screen. One such example is "the Hurley bird." At the end of season one, Hurley, Jack, Kate and Locke were heading to the inland slave ship, the Black Rock, when a large bird swoops by them. Later, in the January 9, 2006 official podcast of the show, writers Damon Lindelof and Carlton Cuse were asked why there were no birds on the show, and they mentioned one bird on the island that they'd dubbed "the Hurley bird" because its call reminded them of Hurley's name. In the second season finale, the bird appears again, squawks twice, and Hurley asks, "Did that bird just say my name?" The writers and producers were paying attention to the audience contingent digging for gold through all the paraphernalia surrounding the show, and in this case threw them a bone. A similar distraction concerns the theory that the Lostaways are in purgatory. Despite the writers firmly denying the purgatory theory,* in the summer of 2006 Hyperion actually published *Bad Twin*, the manuscript of a writer named Gary Troup who supposedly died in the crash of flight 815 (and whose name is an anagram for "purgatory"); Sawyer found a copy of the manuscript

---

*"It's time to actually blow up several theories of the show," writer Damon Lindelof said to *The New York Times*. "People who believe that they're in purgatory or that they're subjects of an experiment are going to start reassessing those theories based on the fact that we are literally showing you the outside world." Kate Arthur, "Dickens, Challah and That Mysterious Island," *The New York Times*, May 25, 2006: E1.

on the beach and was reading it until Jack tossed it in the fire. Hyperion published this fictional-space manuscript in the real world. The audience has become a thread in the fabric of the show, and as we know from the second season, part of the Dharma Initiative's mythology entails psychological tests and games. Through such distractions and clues in both the fictional space of the show, cyberspace and real space, the audience itself becomes part of that mythological fabric, essentially participating in the story similar to the way the characters do.

Am I saying there is no key to unlocking the mysteries of the island? No. Am I saying there *is* some key? Uh-uh. I *am* saying that to focus on solving *Lost*'s puzzles is partly to miss the point of what makes the show so effective and enjoyable, like Samuel Beckett's Godot or Stanley Kubrick's black monolith. The entire enterprise becomes a kind of Rorschach test, reflecting what's already going on in the mind of the viewer, both culturally and historically; that's what makes it all so interesting, and that's what the following pages are about to get lost exploring.

FIRST SEASON EPISODES

Lost (Pilot)
Tabula Rasa
Walkabout
White Rabbit
House of the Rising Sun
The Moth
Confidence Man
Solitary
Raised by Another
All the Best Cowboys Have
Daddy Issues
Whatever the Case May Be
Hearts and Minds
Special
Homecoming
Outlaws
…In Translation
Numbers
Deus Ex Machina
Do No Harm
The Greater Good
Born to Run
Exodus (3 Parts)

SECOND SEASON EPISODES

Man of Science, Man of Faith
Adrift
Orientation
Everybody Hates Hugo
…And Found
Abandoned
The Other 48 Days
Collision
What Kate Did
The 23rd Psalm
The Hunting Party
Fire + Water
The Long Con
One of Them
Maternity Leave
The Whole Truth
Lockdown
Dave
S.O.S.
Two for the Road
"?"
Three Minutes
Live Together, Die Alone
(2 Parts)

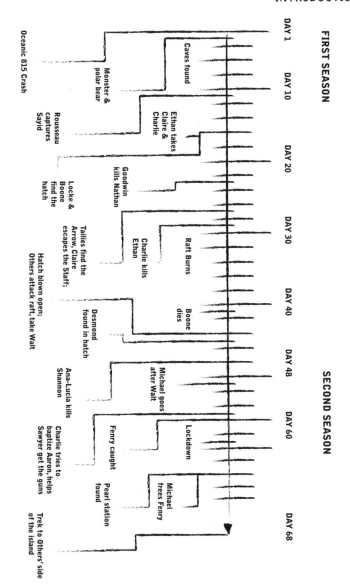

FIRST SEASON

SECOND SEASON

DAY 1
DAY 10
DAY 20
DAY 30
DAY 40
DAY 48
DAY 60
DAY 68

Caves found

Monster &
polar bear

Oceanic 815 Crash

Ethan takes
Claire &
Charlie

Rousseau
captures
Sayid

Goodwin
kills Nathan

Locke &
Boone
find the
hatch

Charlie kills
Ethan

Raft Burns

Tailies find the
Arrow, Claire
escapes the Staff;

Hatch blown open;
Others attack raft, take Walt

Boone
dies

Desmond
found in hatch

Michael goes
after Walt

Ana-Lucia kills
Shannon

Lockdown

Fenry caught

Charlie tries to
baptize Aaron, helps
Sawyer get the guns

Pearl station
found

Michael
frees Fenry

Trek to Others' side
of the island

LIVING LOST

NARRATIVES AND NODES
A QUICK INDEX

Nearly everyone who follows *Lost*, even some of the cast, has their theories of what's really going on in the narrative. The reason theories are difficult to take into account, yet nearly impossible to avoid, is at least two-fold: The show's writers have claimed that all the clues to the show, the framework per se, were laid out in the pilot. "We realized early on we needed to know where the polar bear came from, what the source of the French transmission was, that note Sawyer was holding in his hand, that photo Sayid is looking at. We needed to know those things going into it in order to write the show," says writer/ producer Carlton Cuse. "We did not know where we were going to reveal those things or if we were going to reveal them at all."[+] The pilot and ensuing episodes were back-loaded by producer Lloyd Braun against the wishes of ABC executives Michael Eisner and Bob Iger; Braun hoped that if enough was already in production, the show would have to go forward whether ABC execs wanted it or not: "If we are pregnant enough, they won't shut us down," said Braun.[*] The show's resulting mythology had to be structured on the original framework in the pilot; it's not quite fair to say that it was being created on the fly, because the roots of the mythology were there, but neither is it accurate to say that it was all worked out ahead of time. You could say the "genes" of the mythology were present in the pilot: they don't precisely prescribe how the show will grow, but they do provide a certain direction, similar to the manner in which people born as albino or colorblind (or even people born with only four toes on each foot) have certain predetermined directions.[*] It's fair to consider the

[+] Michael Idato, "Asking for Trouble," *The Sydney Morning Herald*, August 25, 2005.
[*] Craig, "The Man Who Discovered Lost."
[*] Needless aside: When thinking of some genetic anomalies for this analogy, I *really* wanted to use human chimerism, which occurs when someone is born with their own twin inside them,

trajectory of the narrative, but beyond that, we're really walking in the fog, and possibly getting wildly off-track.

Rather than considering any specific theories outright, let's consider the trajectories the narrative has offered and see where they lead. Usually books, films, and television programs have specific themes running through the text of the overall narrative, carrying the audience along in a fairly painless way. *Spider-Man* is about young-adult angst mixed with tons of responsibility and super villains; *Heart of Darkness* is about the thin line that divides civilization from savagery; *Seinfeld* is about nothing. *Lost* doesn't necessarily follow any overarching theme in every episode, beyond trying to survive on an increasingly treacherous island. Indeed the narrative weaves together a tapestry of themes that intersect at certain points and in particular ways. These points of intersection are the thematic "nodes," or hubs from which story-lines emerge, intersect and create tensions that drive the narrative.

Before jumping into the nodes and seeing how they operate, it will help to have a greater understanding of the way the narrative has taken shape. The drama is immediate and violent: a plane explodes, leaving a group of people seemingly isolated from the rest of the world, representing a widely multi-ethnic group – Americans (white, black, Hispanic), English, Australian, Korean, Iraqi, Nigerian, Scottish, (Others claiming to be) Canadian, and trans-nationals. This group has to look at each other closely, take each other's measure, and figure out a way to live together while

and some of their body parts actually come from the twin. When it occurs, it's most often only at a cellular level: in the case of Lydia Fairchild, she carried two different lines of DNA. But then there are cases like Mourat Zhanaidarov of Kazakhstan, who was born with his own conjoined twin inside his stomach. His twin never developed, but grew as a parasite inside him until Mourat looked like he was pregnant when he was just seven years old. The idea of twinning is important to the overall narrative of *Lost*, but this anomaly would have taken too much explanation. It's rather grotesquely fascinating, like a car wreck or an extra limb.

dealing with the natural urges of distrust and need for a leader after such a trauma. Just as they have begun to accept their new reality, the group is attacked; something mysterious that can't be seen (the smoke monster) attacks at random points and in surprising ways. More attacks come courtesy of polar bears, creatures that just shouldn't be on the island, zoologically speaking. The group finds that it has been infiltrated by an outsider who appears to be one of them (Ethan), and at the same time finds that not everyone in the original surviving group can be trusted (Sawyer, Michael and Charlie). There are rumors of a communicable disease, possibly requiring quarantine. The threat of another attack, complete with clear and present warning signals (the smoke column), is not only a false alarm, but a possible ruse by a potentially harmful individual (Danielle, who eventually took Aaron). Members of the group are killed (Ethan kills Scott, Ana-Lucia kills Shannon); others die trying to help the group (Boone is fatally injured trying to make radio contact); and members are abducted by the Others (the children from the tail section are taken; Walt, Claire, Michael, and eventually (with Michael's help) Jack, Sawyer, Hurley and Kate). An entire underground, hidden infrastructure is discovered in the Swan and other stations, and according to the Swan's orientation film, if this infrastructure isn't maintained, a devastating "incident" will occur. Members of the group turn on each other (Kate tries to poison Jin to get on Michael's raft, Sawyer steals from the group, Charlie takes revenge on Locke and Ethan, and Michael turns members of the group over to the Others). Even the underground infrastructure provides contradiction (the Pearl station secretly observes the Swan station, but the Pearl observers may actually be the experiment's unwitting subjects). Members of the group lose the faith they gained from the originating trauma: Jack's faith in science and Locke's faith in destiny are both challenged. And the status of the "bad guys" is thrown into question when Ben claims the Others are "the good guys."

If this rough abstract sounds familiar, it's probably because it could also fit the U.S.'s own national narrative since the attacks of September 11, 2001: from plane crashes out of the clear blue to a frightened group under attack to the rallying around a leader figure and the simultaneous distrust of some members within the group – sometimes justified, sometimes not – to the seemingly random Al Qaeda terrorist attacks in Spain, England, Bali, and the more than 110 other terrorist attacks that have occurred across the globe in every continent since September 11.☆ Like *Lost*'s survivors, the real-world group that perceives itself under attack (sometimes correctly, sometimes not) is a diverse, multiethnic group – cosmopolitan populations in large cities like New York, London and Madrid. And Americans learned that there were those in the Western world who seemed to be "one of them," but weren't (the American Taliban John Walker Lindh, the English shoe bomber Richard Reid). With the lack of clear information and our leaders constantly reminding us of looming threats – in the U.S., this was amplified by the ridiculous specter of the color coded terrorist threat meter – conspiracy theories grew unchecked, and were rarely met with anything more than out-of-hand dismissiveness, even when countervailing facts existed.

If you were really digging and paying attention, you might have discovered former U.S. Defense Secretary Don Rumsfeld's

☆If you want a bit of a reality shock, try doing a search for the terrorist attacks that have occurred since 9/11 - not counting the tactical ones that generally occur as guerilla tactics in lopsided warfare.

Proactive and Preemptive Operations Group (P2OG), an alternative intelligence agency established in 2002 by Rumsfeld to gather intelligence which agreed more readily with the administration's foreign policy plans and could be used to challenge the other established intelligence agencies' findings. Defense analyst William Arkin reported in the *Los Angeles Times* that P2OG's mission was to "stimulate reactions" from terrorist cells so the U.S. military would have a reason to respond and attack; in other words, P2OG, an entity within the group, was established to help create attacks on that group to which they could then react.❖ Couple this with the civil-liberty-eroding 2001 Patriot Act and the 2005-06 revelations that the National Security Agency had been conducting illegal surveillance operations of its own (U.S.) citizens by collecting phone and computer data, and Americans had incentive to believe some kind of shadow government was forming and running things, Oz-like, behind the curtains. We were being watched and tested, similar to the way the Dharma Initiative ran its own literal underground operations that included creating tense, dangerous situations, spying and surveillance.

The real-world echoes continue. The national torture debate came to the fore after the 2003 Abu Ghraib scandal in Iraq. In November of 2004, White House Counsel Alberto Gonzales's nomination to the post of Attorney General was being debated. In Senate confirmation hearings, it became clear that he authored a memorandum "that asserted the President's right to order the torture of detainees and redefined torture itself so that pain short of organ failure, death or permanent psychological damage did not qualify."❑ The same month, "Confidence Man" aired,

❖William Arkin, "The Secret War," *Los Angeles Times*, October 27, 2002: M1.
❑ Editorial, "Mr. Gonzales's Record," *The Washington Post*, November 22, 2004: A18.

and we saw Sayid torturing Sawyer for Shannon's asthma medication; in the next episode, "Solitary," Sayid himself was tortured by Rousseau. At the end of 2005, Senator John McCain (R-Ariz.) worked the Detainee Treatment Act banning torture of detainees into a defense appropriations bill; McCain was himself a torture victim during the Vietnam War, and argued in part that torture fails to yield useful information because the victim will say anything to make the torture stop.✧ That bill was signed into law in December, 2005 by President Bush, but with the signing statement claiming that the President could ignore the law if he saw fit.◌ Just weeks after these real-world national events took place, "One of Them" hit the screen, where Rousseau and Sayid captured Ben and held him as their prisoner in the Swan hatch (a fact they hid from the rest of the survivors) and tortured him for information. (Further, the episode's back-story details Sayid's own experience as an American prisoner of war in Iraq.) McCain's argument was supported by the show: None of *Lost*'s torture yielded anything useful (Sawyer never had Shannon's asthma medicine, Sayid didn't know where Alex was, and Ben only lied to, misled and divided his captors). In January of 2006, the U.S. Congress initiated resolutions to investigate the National Security Agency's spying on Americans, raising a national debate that we were being flimflammed by our own government. One month later, in February 2006, ABC broadcast "The Long Con," which detailed the depth of the survivors' duplicity.

It'd be too easy – not to mention wrong – to suggest that the show's writers are responding directly to our own national situation in such a literal way. They don't need to; the writers and the

---

✧John McCain, "Torture's Terrible Toll," *Newsweek*, November 21, 2005: 34.
◌Charlie Savage, "Bush Could Bypass New Torture Ban," *The Boston Globe*, January 4, 2006: A1.

audience are all influenced to a degree by what is happening in our broader culture, and the elements of those events naturally work their way into our cultural productions. There would have been no *M.A.S.H.* without the foul taste that Vietnam left in the mouths of many.♦ The national craze for celebrity that led to paparazzi court cases certainly plays into the everyday schlub's desire to be a celebrity for a short while, hence the vomit of reality television that has taken over much of prime-time TV. Samuel Beckett's *Waiting for Godot* doesn't seem to have much to do with World War II per se, or anything for that matter, but couldn't have been fathomed by Beckett until he'd gone through the experience of working with the Resistance in Paris during the war and spending nights in ditches, not knowing if he would need to kill or be killed. Stanley Kubrick's *2001: A Space Odyssey* just wouldn't have happened without the Cold War-fueled space race. Such political and social realities are always peppering our cultural artifacts. So when the world witnessed the bird flu scare build over 2005-06, resulting in sensationalist made-for-TV movies, it should have come as no surprise that *Lost* was also riding that zeitgeist, increasing the references to the possible quarantine on the island and raising the specter of infectious disease.

So what does this narrative look like? It's starting to look like something that is reflecting a lot more of what we deal with in our everyday lives, which pushes it past the traditional realms of TV fiction as we know it. Director Jack Bender discussed this during a seminar held at the 2005 Hawaii International Film Festival:

Well, you know, so much of life is timing, and I

♦*M.A.S.H.* didn't even deal with Vietnam; it dramatized the Korean War from twenty years earlier.

8

think this was the right show at the right time. I think that post-9/11, in the world we're all living in, I think this show speaks to "how could you survive with a group of people you've never met before." Y'know, they're creating this brave new world; everybody has their luggage and their pasts that they carry on to this island, but this island is their future, the island is the life they're living now, and that's true of all of us. And I think that this show, in a lot of ways, aside from being terrific and entertaining, speaks to those issues, which means it's right on the pulse of people's concerns and desires. [...] It's the right time in the world for this show.

Something strange began to happen in the first month on the island (season one), and was developed through the second season: the narrative began to bleed into the reality outside the show. In the latter part of the second season, this interaction with the audience's daily lives went a step further into something completely original: *The Lost Experience.* In the second season episode "Orientation," the Swan station's orientation film introduced the Dharma Initiative, the group funded by Danish industrialist Alvar Hanso and established by Ph.D. candidates Gerald and Karen DeGroot in 1970 to pursue studies in "meteorology, psychology, parapsychology, zoology, electromagnetism, and utopian social —." (The film then jumps and misses the end of the sentence.) The last image of the film is a logo for "The Hanso Foundation." Later in 2006, a strange ad started airing during the last commercial break of the show on ABC (first aired in the U.S. in the episode "Two for the Road"). The commercial's production style resembled the kind of ad you see on the Sunday morning news shows, one of those slick promos created by a large, established corporate entity like Exxon or ADM or Price Waterhouse Cooper. *Lost*'s commercial was for The Hanso Foundation, complete with a website and toll-free telephone number displayed at the end of the ad. Viewers could actually call the spot's working phone numbers to get further information, or go to the websites. But nothing was simple: Not only did the numbers and websites change from week to week, new information appeared, including dead ends on some of the websites. In some cases, viewers needed a password to enter the page, but it wasn't clear where to find that password. At www.hansocareers.org, there are descriptions of job openings that require a nearly impossible combination of qualifications. For example, the description for "Art Therapist/ Psychologist" required experience working with "highly gifted but unstable minds," fluency in "Eastern European languages" (which ones, it doesn't specify), knowledge of applied mathematics, and a willingness to relocate to Vik, Iceland. But if the interested applicant looked closely, they could see that a couple of letters on each description appeared slightly grayer than the rest of the letters. The gray letters taken together were an anagram for "inmate asylum," which was a password for another Hanso website. This is the alternate reality game *The Lost Experience*, a development that boldly took the show where no show had gone before – straight into new zones of our everyday experience. Not only was *Lost* responding as a TV show to our experience in the age of the War on Terror(ism), but it was now actually insinuating itself into real space, in ways that required sharp eyes, exposition, and technical savvy. Designed by Damon Lindelof, Carlton

Cuse and the other writers and producers in conjunction with seven television networks in three countries, the game went worldwide in May of 2006. Different clues were presented to respective audiences in the U.S., Britain and Australia. To solve the puzzles, people who played the game gathered in virtual online communities and traded clues; these clues led to secrets that didn't necessarily solve the mysteries of *Lost*, but did help to broaden its depth and deepen its mythology. And in a very real way, *The Lost Experience* audience-players performed the way the characters in *Lost* do: they came from a variety of geographical and cultural zones, they had to find ways to work with each other, share information, and overcome obstacles either intentionally created by the designers of the game or caused by their various geographical and cultural differences.

And in another way, *Lost* is doing what Walt does: manifesting ideas into reality. Things that begin in Walt's imagination have a way of worming their way into the real world – the bird he was studying in a book while still in Australia flew into his home's window; the polar bear he read about in the Green Lantern comic appeared on the island (although there are indications that the polar bears were already on the island before Walt imagined them); and Walt himself began appearing in places he just shouldn't have been, usually soaking wet and talking backwards.▼ The point, though, is that elements from a fictional, imagined space end up in reality, and that's just what *The Lost Experience* accomplishes outside of the space of the box. The game has given no end to the pontification and conspiracy theories put forth by followers of the show. Who is Alvar Hanso? What is Thomas

▼This quality was something the Others were interested in knowing about.

Mittelwerk, the president of the Hanso Foundation, really into? What did the Dharma Initiative really set out to do, and who are Karen and Gerald DeGroot (and where are they now)? What is that conspiracy nut Rachel Blake up to, and does she provide solid information or distractions and wild goose chases?

Many alternate reality games tend to be advertising vehicles that take the experience of how we read advertising to new levels. Games have been produced for the likes of AOL, Microsoft, the Stephen Spielberg film *A.I.*, the television show *Push, Nevada,* and a number of video games.※ Clues for an alternate reality game can appear in commercials that aren't necessarily associated with the show, on billboards, on tie-in websites, in all kinds of places that serve to draw eyeballs to a product. But such games also provide the commercial audience with a measure of agency in the advertising experience that they'd not previously had.✳

So what does all of this mean for the narrative of *Lost* itself? The writers abstract the experience of the War on Terror(ism) and crystallize that experience in the show's narrative, and *The Lost Experience* impresses the fiction of the show into real space. In the first case, reality works its way into the fiction; in the second, fiction works its way into reality. The result is that the performance/audience borders start to collapse, and what at once seemed like two distinct sides – one of performance, and one of audience – becomes the same side. If you want to see a model of such a thing, a visual symbol of the concept, it's the Möbius Strip:

※A 1997 episode of *The Simpsons* featured something like an alternate reality game. The episode "Lisa the Skeptic" had Lisa finding a skeleton with wings in an archeological dig. Everyone except for Lisa believed the skeleton was of an angel, but it was in fact part of an ad campaign for a new shopping center.

✳ None of the companies are advertising in this book, so there's no need to mention any tie-ins and their lemony-limey flavor.

Follow the strip on one side, and you'll find that you end up on the other side, without ever having changed sides. The design is the product of a mathematical function discovered by August Möbius in 1858. We'll look at the Möbius function in greater detail later.

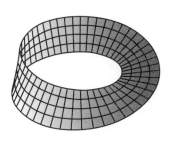

In this two-to-one-sided narrative, there are a number of thematic nodes. The following will give some sense of the framework of the narrative.⊘

Twins & Twinning: Throughout the *Lost* narrative, storylines and characterizations are twinned in several ways. In fact, many ancillary characters are named Tom, which comes from a Greek translation for twin.⊳ But in *Lost* we're dealing with a certain kind of twinning: In the Gary Troup book *Bad Twin*, two of the protagonists, Cliff and Zander Widmore, are mirror twins, meaning they're genetically identical but with opposite features – one is right handed, one is left handed. Mirror twins may share features like curly hair, but their respective curls go in opposite directions; they may appear to display the same crooked nose, but the noses crook to opposite sides.

This kind of mirror twinning has occurred at the plot level,

⊘For a more detailed discussion of *Lost*'s characters, see "Appendix: The Manifest's Destiny." For clarity, the survivors from the middle part of the plane (the focus of the show's first season) are called the Lostaways. The group from the back of the plane are referred to as the Tailies.

⊳"Thomas" is the Greek translation of the Aramaic word Te'oma, which means twin (in Greek twin is *dydimus*). It's referenced in the New Testament Gospel of John, where the writer notes "Thomas, who is called Dydimus."

especially in the characters' back-stories: Jack became the de facto leader of the middle section. His once-boss was his father, and Jack's outing of his father killing a pregnant woman on the operating table led to his father leaving his job. Ana-Lucia became the de facto leader of the Tailies. Her once-boss was her mother, and Ana-Lucia's getting shot and losing her baby and tension with her mother led to Ana-Lucia leaving her job. Walt and Aaron, two children from the plane's middle section, are both } considered to be "special" in some way, and one is black and the other is white. Locke (who is white) has a kind of spiritual mirror twin in Mr. Eko (who is black), but while Locke's belief is a kind of naturalism, Mr. Eko's is deeply Catholic. Michael lost his son Walt to the Others as Rousseau lost her daughter Alex; both parents go a bit mad, and in this case the black/white mirroring includes a male /female element. Both Rose and Locke believe they were healed by the island, and again, they denote both black/white and male /female mirroring. Moreover, the established narrative of *Lost* the audience experiences on television is mirrored by the alternative narratives being developed in real time and space with *The Lost Experience* alternate reality game. This mirror twinning can be seen as a device used by the writers to help organize the narrative, and if you're obsessive for balance, the mirror-twinning narrative technique provides instances of aesthetic harmony and balance that can elevate the narrative from simple passive TV entertainment to something that, upon reflection, takes on a kind of more sophisticated formality. This is the kind of balance Aristotle stresses throughout his *Poetics* (a standard text for anyone who studied writing in college); incidentally, an 18th century translator of Aristotle's *Poetics* was a scholar named Thomas Twining.

The mirror twinning idea is even reflected in the yin/yang of the Dharma Initiative logos; the logos for each station are based on the Chinese bagua, an eight-sided figure that is a fundamental concept in Chinese philosophy (Taoism, the *I Ching*, martial arts, feng shui, and more). Each side of the bagua represents a set of concepts, like natural elements, personality, or direction. In the center of a traditional bagua one finds the yin/yang symbol, opposites that are intertwined and that partially contain each other. Because the symbol's white and black waves wash over each other, part of the yin is always already present in yang as a dark circle, and part of the yang is always already there in yin as a light circle. They are each other's mirror image, at once separate but part of each other, and the Dharma Initiative's logos are based on this fundamental mirror-twin symbol. This image will also become important when considering the electromagnetic properties of

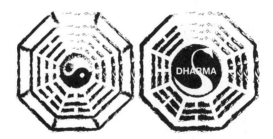

the island.

Finally, the title of Gary Troup's book *Bad Twin* may also have a broader meaning. In 1984, University of California-Berkeley physicist Richard Muller introduced a theory that helped to explain periods of global animal extinction. The Nemesis theory, as it's called, posits that our sun has a twin dark star somewhere in the galaxy. This isn't uncommon; many stars have twins. What Muller suggested was that if our sun has a twin, the twin could pass through a bank of comets called the Oort cloud every 26 million years as it orbits the galaxy. When it passes through the Oort cloud, it knocks comets out of the cloud's orbit, some of which crash into other planets in the galaxy. The theory was first developed in response to evidence that a giant comet or asteroid collision with the earth caused the extinction of the dinosaurs. Isaac Asimov's 1989 novel *Nemesis,* one of his last books before his death in 1992, is about the Nemesis theory. In the episode "The Long Con," Charlie attacked Sun as part of Sawyer's plot to capture the guns. When Charlie told Sawyer that he wanted to make Locke look like a fool, Sawyer said, "Well, well. Looks like Johnny Locke's got himself a nemesis." Charlie replied, "Sun can never find out what I did to her." The proximity of the words "nemesis" and "Sun," coupled with the recurrent theme of twinning and the book *Bad Twin,* has led many in the greater *Lost Experience* community to bring up the Nemesis theory as related to various other extinction theories.

In a May 19, 2006 *Entertainment Weekly* interview with Josh Holloway (Sawyer), Jeff Jensen theorized that perhaps some sort of mass extinction was occurring at the time of the crash, and the island is where civilization will begin again. Jensen also noted that one such Nemesis mass extinction was called the K/8 Event, and he related that to the character Kate. Actually, it was called the K-T Event, for Cretaceous-Tertiary (from the Greek *kreta*), but you still might pull Kate out of K-T (and Kate's old boyfriend Tom did call her "Katie"). The extinction idea gets a little more play when one looks back at *Bad Twin* author Gary Troup, who supposedly died in Flight 815's crash. Before *Bad Twin,* the fictional Troup wrote a non-fiction book (that's now conveniently out of print) called *The Valenzetti Equation.* In brief, Valenzetti was a Cold

War-era mathematician who developed a theorem that could predict the end of the world. A reference to "Valenzetti related research" was visible on the blast door wall during the lockdown incident. And Valenzetti, who is part of the show's mythology, seems to be a figure of mysterious scientific understanding like Milo Rimbaldi from *Alias*. In one of Rachel Blake's video entries from the Vik Institute in Iceland, she explained that she learned that The Hanso Foundation employed a staff of autistic savants in the basement of the institute in an attempt to manipulate the Valenzetti equation. The hieroglyphs seen on the timer in the Swan station figure into the equation as symbolic notation; Damon Lindelof and Carlton Cuse stated at the 2006 International Comic Con that the hieroglyphs all together basically mean "underworld."

Such a prediction of the end of humanity echoes the ancient Mayan calendar, which is made up of two calendars, the Tzolk'in and the Haab'; their combination worked like a kind of computer to calculate the Long Count, or time since the beginning of time. The Long Count also predicted the end of the world – mark your calendars for December 21, 2012, and let's see what's going on January 1, 2013. This echo will return.

Black & White: This is one of the more obvious thematic nodes to which the narrative returns. These counterpart colors also relate to the idea of mirror twinning in the way they are put to use in the narrative. For instance, Locke taught Walt backgammon shortly after the crash. In his explanation of the game, Locke held up two game pieces and told Walt, "Two players. Two sides. One is light, one is dark." But the game does not work without one side reacting to the other; in other words, both sides need to exist for the game to go on. As opposites functioning together, black and white are familiar in the yin-yang symbol, which is reflected in the Dharma Initiative logos. In one of Claire's dreams, she saw Locke playing solitaire; he had one black eyeball and one white. This foreshadowed Locke's own inner struggle to be a man of faith and maintain that faith against the realities (Boone's death, the code entry) which challenge it. In another example, when the Lostaways found the caves where they would eventually seek shelter, they also found the bodies of two previous inhabitants and a small sack with two stones in it, one black and one white, looking not unlike Locke's eyeballs in Claire's dream.

Of the characters, plenty of black/white ethnic mirror twinning has existed, as noted previously. Walt and Aaron, the two supposedly-special middle-section children are, respectively, black and white.* Walt's mother and stepfather are another black and white couple. (Susan is black; Brian is white.) An interracial (black-white) marriage formed the strongest connection between the Lostaways and the Tailies: Rose, who is black, landed with the middle section, while her (white) husband Bernard was with the Tailies. And where Rose and Bernard represent romantic counterparts, Mr. Eko and Locke embody the black white convergence of spirituality on the island, as well as two different aspects of spirituality: Mr. Eko's Catholicism and Locke's more pagan naturalism. Michael's search for Walt, who was taken by the Others, is echoed in Rousseau's search for her daughter, Alex – one black parent, one white. Beyond the human characters, there are black-white counterparts in the creatures who hunt on and protect the island, specifically the black smoke monster and the white polar

---

*We've seen why with Walt is special, but the infant Aaron is still an unknown quantity.

bears. And finally, there is the Black Rock, the 19th century slave ship that somehow ended up perched on a hill in the middle of the island; the ship appeared to have been run by(white) slavers carrying (black) slaves that somehow got way off track.

Cons: The word *con* derives from "confidence game," a ruse to financially defraud a gullible victim; a "confidence (con) man" is one who gains the faith of a dupe by convincing them that they are investing their cash with the promise of a significant return that never comes. Cons are rife throughout the *Lost* narrative. Sawyer makes his living as a con man and shows no signs he's interested in getting it out of his system. When he was a child, his mother was conned by a professional; when his father discovered that his wife had been unfaithful and that his fortune was lost, he killed his wife and then turned the gun on himself. Sawyer eventually vowed to find and kill the con man who ruined his life, but not until he had adopted the man's name and profession for himself. (Season One, "Confidence Man.") He was in Australia under the mistaken belief he'd finally found the original Sawyer, but was in fact being conned himself by one of his past partners.

But Sawyer isn't the only one running cons. Kate tried to con an insurance company when she killed her father, then took to crime to stay on the run. (Season Two, "What Kate Did.") On the island, she continued conning, trying to steal U.S. Marshal Edward Mars's keys through sleight of hand and conspiring with Sun to poison Jin to obtain a spot on Michael's raft (carrying a passport she stole from another crash victim). (Season One, "Born to Run.") In a flashback, Charlie too had resorted to conning, in an attempt to feed his heroin habit. (Season One, "Homecoming.") Shannon conned her own stepbrother Boone (as well as his mother) for money, which led to Boone traveling to Australia to rescue her. She was accustomed to living in the lap of luxury, but after her father died (at Jack Shephard's hospital), her stepmother denied her any inheritance or other financial support, so Shannon began conning in order to support herself and get the money she felt she deserved. (Season One, "Hearts and Minds.")

One of the more pernicious con men, though, was Locke's father, Anthony Cooper. Much of Locke's inner distress was caused by his relationship (or lack thereof) with his father. Cooper first abandoned Locke at birth – before birth, in fact – and later came back into his son's life only to trick him. Cooper feigned interest in his son long enough to establish a temporary bond, got Locke to offer him a much-needed compatible healthy kidney, then left before Locke's anesthesia wore off. (Season One, "Deus Ex Machina.) After cutting off all communication with his son, Cooper faked his own death, only to return to Locke when he needed an ally in another ruse. Locke, ever hopeful, agreed to help his father collect money that Cooper had swindled in a retirement scam. Cooper offered Locke $200,000 of his ill-gotten funds for his trouble, and managed to get him to go along with the con, effectively ending Locke's only authentic relationship with his great love, Helen. (Season Two, "Lockdown.")

Richard Malkin is one of the more puzzling examples of *Lost*'s con men. Malkin first had a violent reaction to Claire when she went to him for a psychic reading. He told Claire that she must raise her own child; later, Malkin changed his tune, telling Claire that he had arranged for her child to be raised by "good people" in Los Angeles, which led to Claire being on Oceanic flight 815, and ultimately on the island with Aaron. In a seemingly unrelated matter, Malkin appeared in an Eko flashback; Malkin's daughter Charlotte had fallen into a mountain river and apparently drowned, but when she was on the autopsy table, she coughed back to life. Charlotte had been in the water for two hours; Malkin's wife claimed her daughter's recovery qualified as a miracle, and wanted it declared as such by the Catholic church. Mr. Eko (who at the time was posing/living as a Catholic priest in Australia) was selected by the monsignor to investigate the supposed miracle; Eko told his monsignor that he didn't believe Mrs. Malkin's story about her daughter, to which the monsignor replied, "Why do you think I chose you?" Eko's investigation was stymied by Malkin; the psychic explained that he was in fact a fraud, and that his wife was a religious zealot. He believed his wife was only claiming Charlotte's revival was a miracle to get back at him. "Because she knows I'm a fraud. Because I make my living as a psychic. You see, that's what I do; I gather intelligence on people, and I exploit it. Everyday I meet people looking for a miracle, desperate to find one. But there are none to be had. Not in this world, anyway." (Season two, "?") While Malkin admitted to Eko that he was a con man, there is reason to question him: If Mr. Eko had not been sent to investigate the miracle of Charlotte Malkin, his trip to the United States would not have been delayed and he would not have been on Oceanic 815. Without Malkin's intervention, Claire would not have been on her way to L.A. to meet her baby's adoptive parents. Because he admitted to being a con man, and because of his direct connection to two seemingly unrelated victims on Oceanic flight 815 (three, if you count Aaron), the exact nature and extent of Richard Malkin's role remains unclear.

And then there are the Others, the enigmatic raiders/pirates/assassins/scientists who are nothing like what they seem.

Ethan and Goodwin pretended to be flight 815 survivors in order to infiltrate the Lostaways' and the Tailies' respective camps.⊗ Tom (a.k.a. Mr. Friendly) wore a disguise to appear more like a haggard pirate than the more refined and powerful man he really was. Ben's ruse was even more sophisticated: In order to infiltrate the survivors' camp, he allowed himself to be caught in Rousseau's net, claiming to be "Henry Gale," a man he (or one of the Others) murdered. Ben showed total commitment and risked severe bodily harm to carry out his con, maintaining his commitment even after he was exposed as a liar. But the Others continue to claim they are "the good guys." If so, their "good" actions have led to the deaths of some of their own group as well as several of the survivors.✦

Finally, there's the Dharma Initiative. What started as just some rudimentary button-pushing revealed itself possibly to be its own experiment in human behavior. According to the Pearl station's orientation film (discovered by Locke and Eko), its inhabitants were supposed to secretly monitor the Swan station via video feed. Their observations were entered in logs, which they sent up a pneumatic tube. As Michael, Jack, Kate, Hurley and Sawyer made their way to the Others' camp, they discovered a pile of unexamined log books in the jungle. It was clear to the audience that no one was collecting the information recorded in the Pearl; in fact, the Pearl workers may themselves have

---

⊗And perhaps Nathan? We still don't know enough about him.

✦Since the Others' methods and purposes are still largely a mystery, it'd be rash to ascribe reasons at this point, but the vague references to them being good recall the Manichean rhetoric used in the War on Terror(ism). This rhetoric is seen when the subjects articulating a position (the U.S. and coalition forces, politicians, fundamentalist religious voices of any stripe, etc.) posit themselves as de facto good, making that which is not them, bad. Fallacious logic, no doubt, but it makes for great soundbites.

unwittingly been the test subjects. Through playing along with *The Lost Experience*, insatiable fans have learned that "Dharma" doesn't just mean *"the one true path"* (its Buddhist meaning), but is also the acronym for "Department of Heuristics and Research on Material Applications." And this Dharma con, funded by The Hanso Foundation, carried over into the space of reality when the alternate reality game started. The game includes a large-scale ad campaign that ties *Lost* to other products, which will in turn advertise during *Lost* broadcasts; when audience members follow the game, call the phone numbers, go to the websites and fuel the fervor for the show, their actions are being watched and recorded just like the Swan (and perhaps the Pearl) inhabitants' actions were.

Parents & Children: Stress between parents and children drives many of the personal histories of the characters on *Lost*, and is the reason many of these people were on Oceanic 815 in the first place. Locke and Hurley were both in Australia to find some sort of panacea for the pain they experienced through their parents. Locke had become wheelchair-bound since his last encounter with his father, and he traveled to Australia believing the spiritual journey would help him reconnect and heal after the pain caused by his father's betrayal. Hurley went to Australia to find the origins of his winning lottery numbers which he believed had led to his mother's injuries and his grandfather's death. Michael was returning to America with his estranged son Walt, whom he'd not seen since Walt was a small child and whose first words to Michael were "you're not my father!" Just as Walt lost his mother, Shannon lost her father, and just as Michael lost his son, Rousseau lost her daughter. The obverse of Michael's situation was Jack's: Jack was returning with a dead father (as opposed to Michael returning with a live son). Jack wouldn't have been in that situation if he hadn't reported his father for causing the death of a pregnant patient by operating while drunk.

The mirrored twin of Jack's situation may be Ana-Lucia's. She was returning from Australia to be with her mother (and boss) again. And she would not have been in Australia were she not running from the retaliatory murder she committed after the loss of her own unborn child. But Ana-Lucia wasn't the only one running to Australia to escape a murder: Kate was on the run after killing her father (for which she was turned in by her own mother). And the obverse of Kate's situation – running from her parents – was Claire's, a parent who was running to L.A. to give away her unborn child.

Jin was ashamed of his humble fisherman father and tried to divest himself of this baggage, whereas Sun's father Mr. Paik was a powerful and shady businessperson, the opposite of Jin's father. Jin's father is a forgiving man who welcomes Jin back; Sun's father is a hard man who will kill to achieve his agenda. Sun's mother pushed her to find a husband. Mr. Paik has a counterpart in Charles Widmore, the father of Desmond's great love, Penelope; but while Charles Widmore tried to keep Desmond away from his daughter at all costs, Mr. Paik employed Jin, keeping him close, yet keeping Jin so busy they were in effect far apart.

Finally, Charles Widmore brings us back into *The Lost Experience* with *Bad Twin's* Arthur Widmore, the patriarch of the American Widmore line and a wealthy industrialist who has strained relations with his (mirror-)twin sons. Clifford, Arthur's son, plotted to take over his empire, all the while acting as his confidant. Zander, Clifford's twin, continually argued with his father, but was at least honest with him. The quick-eyed (or those good with a TiVo pause button) may have noticed that the pregnancy test Sun got from Sawyer's stash on the island was made by the Widmore Company.

Faith & Fact: This thematic node was already initiated by the time Boone died, but that event cemented the tension between Locke, the man of faith, and Jack, the man of science. Their essential divide led them into a kind of subconscious pissing contest for leadership over the group, one form of leadership based on intuition and belief, the other based on empiricism. The show's writers have noted that they wished to explore such issues of faith because of their own experiences, and they've done so in a way that invites the audience to witness matters of faith without proselytizing. Carlton Cuse is known for having come from a more Catholic point of view, whereas Damon Lindelof came from a more empirical point of view, and these polarities are exploited in the fabric of the narrative. But matters of faith are mostly raised as challenges; faith in *Lost* is hard-earned and hard-kept.

The other spiritual polarity is between Locke, the man of natural faith, and Mr. Eko, the drug lord turned Catholic priest. Even Boone's death did not deter Locke from believing in his destiny and its connection to the hatch; Locke felt that Boone's loss was "a sacrifice that the island demanded." (Season One, "Exodus.") Ben's con finally shook Locke's faith in the hatch, and Locke decided to stop entering the code. Mr. Eko's faith, however, was maintained and even strengthened after he and Locke discovered evidence that led them to believe that the Swan hatch may have just been an experiment in human behaviorism and not a matter of Locke's personal destiny. Locke and Eko discovered the hard way that Locke, in his own words, "was wrong."

(Season Two, "Live Together, Die Alone.")

But matters of faith don't end with Jack, Locke and Eko; Charlie and Sayid also struggle with their beliefs. Charlie is a lapsed Catholic whose drug habit is the smack of fact that interrupts the flow of his faith. Even when Charlie got clean on the island (with the help of Jack and Locke – "reason" and "faith"), the specter of his heroin habit constantly overshadowed him, symbolized by the heroin-stuffed Virgin Mary statue he kept nearby. Sayid, on the other hand, did not at first seem religious and behaved more along the lines of a "man of science": he understood applied mathematics, could repair communications equipment, and used his military logistical skills to better the group's chances of survival on the island. Initially, he was not seen praying or observing any religious faith (indeed, the Ba'athist Party he belonged to as a member of the Iraqi Republican Guard was secular). We later found out that Sayid's college roommate, Essam, was a fundamentalist Muslim who had joined a terrorist cell in Sydney after his wife was killed in a bombing during the invasion of Iraq. When he helped the CIA infiltrate Essam's cell, Sayid gave him a chance to escape, but Essam shot himself in despair in the wake of discovering his friend's duplicity. Sayid made sure that Essam received a proper burial according to his Islamic faith and thereby delayed his own departure from Sydney (and his reunion with Nadia, the very reason he cooperated with the CIA). (Season One, "The Greater Good.") This action implied that Sayid was respectful of Essam's faith, and that he was at least versed in Islam, if not a practitioner. When Shannon was killed, he laid prayer beads at her grave, suggesting a more spiritual side to this soldier, which was confirmed when Sayid dropped to his knees and prayed on the deck of Desmond/Libby's sailboat.

(Season Two, "Live Together, Die Alone.")

Finally, there are those who commune with some other world, outside of and among the survivors. Not only do we encounter a psychic and a spiritual healer, but both Locke and Eko have prophetic dreams, and Walt actually seems to move between realms of existence. Richard Malkin first told Claire, "You mustn't allow another [an Other?] to raise your baby," and later told her he had found a couple in Los Angeles to adopt her unborn baby. This contradiction may have been a way to get Claire out of Australia and the baby away from danger – even with the Others on the island, Claire and Aaron would be hidden from the rest of the world. Or it may have been a ruse to get Claire's baby to the Others. However, as noted above, when Eko went to Malkin's home to investigate his daughter's recovery, Malkin confessed to Mr. Eko that he was a fraud. Perhaps Malkin's purposes were more practical than parapsychological.

Isaac of Uluru is the spiritual healer in the Australian Outback whom Bernard hired to cure Rose's cancer. Surrounded by the crutches and wheelchairs left behind by the people he'd helped, Isaac claimed to draw his healing powers from the energy of the Uluru (Ayer's Rock), and channeled that energy in order to heal people. Isaac told Rose, "There are certain places with great energy. Spots on the earth like the one we're above now. Perhaps this energy is geological – magnetic. Or perhaps it's something else. And when possible, I harness this energy and give it to others." (Season Two, "S.O.S.") Soon after he began his session with Rose, however, he recoiled, reacting much the way Richard Malkin had with Claire, telling Rose that he couldn't help her, that "some other place" was for her, and offered to return Bernard's generous donation. We have no evidence one way or the other if Isaac is a fraud – he never claimed to be one, as Malkin had – but if it had not been for their visit to Ayer's Rock, neither Rose nor her husband would have been in Australia, let alone on Oceanic 815.

Regardless of whether Malkin and Isaac are legitimate seers/healers, both Locke and Rose were healed of their physical ailments after the crash. Rose is the only person on the island who knows that Locke was once in a wheelchair. When Locke fractured his leg in the Swan hatch, Locke told Rose he was supposed to be in a splint for at least four weeks; Rose simply looked at him and said, "But honey, you and I both know it's not gonna take that long." (Season Two, "S.O.S.") Something on the island seemed to heal both of them, and it ostensibly had nothing to do with faith. Perhaps Isaac was right, and the island's "energy" was the cure for what respectively ailed them.

Good & Bad People: The Others, like Ben, Ethan and Goodwin, often spoke in terms of good people and bad people. Ethan tells Claire that they are a "good family." (Season Two, "Maternity Leave.") The list that the Others use to indicate the Tailies and the Lostaways they planned to abduct indicated the survivors they considered to be good. But the standard the Others used to determine "good" isn't explained: Morally good? Physically healthy? Possessing some quality the Others needed to study? It's far from clear. But Goodwin ("good one") told Ana-Lucia that as well as children, the Tailies that were kidnapped seemed to be the strongest and healthiest, suggesting there was a kind of physical profile involved. Goodwin also told Ana-Lucia that Nathan had to be killed because he was not a good man; Nathan seemed healthy enough, but he was going off to the bathroom for hours at a time, so maybe he wasn't, or just maybe there's another definition for his badness. Shortly after the crash, the Others tried to take Mr. Eko, but they failed when he killed two of them in the process. We were later told (by Ben, who became known for his habitual lying) that Goodwin had told the Others that Ana-Lucia could become a "good person."

Which of Ben's tales do we believe? Did he tell Ana-Lucia she could be a "good person" because he sensed she wanted to kill him? (Season Two, "Two for the Road.") Earlier in the same episode, Ben referred to Others that were killed by the Tailies as "good people who were leaving you alone," and added that the Others wanted Locke because he was "one of the good ones." (Season Two, "Two for the Road.") Then again, Ben was trying to manipulate Locke from within his armory prison cell, and had already managed to get inside Locke's head. When Sayid interrogated Ben and threatened to shoot him, Ben screamed, "You can't do this! I am not a bad person!" (Season Two, "Dave.") And when Michael led Jack, Kate, Sawyer and Hurley to the Pala Ferry as a trade for Walt, Michael asked Ben who the Others were. Ben naturally replied, "We're the good guys, Michael." (Season Two, "Live Together, Die Alone.") The Others were particularly concerned with a distinction between good and bad (as opposed to good and evil).

Nathan's true identity remains unknown. The Others were careful to identify the "good ones" among the survivors; Goodwin assassinated Nathan. This could have been because Nathan had some bowel problem (since he went on extended bathroom breaks), or perhaps was sick with the quarantine-worthy disease that has been referred to repeatedly on the island. Kelvin Inman raised another possibility: he referred to a group of people on the island as "hostiles." He could of course have been referring to the Others, but their use of the Staff station suggested that they may once have been (or still are) a part of the Dharma Initiative. Kelvin also noted that he joined the Dharma Initiative after the Gulf War, which would have meant that the Dharma Initiative was actively operating into the 1990s. Kelvin himself may have been one of the Others. And if the Others are in fact "the good guys," perhaps there is yet another group of people on the island, the hostiles Kelvin referred to, people Goodwin and the Others would classify as bad people needing their necks snapped. If there really is another group of as-yet unidentified hostiles, they may be renegade Others, or something completely different.

A number of other good/bad references exist, but more as passing conversation among characters than as specific references. Like much of *Lost,* such references have been carefully accounted for and scrutinized with Talmudic intensity and are available online, but it's far from certain how much something like Sayid's saying, "I was a good man; I was a soldier" or Walt's saying, "Good boy; good job, Vincent" had to do with the overarching good/bad mythology of the narrative.

The basic histories of the characters reveal something about their ethical make-up and set up more parallels. Sawyer, Charlie, Mr. Eko, Jin, Kate, Ana-Lucia, and Desmond all have criminal pasts. Sawyer and Charlie were mostly petty thieves. But Sawyer wasn't willing to do to another child what was done to him. He was in the midst of pulling the same "Sawyer" con on a couple when he found out they had a young boy, and he called off the deal, putting himself at risk with his partners. (Season One, "Confidence Man.") He put himself at risk again when he pulled out of a long con with a wealthy divorcee when he fell in love with his mark. (Season Two, "The Long Con.") Sawyer isn't above basic theft and hoarding, but he does have a kind of moral counterbalance somewhere in him. Revenge for the murder of his parents' con man was the reason Sawyer was in Australia. Sawyer's associate Hibbs told him that the original Sawyer was in Australia selling shrimp sandwiches. Sawyer found the man in question and killed him, only to learn as his victim died this he was in fact the wrong man; Sawyer, the consummate con man, had himself been conned by Hibbs into killing a man who was simply late on his payments to Hibbs.

Charlie's thievery was on a much pettier (and seedier) level than Sawyer's; he only wanted to support his rock and roll smack habit, introduced to him by his brother, and which got in the way of Charlie's Catholicism. Charlie went to confession and admitted to having "physical relations" with a girl he didn't know, and then with a second girl, then "straight after that I watched while they had relations with each other." (Season One, "The Moth.") Eventually, Charlie pretended to be interested in a woman named Lucy because her father was a wealthy man from whom he could nick things, such as an expensive cigarette case that had belonged to Winston Churchill. Much as Sawyer did with his own long con, Charlie found himself falling for the woman he tried to scam. Charlie soon glimpsed a better life in the stability he found with Lucy and considered a different ending for the two of them; he even accepted a job through her father selling copy machines (not unlike Jin getting a job through Sun's father). But his heroin withdrawal got the better of him; he vomited inside a copy machine he was demonstrating, was hospitalized, and was caught with Churchill's cigarette case. (Season One, "Homecoming.") Lucy, heartbroken at Charlie's ruse, left him.

Whereas Charlie's brother was a rocker who led Charlie away from his faith, Eko's brother was a Catholic priest. In a kind of reverse-trajectory to Charlie's tale, Mr. Eko performed an act that saved his brother Yemi but led Eko into a life of brutal crime, and eventually back into his Catholic faith after re-encountering Yemi.✞ Gangsters raided Eko's boyhood village and forced Yemi to hold a gun to an old man's head. Eko took the gun from Yemi, took the responsibility on himself, and took his first life (to spare his brother the experience). The gangsters took Eko away with them: "Look at Mr. Eko! No hesitation, a born killer!" (Season Two, "The 23rd Psalm.") Eko grew up to become a violent gangster, while Yemi grew up to become a priest. As an adult, Eko returned to Yemi with a proposition: Eko had taken a load of heroin off two Moroccan drug runners, and needed to get the heroin out of Nigeria, possibly back to Morocco. The only private air traffic allowed in and out of Nigeria at the time was for Catholic missionaries and United Nations aid, so Eko approached Yemi to help him spirit the heroin out of the country inside Virgin Mary statues, with Eko and his henchmen disguised as Catholic priests. He reasoned with Yemi, telling him that his help would ensure the drugs were out the hands of Nigerian kids, and offered his brother a large sum of money that could be used by the Church. Notwithstanding Eko's offer, Yemi refused to provide any assistance, but Eko's associates forced Yemi's hand: they threatened to burn down his church if he didn't sign the papers designating them as priests. Yemi's actions determined the rest of his brother's life (and his own death); he signed the papers, but then informed the military about the gangsters'

✞Eko gave his brother Yemi the cross Yemi wore as a priest when they were young, suggesting Eko had some semblance of faith when he was a boy.

departure. Yemi tried to warn Eko at the airstrip, but was caught in the military crossfire and took a bullet in the chest; a gold-toothed gangster dragged the mortally-wounded Yemi into the plane, but kicked Eko out of the plane and left him on the runway. Eko spent the rest of his days up to the crash of Oceanic 815 as the priest he pretended to be, taking his brother's place and finding his own faith along the way.

If Mr. Eko's life was one of rough-hewn thuggery, Jin's was high-class thuggery. In order to escape his impoverished fishing village in South Korea, Jin went to Seoul to find work. His first job was as a doorman at a large hotel. He was humiliated in the job interview, and warned not to allow "anyone like him" to pass through the hotel's doors. When Jin eventually took pity on a man and his son, it cost him his job. Shortly thereafter, Jin met and fell in love with Sun. He took a job as a brutal enforcer for her father, Mr. Paik, and soon all the compassion that had made Sun fall for Jin was deeply buried.✦ Jin was a perfect indentured servant: to be with Sun he had to be financially successful enough to support her, but that was not possible for him without her father's abusive employment. In one flashback, Jin beat a man at the man's own home, telling him, "I just saved your life." (Season One, "...In Translation.") Jin either held back, falling short of orders to kill the man, or was instructed to instill the fear that there was more punishment to come if the man did not follow Paik's orders. As Jin grew harder and more distant, Sun grew despondent, and eventually plotted her escape. She learned English, made underground contacts and arranged to leave Jin at the Sydney airport, where she and Jin were preparing to leave together for Los

---

✦Mr. Paik was a Korean businessman who is most likely the man behind Paik Heavy Industries noted in *Bad Twin*, but whatever business Paik was in, he needed hired muscle.

Angeles, where Jin was to deliver Rolex watches to Paik's business associates. As Sun was completing her plan to leave Jin, he surprised her, handing her a flower, just as he had done when they first met and fell in love. It was this small act of kindness in the Sydney airport that made Sun reconsider her escape. Had Sun not wavered, she would not have been with Jin on Oceanic 815. One might note that although Jin has lived a high-class criminal life, all of his actions were taken on behalf of Sun, and unlike Sawyer, Kate and Charlie, Jin does not partake in any duplicitous behavior on the island.◉

Not all violence in *Lost* is limited to the men: Kate and Ana-Lucia have killed before arriving on the island. Kate's first murder was the premeditated explosion of her father's house as he lay passed out in bed. She had taken out an insurance policy on the house before blowing it up, and then handed the policy over to her mother before going into hiding. But Kate's mother didn't appreciate the gesture; she turned Kate in to the police when Kate tried to visit her in the hospital, making Kate a fugitive. The next death she (inadvertently) caused was that of her high school boyfriend Tom Brennan, when she crashed through a police barricade trying to escape in Tom's car. With murder and manslaughter on her record, Kate had to stay on the run, and U.S. Marshal Edward Mars began to track her down. When Mars captured her the first time, Kate escaped after their car crashed when Mars swerved to avoid hitting a horse in the road. Kate began participating in bank heists and other crimes, eventually fleeing to Australia. She lived on a farm belonging to a man named Ray Mullen, performed odd jobs, and was about to escape again when

◉Jin beat Michael not for personal gain, but to protect his father-in-law's property.
◉Kate's reward recalls another occurrence of the code numbers.

Mullen recognized her photo in the post office and turned her in for a $23,000 reward.⊛ This led to Kate's recapture by Mars, who was accompanying her to the U.S. on Oceanic 815. Mars was fatally injured during the crash – presumably leading to another death on Kate's record.

If Kate represents the female personification of the reluctant outlaw, Ana-Lucia is her counterbalance. Ana was a former beat cop – in theory, one of the "good guys." Her first killing, like Kate's, was out of revenge. Ana-Lucia was shot in the line of duty, and although she was wearing bullet-proof armor that saved her own life, she was pregnant at the time and miscarried as a result of her injuries. Ana-Lucia plotted her revenge: When her assailant was captured and brought into custody, she chose not to identify him; instead, she followed him to a bar, confronted him in the parking lot as he left, and shot him six times, point-blank. But Ana-Lucia's boss, the chief of police, was also her mother (the mirror twin of Jack's story with his father). When Ana-Lucia's mother/boss confronted her about the murder, Ana-Lucia left her position on the force and eventually took a job in airport security at LAX. This led to her chance encounter with Jack's father, Christian Shephard, who asked her to join him as his personal bodyguard in Australia. As seen in a flashback, Ana-Lucia was quick to pull her weapon, and especially sensitive to children in peril; when she encountered a crying baby while answering a police call, she immediately overreacted and pulled her firearm on the squabbling couple in order to protect the child. Freud would have had fun with Ana's case; perhaps her life instinct was snuffed with her miscarriage, and that life instinct came into conflict with a strong death instinct, which she acted on when she took the life of the man who shot her. The life

instinct would be sparked again by her attempt to protect the surviving children after the crash of 815, but this wasn't to be (the
Others kidnapped the children soon after the crash), and her
death instinct led her into increasingly destructive and reckless
behavior. She took the lives of Goodwin (intentionally) and
Shannon (accidentally), became erratic with her domineering
control, and eventually was shot by Michael in the stomach, not
unlike the way she was shot when she lost her baby.

Two more significant mirror-twinned narratives of good and
bad people concern the former soldiers, Sayid and Desmond.
Desmond's back-story is still largely unknown. He was in a British
military prison, dishonorably discharged for (according to the
prison guard's discharge statement) "failing to follow orders."
Des may have actually refused to follow an unjust military order,
or his imprisonment may have been finagled by Charles
Widmore, the powerful businessman who wanted to keep
Desmond away from Widmore's daughter Penelope. If Desmond
did commit some kind of incarcerable offense, it would seem to
be in conflict with his own personal nature, as he is exceedingly
concerned with honor, and is strong in his faithfulness to Penelope.
In fact, if it weren't for this concern with his honor, Desmond
never would have entered Charles Widmore's sailboat race around
the world, and never would have ended up on the island.

Sayid is in a similar situation, again in the mirror-twinned
paradigm. As an Iraqi communications officer, Sayid did his job
well, but he couldn't bring himself to interrogate Nadia, a woman
he knew from childhood who as an adult became involved with
insurgents during the Gulf War. Rather than harm Nadia to get
information, Sayid arranged for her escape, killing another officer
in the process. His act was ethically good – he protected his

friend – but also directly defied his orders as a soldier. Later, Sayid was captured and chosen by Sergeant Major Sam Austen (Kate's stepfather) to interrogate Sayid's commander, Tariq. In doing so, Sayid was given a new skill set by DIA agent Kelvin Inman, who taught Sayid how to torture: "One of these days there will be something you need to know. And now you know how to get it." (Season Two, "One of Them.") The conflict his new "skills" created was double-edged; Sayid believed he was once a good person who had been twisted by Kelvin, but it was the very skills Kelvin taught Sayid which allowed him to get information from Ben and deal with Rousseau when she tortured him, thereby helping to protect his group. However, when he tortured Sawyer for Shannon's asthma medication and got nothing, the ineffectiveness of torture was shown; a strong-willed person will find ways to sustain the pain damage until the torturer relents, ending the torture without giving up their position of authority over the wanted information.

Additional characters who walk the good/bad tightrope include Jack's alcoholic father Christian Shephard, Locke's con man father Anthony Cooper, Kate's dead father Wayne, Sun's father Mr. Paik (there seems to be a father issue here...), and certainly more characters to come.

Games: From the pilot episode forward, games have become a major theme of the *Lost* narrative. The games aren't just there for show; they have interior meanings that relate to the larger game being played out in the narrative. The first obvious instance is with Locke and his backgammon set: "Backgammon's the oldest game in the world. Archaeologists found sets when they excavated the ancient ruins of Mesopotamia – 5,000 years old. That's older than Jesus Christ." Backgammon is a game that blends chance with strategy. As Locke describes, there are two sides, one dark and one light. A player rolls the dice and moves his pieces from one end of the board to the other, but can be blocked by the opponent's pieces. The idea, then, is to make the most effective decisions with whatever options chance allows, and work within those options to get across to the opponent's side of the board. It's a fantastic metaphor for the first season of the narrative, where the characters are learning how to adjust to chance events and work off the options left for them. By the end of the season, they have worked their way across the island from the beach to the caves to the hatch.

Games figured into the lives of the characters long before they arrived on the island. When Hurley was in the Santa Rosa Mental Institute, he played regular games of Connect Four with another patient, Leonard, who used to be in the Navy but now just mumbles the same sequence of numbers (4 8 15 16 23 42) to himself. (Hurley later used these numbers to play a much more profitable game: the lottery.) Connect Four, like backgammon, is a game of strategy, but lacks backgammon's element of chance, and instead of black and white pieces, Connect Four's pieces are black and red, like the hieroglyphs that appeared on the timer in the Swan station when the code isn't entered in 108 minutes. In Connect Four, the goal is to predict your opponent's moves within a circumscribed playing area (a grid with 42 spaces) in order to line up your own pieces without your opponent catching on. The idea of setting things in place without being caught develops across the narrative after the crash, from the local level with characters like Sawyer amassing capital and Kate keeping her identity secret, to the broader level with the Others taking Walt and organizing the hand-over of Sawyer, Kate and Jack.

The black and red color theme is picked up again in the poker games played on the island. Rather than a circumscribed space, poker focuses on circumscribed options (as do card games in general).◻ Chance is at play, but it's internal rather than external; a player makes choices and decisions based on his best guesses of what the other players are holding. The guesses are educated to an extent, based on what he is holding and his understanding of odds. Poker is also about putting forth the best front; the self you present to your opponent is never the real self, and much of the game comes down to calling other players' bluffs. Tom (Mr. Friendly), Ben, and the Others in general are all about false fronts, as are the Dharma Initiative stations. And as far as the Dharma Initiative and their orientation films go, we don't know when the films are bluffing, or whether they're bluffing the participants, an outside bluff, or when (if ever) they're for real. Even the speaker in the orientation films is a mystery. In the Swan film, the doctor introduced himself as "Dr. Marvin Candle" and seemed to have a false left arm, whereas in the Pearl station, a man who appeared to be the same person introduced himself as "Dr. Mark Wickmund," and his arm seemed just fine.✤

The final sit-down strategy game in *Lost* is chess, which makes an appearance in the arctic listening station in the final episode of season two. Aside from the key factors (pure strategy and prediction in a circumscribed space), and the black and

---

◻Although not directly referenced in the show like many of the other books in the narrative, Stendahl's 19th century masterpiece *La Rouge et le Noir (The Red and the Black)* deals with the hypocrisy of having to pretend to be something you're not as its major theme. This is also a major theme of *Lost*, with characters like Kate, Sawyer, Locke and the Others all at turns concealing their true identities.

✤It's not easy to catch, but he grips his right hand with his left near the end of the film, proving that this time the arm is for real.

white color scheme, the two goals of chess are to capture your opponent's pieces and infiltrate your opponent's part of the game space. If one's pawn makes it across the board, he is able to return a lost piece into play. The Others played this (figurative) game better than the Oceanic survivors; they managed to infiltrate the Tailies' and the Lostaways' camps, twice. If they were able to retrieve a pawn, it was in the mode of Michael, who is sent to infiltrate the Lostaways yet again. When some of the Lostaways did manage to infiltrate the Others' territory (Kate, Michael), they were easily captured.

And of course there is golf, a game that, like backgammon, is a combination of strategy and chance. Golf is about adjusting to the conditions at hand in order to improve a player's own conditions as efficiently and in as few strokes as possible, and finally tap the ball into a hole in the ground. Aside from its clear connotations of strategy and chance, golf is an old Scottish game, originally played by shepherds with their herding crooks (which puts a little ironic spin on Jack *Shephard* being a decent golfer). Golf is also one of several *Lost* plot points associated with Scotland.*

But Locke seems to have cornered the market on games in this narrative. In flashbacks, we saw Locke putting together a game of Mousetrap, a game which became another metaphor for the narrative over the first two seasons. Mousetrap is basically a

*Aside from Desmond and the Widmore family being from Scotland, the purpose for such ethnic connotations found in the narrative is still a bit of a mystery. There are names that recall Scottish Enlightenment philosophers (Hume, Carlyle); Kelvin recalls the Irish-Scottish physicist who developed the scale to calculate absolute temperature (and absolute zero); there's golf, of course; and in *Bad Twin*, the plot of one twin searching for the other revolves around the old Scottish law of primogeniture, where property inheritance goes to the first-born. The law of primogeniture was still in effect in Scotland until it was abolished by Act of Parliament in 1964.

small-scale Rube Goldberg contraption demonstrating cause and effect out of chaos. From the last-minute flight changes (Hurley, Jack, Sayid, Sun, Eko) to the crash itself to the abduction of Sawyer, Kate and Jack on the island, events seem random, but in retrospect show a definite predetermined pattern. After all, how did the Others get lists of the survivors' names? Locke also played Axis & Allies, which is a kind of glorified version of the military strategy board game Risk. Axis & Allies attempts to have the players re-enact World War II by moving troops, tanks, and sea and air support in a kind of global chess match, but with the added chance of dice. Finally, Locke was working on a cross-word puzzle when Mr. Eko brought Sawyer back to the survivors' camp. (Season Two, "Collision.") The clue Locke was working on was a nine-letter word for "Enkidu's friend." The correct answer should have been "G-I-L-G-A-M-E-S-H," which suggested the parallel between Locke and Mr. Eko that would develop after they met; Gilgamesh was a Sumerian hero-king who became best friends with Enkidu, the wild man sent from heaven to challenge him. However, if "Gilgamesh" is the answer, the crossing words don't work, and just enough of the clues and the other answers are covered to keep us guessing what's what.

Names: Names in this narrative are not to be ignored. Many names are rife with internal and external reference that, if you were up for it and did a little research, revealed layer upon layer of meaning in the *Lost* narrative. Like the literary references throughout the show, the references found in the names have led to an entire additional dimension of readerly work the likes of which Oprah would envy, and English departments all around the world should be tapping into. As long as the parallels can be drawn, the reference a name suggests isn't limited to that character's experience, but can relate to the overall narrative.

• Jack Shephard, as a leader and caretaker on the island, tried to live up to his name. He focused on keeping the group together and bringing the strays taken by the various jungle wolves (or who just wandered), which put him squarely in shepherd mode. Ironically, though, Jack's father has almost too much to live up to – Christian Shephard! – and though he was chief of surgery, the weight of such a responsible-sounding name seems to be just too much for him.

   • Sayid's name may recall the 20th century literary critic Edward Said, whose contributions to scholarly thought include how the "Other" is psychologically construed as the opposite of what one imagines oneself to be like, whether true or not.※ So we saw things like Sawyer's assumption from the beginning that Sayid must be a terrorist, even though Sayid had helped infiltrate a terrorist cell and tortured his own commanding officer on behalf of the American forces (although Sawyer wouldn't have known that). Likewise, Sayid assumed Sawyer is a simple hot-headed redneck who automatically acted out of prejudice.

   • Sawyer's real name is James Ford, but his chosen name of course recalls another great literary con man, Tom Sawyer. Tom Sawyer was known for being a scalawag who could usually get what he wanted out of people, taking advantage of either their capital or their labor. Tom Sawyer's author Mark Twain – always good with a snappy line – also had some very specific feelings about Jane Austen (see below). The "Ford" in his real name can also

---

※Locke hinted at this problem of 'the other' when he observed to Jack, "To Rousseau, we're all Others. I guess it's all relative, huh?" (Season Two, "One of Them.")

be seen as emblematic of Sawyer's hyper-capitalist tendencies.

In Kate Austen, there is a bit of an echo of Jane Austen, an author who was influenced by two of the Enlightenment philosophers (Hume and Locke). Jane Austen was known for her deep sense of irony and her progressive use of strong female characters. She was also denounced by other writers for being middlebrow; Mark Twain said that any library that didn't have a book by Jane Austen, even if it had no other book, was a good library by him. Austen also echoes the name of *The Six Million Dollar Man*, Steve Austin, and writers Damon Lindelof and J.J. Abrams are confessed 1970s TV culture-vultures. The president of *Lost's* production company, Bad Robot, has stated that he, J.J. Abrams, and post-production manager Brian Burke hope in thirty years people will talk about *Lost* the way they do about shows like *The Six Million Dollar Man*.△

• As far as Hurley goes, his real name is Hugo, and without pushing it too far, the name "Hugo" recalls Victor Hugo. His *Hunchback of Notre Dame* protagonist was shunned because of his physical grotesqueness, and Victor Hugo himself spent his later years exiled on an island. While certainly no hunchback, Hurley's size is an issue for him and for some of the other survivors; he's a kind of grotesque-lite. And Hurley's taking a census of the island might recall a character from another program that has influenced *Lost*, *Twin Peaks*. Big Ed Hurley was the town's unofficial deputy.

• Boone's surname Carlyle might refer to the Victorian-era Scottish essayist Thomas Carlyle. Carlyle's first book *Sartor Resartus* was intended to be both factual and fictional, again recall-

△Interview with Bad Robot Productions president Thom Sherman, "Spotlight," *Media Exchange*, June 2005 (www.mediaexchange.com).

ing the way *Lost* has articulated itself both in the fictional space of television and in the real space of everyday life. *Sartor Resartus* followed a narrator who was disgusted with the direction of human society, not unlike Jonathan Swift, and Carlyle's later works developed his concern with the dehumanization of society (some of those essayists from the 17th century to the 20th century Celtic world could get downright apoplectic about the absurdly dangerous contradictions in human nature). Carlyle espoused communal values over individualism, which sounds very Dharma Initiativish, and while his early thinking influenced socialism, his later thinking tended more toward conservative hero-worshipping ideologies which would later influence fascism.

• Locke's full name directly points to one of a trifecta of Enlightenment philosophers clearly referenced on the island, John Locke. Locke the philosopher was an empiricist and a major figure in the development of liberal political theory (in its original sense) and the social contract. A social contract is an implicit agreement between a government and its citizens. For Locke, the government was only legitimate when it operated with the consent of the governed, and when it protected their natural rights (such as life, freedom and property). Locke's version of the social contract was in opposition to Thomas Hobbe's version: Hobbes saw unbridled freedom in nature, which he believed led to a dangerous lack of limits, and he understood the social contract to impose limits on those heathens who couldn't limit/govern themselves. It was the classic "I'm willing to give up some freedom for some protection" model that we hear so much about since the War on Terror(ism) began, and for Hobbes, his social contract advocated absolute monarchy. Locke didn't see nature as inherently bad; he argued that people were born naturally good and had natural rights that a government's function was to protect. Locke's approach to the social contract influenced many of the founding fathers of the United States, especially Thomas Jefferson, and led to models of representative democracy. The 42 middle section survivors and the 23 Tailies have all seemed to organize themselves around a kind of representative model of governance. Everyone is represented by the stars of the show, even though some aren't too cool with this; one survivor named Chris was keeping a diary that could be read online, and in some of his entries he complained about the clique of people leading the rest.✸ If the philosopher Locke is somewhat represented by the character Locke, we might say that the island represents Hobbes's view of nature, but rather than attempting to defeat nature, Locke finds a kind of balance with/acceptance of it.

   • Danielle Rousseau calls up the next Enlightenment figure, the Swiss philosopher Jean-Jacques Rousseau. J.J. Rousseau espoused another form of the social contract, one based in popular sovereignty; Locke's social contract could function through *representative* democracy, but Rousseau felt that *direct* democracy was the way to go, and that the individual's job was to work out one's own will with the wills of others and come to some consensus that would be the general will. Rousseau felt that popular sovereignty was an inalienable right, and that people would have to be forced to be free, but any deeper meddling in the affairs of people by government would twist them. Rousseau's thought was influential on the French Revolution, and later incarnations of socialism.

✸ This diary is part of *The Lost Experience*, and appeared on the official *Lost* website. Chris was the second writer in the diary; he took over from the original writer Janelle after the hatch was opened. The diary idea, though, was not adding much to the mythology of the show, and was ultimately dropped.

J.J. Rousseau, however, like Danielle Rousseau, spent his later years in questionable mental health, showing signs of paranoia.

• The Scottish soldier Desmond Hume points to the third of the Enlightenment trifecta, the Scottish philosopher David Hume. David Hume had hoes in all kinds of philosophic fields: phenomenology, empiricism, economics, liberal political theory, ethics, reason, free will versus determinism – he even took on intelligent design.ϒ Hume is notable for his rigorous analysis of empirical experience (what we see/hear/otherwise perceive in our daily lives), without recourse to previously existing principles or ideologies, in order to understand events and reality. He argued that our impressions of causation – that one event leads to another – are in fact projected onto events by the individuals that perceive them, and don't necessarily exist in reality. In other words, when events *seem* to be connected, take a second look; it may be just your own psychological need for a complete narrative. Or, just because entering the code into the computer *seems* like a behavior experiment, doesn't mean it is one, even when evidence (the Pearl film) indicates it might be so. Those who are observing may be that actual experiment. In 1766, Jean-Jacques Rousseau was being run out of various Swiss towns and his work was suppressed, so David Hume accompanied the philosopher to London, where he secured him a place to stay and a pension. But Rousseau began showing signs of his paranoia, and believed that some British intellectuals – including Hume – were besmirching him and making him a laughing stock. Rousseau went to France,

---

ϒHe wasn't for it. For one thing, Hume believed we don't have enough experience with other universes to know if all are as well-ordered as ours, so we can't be sure that a well-ordered world necessarily means an intelligent designer. And anyway, that intelligent designer would have needed a designer, unless you presume one sole designer of a well-ordered world, in which case you could assume simply a well-ordered world in itself without a designer.

and Hume responded to the accusations by publishing his correspondence with Rousseau, *A Concise and Genuine Account of the Dispute Between Mr. Hume and Mr. Rousseau, 1766.*

• Kelvin Inman, Desmond's first partner in the Swan, has an especially evocative name. Inman is the "in man" as an intelligence agent. The name Inman also recalls Charles Frazier's protagonist W.P. Inman from his 1997 novel *Cold Mountain.* W.P. Inman was a deserter from the Confederate Army who was trying to return to the woman he loved by walking across the Blue Ridge Mountains. W.P. Inman's story more closely parallels Desmond's, but it would be interesting to learn if Kelvin Inman was also a deserter. The name *Kelvin* is also the name of the standard international unit of temperature that marks the point where all kinetic motion ceases and no heat is transferred; in other words, a point where everything freezes. The 19th century British physicist William Thomson, who had a barony named after the River Kelvin Glasgow, Scotland, theorized that point where all motion stopped as *absolute zero*, and that point has since been called 0° *Kelvin* (-273.15 °C, -459.67 °F). Kelvin temperature is important for superconductivity. Superconductors are materials that have no electrical resistance and no interior magnetic field when their temperature is low enough; they make the strongest electromagnets in the world, and can be used to separate weakly magnetic materials from even weaker or non-magnetic materials. From what's known about the geologically unique electromagnetic properties on the island, it's not a far stretch to imagine the Dharma Initiative using those properties and the principles of superconductivity to create some kind of massive electromagnetically-run motor that powered the island. Stretch this: Electromagnetic radiation also makes up the entire spectrum of light, and if some device existed that was powerful enough to manage electromagnetism, it might be able to bend light around an object, effectively making it invisible; this could explain why the island can't be seen. Finally, since super-cold temperatures are required to achieve the superconductivity necessary to make the most powerful electromagnets, it wouldn't be outside the realm of fiction to have the island geographically located someplace very cold, but the motor which powered the island also kept it warm; this might also explain the presence of polar bears.

• Mr. Eko's name might recall the Italian writer and semiotician Umberto Eco. Eco was a pioneer of reader-response theory in the 1960s, and his subsequent work remains very interested in popular culture, has an archival knowledge of Catholicism, and is known for the convoluted puzzles he works into his narratives. His novel *Foucault's Pendulum* deals with the Freemasons, the Knights Templar, the Illuminati, Kabalah, Catholicism and conspiracy theories that in comparison makes *The Da Vinci Code* look like *The Hardy Boys*. Eco and Eko's Catholicism aside, reader-response theory is the study of how audiences experience and respond to the performance of a text, and Eco proposed the idea that understanding was produced in the play between expectation and fulfillment of meaning. In other words, meaning lies somewhere between what we see and what we think we're supposed to see. By the 1990s, reader-response theory and psychological/cognitive science merged with B.F. Skinner-like behavioral experiments, where audience responses to aesthetic creations were monitored and analyzed not just for aesthetic

◆See for instance Richard Gerrig's *Experiencing Narrative Worlds: On the Psychological Activities of Reading* (Yale University Press, 1993); or consult the International Association of Empirical Aesthetics for about two decades of work in this area.

reactions, but for mental processes.♦ This should sound familiar: the Pearl station seemed to be part of a behavioral experiment. And part of what's happening with *The Lost Experience* alternate reality game is a reader-response experiment where the audience members/players move from the text of the show to the text of the game in order to create the broader meaning of the narrative. Finally, we know that the audience was being watched as the writers responded to the audience's responses by acknowledging their reactions and comments in some of the show's dialog; in the way the alternate reality game develops and what clues are presented to audiences in different parts of the world; and indeed what kind of product placement tie-ins will work their way into this game-space. After all, you'll be more likely to find a soda company tie-in to the game than one for a savings and loan.

• Locke's father Anthony Cooper refers to yet another Enlightenment-era politician and philosopher, the 3rd Earl of Shaftesbury, Anthony Ashley-Cooper. Ashley-Cooper's wedding was overseen by John Locke, with whom he shared a number of principles. His philosophy stemmed from two main principles: An individual could not be moral until all of the various passions and appetites were in balance, and one must balance individual interests with the interests of the greater social body. At first blush Locke's dad didn't seem to have balanced his interests, since he selfishly conned his long-estranged son out of a healthy kidney only to once again abandon him; but the key here is balance, and he does try to set things right with his son eventually by cutting him in on $200,000 dollars from another con he pulled.

• Richard Malkin has a bit of a double-edged name. Many in the broader *Lost* community have suggested his name suggests "bad family" – *mal kin*. Maybe, but that would be easier to believe were Malkin an exceedingly rare name, like Alvar Hanso, and Malkin isn't an exceedingly rare name. It does, however, have another echo that may be more appropriate. In Scottish and Anglo-Saxon, a malkin (also maukin) was a hare and also known as a "witch's familiar" (similar to a cat, which is also sometimes called a malkin). Hares are also known as tricksters; when they seem to be doing one thing, they're doing something else. And we have no idea what Richard Malkin really is: he's a psychic in one episode and a fraud in another; first he says Claire must raise her own baby, and then he finds an adoptive family in L.A. He also tells Eko that he is a fraud. He fits the trickster modus operandi.

• Among the Others: Ethan Rom's name is an anagram for "Other Man," and Goodwin's name suggests "Good One," recalling the concern the Others seem to have with good and bad people. The name Ben adopts, Henry Gale, recalls Dorothy's Uncle Henry in Frank L. Baum's *Oz* books. In Baum's book *Ozma of Oz*, Uncle Henry takes Dorothy with him on a vacation to Australia, and fantasy craziness ensues. Aside from being a place reached by hot air balloons, Oz is significant as a utopia in crisis because of "the man behind the curtain." Ben's last name, Linus, is also the first name of Nobel Prize-winning quantum chemist and noted polymath Linus Pauling, and Linus Torvalds, the creator of the Linux open-source computer operating system kernel and the Benevolent Dictator for Life (like Ben?) of the kernel.* Both of these historical figures seem to share some sort of intellectual traits with Ben.

• Alvar Hanso's name is too interesting to leave alone.

*This book was largely written on a Linux box.

There is plenty of online speculation about who he is, if he's a personification of various historical scientists, if he's alive, just how far his power reaches, and his name reflects his enigmatic qualities. The orientation films and *The Lost Experience* have shown Alvar Hanso to have been a Danish industrialist who provided munitions to resistance movements in Europe during World War II, and then provided high-tech weaponry to NATO. The Cuban Missile Crisis and its fallout led him to establish the Dharma Initiative; after the crisis, the U.N. commissioned a mathematician named Enzo Valenzetti to develop a theorem that could predict the extinction of humanity. Alvar Hanso bought all the copies of Gary Troup's book *The Valenzetti Equation,* and the Dharma Initiative was established in part to manipulate the equation's factors in order to change its outcome. As of 2002, Hanso has not been seen, and The Hanso Foundation has been run by a man named Thomas Mittelwerk. Hanso's first name is Scandinavian, yet Statbank Denmark shows no one in Denmark with the last name of Hanso.✾ Be that as it may, in 1820, the Danish physicist Hans Christian Ørsted – Hans Ø (or *Hanso*) – discovered electromagnetism when he noticed a compass that would veer off magnetic north whenever he turned a nearby battery on and off. And a Swedish Nobel-winning physicist who received the award in 1970 for his theory of magnetohyrdrodynamics is named Hannes Alfvén.✛ But the name Alvar also has a few odd connotations. It's not a common name – the Statbank Denmark shows only ten Alvars in the whole country – but Alvar is related to "alf"

✾Statbank Denmark is the website for Danmarks Statistik, Denmark's governmental statistics organization under the Ministry of Economics and Business Affairs.

✛Magnetohydrodynamics is basically the study of fluids that conduct electricity (plasma, salt water); and if something conducts electricity, it has a magnetic field.

(Danish), "alv" (Swedish , Norwegian), "älva" (Swedish), "álfr" (Old Norse), and "ælf" (Old English/Anglo-Saxon), all words which mean "elf" and are derived from the Indo-European root for "white." In the Scandinavian world, elves aren't the little fellas who make cookies in trees. They're big, powerful, wise, tricky, and in the Old Norse mythology which informs that part of the world, they are minor gods.

Moving from the influence of mythology on Alvar's name, we can see a number of names hearkening back to Greek mythology. There is Penelope (Widmore), whose name recalls the wife of Odysseus. The Greek Penelope waited for her husband to return from his voyage, just as Penny waited for Desmond to return to her (although Penny Widmore is a bit more proactive in her waiting). The great Greek beauty whose face launched a thousand ships and whose abduction led to the Trojan War, Helen of Troy, is recalled by Locke's great love that launches him on a certain trajectory in life that ends up on the island.* It would be interesting to see if in some flashback way we see Helen and Locke's relationship somehow affecting Desmond and Penelope's relationship, just as *The Iliad* led to *The Odyssey*. Rousseau's map had song lyrics from *Finding Nemo*, and "Nemo" is what Odysseus told the Cyclops Polyphemus his name was after he put out his eye; the word means "no one," and in the context of Rousseau's not finding Alex, *Finding Nemo* becomes Rousseau's finding no one. On the blast door map, the name Cerberus can be seen; Cerberus is the guardian of the gates of Hades in Greek mythology, and the Cerberus on the island may be the smoke monster security system. Finally, the protagonist's dog in the Gary Troup book *Bad Twin* is an old, diabetic chocolate Labrador retriever named Argos; this was also the name of Odysseus's loyal dog

---

*At this point, we still don't know why Locke was in a wheelchair and/or if Helen factors into it.

who was the first to recognize Odysseus after his being years at sea. Argos being an old chocolate lab makes him a kind of mirrored twin to Vincent, Walt's healthy yellow lab.

• Then there's the name "Tom." As noted above, the name is repeatedly associated with supporting characters: Tom Brennan is Kate's old boyfriend from Iowa; Christian Shephard has Ana-Lucia call him Tom when they go to Australia; Claire's ex-boyfriend in Australia is named Thomas; Tom is an Other; Charlie's dealer in England was named Tommy; and the president of the Hanso Foundation is named Thomas Mittelwerk. As noted in the Twins & Twinning section, the name Thomas comes from the Greek translation of the Aramaic word for "twin," and the theme of twinning runs through the entire fabric of the *Lost* narrative.

Psychology: From the Dharma Initiative experiments on the island to the broader reader-response experiment of the alternate reality game, psychology is always being tested and tampered with in *Lost*. At the level of the original narrative – which emanated from the pilot episode – there is the basic problem of how a group of people responds together and individually after a devastating trauma. For the first 48 days on the island, the survivors spent much of their time trying to literally pick up the pieces: to determine what they had left and what they had lost, and re-shape their world in a way that at once acknowledged and accepted the event while moving on and establishing a new life. How many people are actually able to "move on" a month after a tragedy? We all know people who are hanging on to some symptom of psychological damage and organizing their lives around that damage, because after not being able to work through it effectively, hanging on to that damage becomes familiar, and thus comforting.

But what the survivors have that most people don't is a group that has all survived the same unbelievable trauma to support both the individual and the individual's need to be part of the group. One of the reasons they're able to get on with tasks like finding and managing allotments of food, dividing labor, protecting the group, and even working out shifts in the hatch, is because they acknowledge the rest of the group's trauma. This aspect of the psychology of the show shouldn't look unfamiliar because it's what most people think happened after our own big plane crashes on September 11, 2001. But that kind of response doesn't just automatically "happen." People – leaders and individuals – look for a way to positively respond. The Red Cross had to turn away potential blood donors because they had more than enough; others joined the military; still others wanted to organize forums to discuss the situations and motivations that lead to such attacks and how they could be addressed. During World War II, sacrifice was shared, as food and materials were rationed and an entire generation looked for and was given ways of aiding in a national effort. Those things didn't really happen after September 11th, as we were told that our comfy lifestyles would not have to change and no sacrifices beyond simple symbolic gestures were necessary – just think of all the flags posted on gas-guzzling cars in the months after September 11th, while next to nothing was done to lessen U.S. dependence on a fossil fuel economy and its crazy market fluctuations due to events in the places that provide a good deal of those fossil fuels. In its own manner, *Lost* became a model for how we could have responded as a group after a trauma, but weren't able to or chose not to.

But then there are the Dharma Initiative's experiments: From what we've seen so far, the Swan and the Pearl stations were part of some larger experiment in behaviorism (it's not yet clear if the Staff station was also part of that experiment). The code "4 8 15 16 23 42" had to be entered into an old green-screen computer terminal every 108 minutes, but the computer was useless until 4 minutes before the countdown ended. (The narrator in the orientation film warned that the computer could not be used for any other function, but Michael's communication with Walt seemed to indicate it was capable of other applications.) When the timer ran all the way down (as happened at least three times: the afternoon of 815's crash, the Swan's lockdown, and finally the day Locke and Desmond locked Eko out of the hatch), a timer on the wall switched from digits to hieroglyphs, a large machine from behind the sealed concrete walls kicked in, and a hum was heard.

Jack is the first to question the protocol, asking Desmond, "Did you ever think that maybe they put you down here to push a button every 100 minutes just to see if you would – that all of this, the computer, the button, is just a mind game, an experiment?" Desmond simply responds, "Every single day." (Season Two, "Orientation.") Jack believed this was a kind of operant conditioning, an experiment conducted to see how a group of people would react to a supposed threat that did-

𝔔 The hieroglyphs are also symbols used in the Valenzetti Equation.

n't really exist. The orientation film mentions B.F. Skinner as an influence on the Dharma Initiative's work, and the Swan station seems to be one big Skinner box, complete with buttons to push and warning bells.* How would the subjects organize their lives around this entity? And with its ultimate function unstated, the subjects/participants could project their own internal issues and fears toward the task. This is what Locke did, as he connected pressing the button to some sort of mystical destiny.

The Skinner box model is clearly at play with the polar bear cages the Others use to imprison Sawyer, Kate and Karl in the third season. When Sawyer first wakes up in the cage, he sees a big red Plexiglas button stenciled with a plastic knife and fork – obviously "push for food," there are levers next to the button. But when he pushes the button, a staticky voice comes over a loudspeaker and says "Warning." Sawyer pushes it again and Karl warns him not to push it a third time, but true to character, Sawyer pushes it anyway and is knocked on his can by a jolt of electricity. Later in the same episode, Sawyer has figured out how to put a rock on one lever and throw his shoe at the other lever, causing bear chow and a fish biscuit fall through a chute. This is a prototypical Skinner box. When Tom sees that Sawyer got a fish biscuit, he tells Sawyer, "Only took the bears two hours."

Locke's views about the hatch shifted violently in line with Jack's after he and Eko discovered the Pearl station and watched its orientation film, which implied that the Swan may have been just some kind of Skinner box, an extended experiment in

---

*A "Skinner box," or operative conditioning chamber, is a kind of room or apparatus used in animal psychological experiments. They have two major components: an operandum and a primary reinforcer. The operandum would be something like a lever – a rat pushes a lever in the box. The primary reinforcer would be something like a hunk of cheddar – the rat pushes the lever and gets the cheddar.

behaviorism. But the Pearl itself could have been its own experiment, something along the lines of the Milgram Experiment of the early 1960s. These experiments involved enlisting people off the street and paying them to participate in tests. The volunteers were all men, from all kinds of backgrounds and educational levels. They were told they would be participating in an experiment to examine "punishment and learning," and that they would be the teachers. Their job was to read off a list of paired words, then repeat the first word of each pair and have the "learner" (actor) finish the pair. If the learner could not finish the pair, the teacher was to press a button that administered an electric shock. The shocks started at 45 volts and went up to 450 volts. The teacher was given a short 45 volt shock just to know how it felt, and was also told that the learner had a heart condition. When the teacher gave the learner a shock, the actor's job was to play prerecorded screams, and as the shocks grew more powerful, to start banging on the walls and complain about his heart. The teachers could choose to stop at any time, but were warned by their instructors to go on four times before being able to stop, once even being told, "You have no choice, you must continue." Of course, the real subjects of the experiment were the teachers themselves: The instructors wanted to observe just how far they would follow orders which clearly harmed someone else for no reason beyond being told to do it by an authority figure. The pre-experiment predictions were that only 0.1% would follow the protocol up to the end, which meant administering three 450 volt shocks. In fact, in the first round of 40 participants, 67.5% followed the protocol to the end (27 out of 40).

Like the Milgram "teachers," the workers assigned to the Pearl station had been told that what was going on in the Swan station was a psychological experiment in behaviorism, to see if the Swan inhabitants would continue to enter the code every 108 minutes for 540 days (about 7200 times). According to the training film, the Pearl station residents only spent three weeks at their post, as opposed to the year and a half the Swan inhabitants spent at theirs. The Pearl inhabitants could have easily contacted the Swan workers and stopped the experiment but there's no evidence they ever made such contact; it was Locke who finally kept the Swan code from being entered, causing the system failure. And what about the Others – are they part of the experiment? They seem to be self-sufficient, but are they independent of the Dharma Initiative/Hanso? They certainly did not appear to be willing to extend a hand to the survivors after the plane crash. And they have shown a willingness to harm the survivors as well (Ethan hung Charlie and killed Scott, Sawyer was shot as Walt was abducted). Are the Others the "teachers" in a kind of larger Milgram experiment? Or are they monitoring some other experiment in which the survivors themselves are unwitting participants?

Those questions are the kind which draw audiences deeper into the mythology of the narrative. Audiences want answers, but more than that, they want to search for answers, whether they know it or not. Late 20th century psychoanalysis can be a frustrating miasma of shifting terms with one researcher redefining the arcane vocabulary of another in the nonstop race for ever-more prestigious grants, but one clear premise has emerged: desire always desires desire. Want can only be temporarily quenched, but never ended – it's what advertising is built on. According to some psychoanalytic theory, this is the way we're hardwired, and if we submit to the journey of working through the morass of our desires and passions and quirks – our

---

⮒Just check out some of the work by Lacanian psychoanalyst Slavoj Zizek; amphetamines not required, but recommended.

"symptoms" – we'd be happier beings.⌂ So the audience is consistently kept on the edge of an answer. The game is predicated on the audience being given only partial glimpses of answers that inevitably only lead to more questions, and then the broader experiment provides more answers through *The Lost Experience* – but only if you're willing to go down the rabbit hole of hacking culture. The viewers are partially quenched but never fulfilled. For instance, where did that massive statue on the other side of the island come from? How was it reduced to only a foot? And (as Sayid pointed out) why does that foot only have four toes? That frustrating non-fulfillment is actually its own fulfillment. It's all a little sadomasochistic; the content providers love to tie us in knots, and we love being in those knots.

But only to an extent: Yes, viewers/players essentially want to stay thirsty for more, but they need some quenching every now and then, or they become desiccated husks of an audience. We are already dealing with the constant real-world threat of possible attacks on our own "group" by some "others" from somewhere out there, and the few clues we receive are cryptic warnings from behind lecterns and desks. We later learned that the same people warning and "protecting" the group are also spying on and infiltrating our private lives. Getting some actual answers on occasion is necessary; it keeps us from becoming blank shells that give up our critical faculties. The clues, Easter eggs and hints provide answers where the narrative of the show doesn't. In conspiracy-theory fashion, if audiences watch closely and pay attention to the details (as Sawyer says in "The Long Con," "It's all in the details"), they can find an archive of material in literature and pop culture that further develops the mythology of the narrative. These clues provide answers, and help the world of *Lost* seem to make more sense, but those little pieces of the puzzle end up showing that the puzzle is a lot larger than presumed. The puppet-masters seem to become the unwitting puppets of still other puppets.

And this brings us back to the con. Mr. Eko once warned Locke, "Don't mistake coincidence for fate." (Season Two, "What Kate Did.") Many of the clues seem to point toward something, but like in *Bad Twin*, often don't lead too far. A con is designed to give the mark confidence in the person offering the goods; once that confidence is gained, the mark finds that the goods just weren't what he thought they were. And it's not like this fact is hidden. Just because Sawyer was reading Judy Blume's *Are You There God? It's Me, Margaret* doesn't mean *that* novel is a Rosetta stone for *Lost*, but you're more than welcome to try to make it all line up, and you won't be the first to do so.■ Like Ben seeing how far he could push his false story, complete with full dimensional details of the volume of the hot air balloon he supposedly piloted, there is more than enough in the *Lost* mythos that seems like it means something, but just may lead to more questions, or even nowhere. It's all a play on the audience's confidence in the narrator's veracity. And we know the writers are paying attention and responding to their audience. For instance, the washer and dryer in the hatch got all kinds of online scrutiny – because they're new models, and everything else in the hatch is circa 1970s. Theories were developed about the entire island being a kind of artificial environment, with the washer and dryer being the key to unlocking that secret. But the producers finally admitted that when they first were looking for materials to stock the hatch, they just

■Granted, the book is about menstruation, and it did appear in the episode where Sun missed her period and found out she was pregnant. (Season Two, "The Whole Truth.")

thought the washer and dryer had a 1970s retro look, and didn't think people would pick at the detail. This audience observation was acknowledged when Libby asked Hurley if the washer and dryer were newer than everything else in the hatch, and Hurley said, "It washes clothes, that's all I need to know." (Season Two, "Fire + Water.")

So we know the audience is being watched. And we know bits of bait are being dropped to keep us coming back again and again. And every time we go to the web pages of *The Lost Experience*, every time an episode is downloaded on iTunes, every time the ratings come in from a repeat episode during the off-season that fans return to in search of clues, it's all being recorded. It's nothing more nefarious than savvy marketing, but we are in effect just like the inhabitants of the Swan, constantly pushing the button, while the marketing execs in the Pearl are recording it all. There's just one problem: At the end of season two, when Locke and Desmond locked Eko out of the Swan hatch and allowed the timer to run down, it turned out that the Swan had a purpose after all, and the real experiment was in fact with the Pearl inhabitants. This put agency back in the hands of the Swan inhabitants/audience. It's like saying, "OK, if we have to be marketed to, at least make it interesting and interactive;" in effect, with the audience participation and the writers' responses to that audience participation, we get to control an aspect of the marketing that was never before in our grasp. It may seem like we're being conned into generating wonderful numbers for ABC and the affiliated product tie-ins, but the writers and audience have managed to con the company into allowing us to determine the terms upon which we'll be sold their product.

Beasts: Animals and monsters play a recurring and perplexing role in the narrative. First of all, the only time you will see a polar bear that close to a palm tree in reality is in a zoo, but there are polar bears all over this "tropical" island. As for island fauna, there are boars and noisy tropical frogs, but there is also a shark with a Dharma Initiative tattoo, a black horse from Iowa, a noticeable lack of birds for a tropical island (aside from the Hurley bird), and almost nothing to bother the yellow lab Vincent when he goes for walks around the island. And then there's that stomping smoke (and for those in the game, a 105-year-old orangutan named Joop).

The polar bears appeared in the early episodes, shortly after Walt saw a polar bear in the comic book he was reading. For many, this suggested that Walt had the ability to make something from his imagination manifest in reality. Possibly, but Rousseau also acknowledged there were polar bears on the island, which meant they were there before Walt arrived. (Season One, "Solitary.") As Walt showed in Australia when the bird he was studying in a book hit the patio window, his imagination does seem to bring things around; perhaps these are just things that are already in the vicinity. (Season One, "Special.") And since the Swan's orientation film mentions the Dharma Initiative's interest in zoology just as the film shows two polar bears fighting, and the Hanso Foundation notes it uses animals in its Life Extension project, it is possible they brought the bears to the island years earlier. There are probably enough boars and Dharma food palettes to keep the bears fat and happy, if a bit too warm. Finally, there is a note on the blast door map referring to "repatriation accelerated de-territorialization of ursus maritus through gene therapy and extreme climate change;" in other words, the polar bears may have been genetically manipulated to deal with extreme climate change. In the first 48 days (the first season), only two polar bears are seen, the one Sawyer shoots and the one that goes after Walt. Nothing of the bears appears again until the third season, when the Others throw Sawyer and Kate into a couple of polar bear cages which double as Skinner boxes. One of the bears drags Eko off to a cave after the electromagnetic pulse; Locke tracks the bear through the jungle to its cave, which is littered with the remains of past victims. Locke scorches the bear's face and manages to get Eko out of the cave. (Season Three, "Further Instructions.") It's not clear how many polar bears the Dharma Initiative has on the island, but only one has been killed, there's at least one more running around with a damaged face, and there are at least two cages on the island.

And the beasts aren't confined to land. When Michael and Sawyer were adrift on the wreckage of their raft, a shark was drawn by the blood from Sawyer's shoulder wound. A shark in the ocean wouldn't normally be considered so unusual, except it had the Dharma Initiative logo on its belly. This suggested that the shark was at least used in some tests, or possibly even engineered. When Sayid was first taken by Rousseau, he found her fort in the jungle by following a cable emerging from the water and leading into the jungle. This was the power cable Rousseau used to power her place, but it came from someplace in the water. There just may be another Dharma station under the sea experimenting with marine life.

The other known Dharma-associated animal is Joop, the Methuselah of the apes. Joop is an orangutan, and he is the subject of The Hanso Foundation's Life Extension Project, one of a number of projects The Hanso Foundation funds, including the

Dharma Initiative. The Hanso Foundation claims Joop is 105 years old, although Rachel Blake, the conspiracy theorist trying to blow open The Hanso Foundation in *The Lost Experience*, claims the orangutan Hanso presents is not actually Joop. Joop's name echoes the intelligent orangutan from Jules Verne's *Mysterious Island*; that ape's name was Jupiter, but its nickname was Jupe.

When Kate helped Sawyer recover from his septic gunshot wound, Sawyer mumbled in his sleep and seemed to be channeling her father, whom she killed. She later saw what appeared to be the same horse that caused U.S. Marshal Edward Mars to crash his car; it was this accident which led to Kate's escape. How the horse got on the island is still a mystery, but Sawyer saw the horse too, confirming it was actually there and not in Kate's imagination.

Then there's the Hurley Bird. Strangely, birds on this tropical island are a rare sight, although the Tailies did find a wild chicken. But the Lostaways encounter one large, swooping bird in the jungle. It's hard to tell what kind of bird this was – it wasn't a parrot – but its call when it swoops down sounds particularly strange. In a January episode of the Official *Lost* Podcast, Damon Lindelof goosed Carlton Cuse into talking about the bird. They were responding to a question about why we don't see birds on the island, and Damon asked, "Is it an accurate statement to say we have never seen a bird on the show *Lost*? Haven't we seen a bird?" Carlton said that a giant bird appeared in the season one finale as the survivors made their way to the Black Rock for dynamite. "And what did that bird sound like, Carlton?" Carlton croaked out, "HUR-LEE! HUR-LEE!"* The online community of course picked this up and started wondering if the bird was

*The Official *Lost* Podcast, January 9, 2006.

another genetic experiment, and the name Hurley Bird stuck. The bird made another appearance in the second season finale when it swooped down toward Hurley and made its call (it now seems to be a harbinger of each season's finale, as the survivors headed into the deeper part of the jungle): Hurley turned to Sawyer and said, "Did that bird just say my name?" and Sawyer responded, "Yeah it did – right before it crapped gold." The writers used this scene as an opportunity for a shout-out to the fans who had been discussing the Hurley bird.✿

Finally, *The Lost Experience* added to the animal theme with the group Retrievers of Truth (www.retrieversoftruth.org), an organization founded by one Dr. Vincent "Wally" Bolé that researches yellow Labrador retriever clairvoyance. The organization was once sponsored by The Hanso Foundation, but if the secret forum on the website is found, the "sponsored by" line changes to "subjugated by." A timeline on the page features a note about a yellow lab being born to a black lab owned by the Porter family in 1899 Australia; they were about to destroy it as an abomination, but the pup was saved by a servant named Lloyd; Walt Lloyd got Vincent, his yellow lab, from his stepfather Brian Porter in Australia. Bolé's major claim is that yellow labs can read our minds: "Friend. Companion. Soul mate. The yellow lab can read your mind. Hear your thoughts. Sense your pain. They can communicate without making a sound. Are you receptive?" Incidentally, in his photo on the web page, Dr. Wally Bolé looks suspiciously like actor Jeff "Big Lebowski" Bridges with a bad fake beard and moustache.

Obsession: If there's one thing such a diverse group of peo-

✿And may have deflated some of the theories about the bird; watch the episode again; there's no gold anywhere after the bird swoops by.

ple as the survivors share, its their individual issues with obsession. The obsessions of some of the characters become the dams that keep their lives from flowing along, and can blind them from other elements around them. Jack can't keep himself from trying to fix people. This obsession with his work is driven in part by his near-Oedipal drive to outdo his father, who was the Chief of Surgery at Jack's hospital. Jack's obsession got in the way of his marriage, tarnishing the legacy of one of his most successful operations.* As noted earlier, if Jack had chosen to save Adam Rutherford that day instead of his future wife Sarah, Shannon most likely would not have gone to Australia, which would have kept her and Boone off Oceanic 815. Jack's obsession with fixing people naturally evolved into an obsession with protecting the group on the island.

Both Boone and Bernard had similar repair-obsessions. Boone's stemmed from the need to prove he was somehow worthy of being an adult, as well as cleaning up after and taking care of his stepsister. From the moment the survivors were scrambling on the beach after the plane crash, Boone was the island boy scout, always prepared to help; it took Locke's intervention to help him grow and begin to let go of his obsessions. Bernard's obsession was with finding a cure for Rose's cancer (and like Jack, he's in the medical field – he's a dentist). But on the island, Bernard's obsession doesn't branch out as widely as Jack's; he is focused on being saved, whether it's transmitting a distress call or organizing another rescue operation. At one point Bernard tried to create a giant "S.O.S." sign, but only succeeded in irritating his colleagues until they all left him – Bernard is not a natural-born leader. But

---

*It was Jack's belief that the surgery had failed that led him to run the steps of the stadium, where he ended up running into Desmond for the first time.

whereas Jack is upfront about his obsession, Bernard is more surreptitious. He told Rose he had accepted her terminal cancer diagnosis when he asked her to marry him, but then spent much of his free time trying to heal her. In fact, if it weren't for this approach, Bernard and Rose may never have gone to Australia, since he took her there on what he pretended was nothing more than an Australian honeymoon, but actually planned to meet the healer Isaac of Uluru.

Just as Jack transferred his obsession from the mainland into something else on the island, so did Locke. The belief that a special destiny awaited him had carried over from his obsession with his father; his overly-emotional tie to this obsession manifested in his anger problem. When Locke's mother found him in California, she told him he was special (in fact, that he had been immaculately conceived) and that he had a special destiny, and he internalized this concept; when his father conned him out of a kidney, this faith made his disappointment that much harder to deal with. The idea that he had special destiny seemed to be revived when Locke's legs started to work again on the island, and was further developed when he discovered the hatch. Locke then transferred his obsession to the administration of the hatch and entering the code. But when he and Mr. Eko found the Pearl station, which contained evidence that the Swan code entries were meaningless, Locke yelled, "I was never meant to do anything. Every single second of my pathetic little life is as useless as that button!" (Season Two, "?")

Charlie's obsession was obviously heroin, but his addiction stemmed from other problems, which we glimpsed little by little across the narrative. Charlie was a devout Catholic, and blamed his brother for getting him hooked on heroin. But Charlie also had a bit of an inferiority complex that caused him to puff his fragile ego and take criticism poorly. As seen in a dream Charlie had, he thought he was supposed to save his family from squalor through his music, but things didn't turn out as he'd dreamed. (Season Two, "Fire + Water.") In heroin, Charlie found a way to deaden that ego center and just "get along." Without it, we saw Charlie acting petty and even vengeful whenever he felt his fragile ego was being attacked. This was seen in his casual lies about the heroin he continued to hold (but not use), when he attacked Sun in order to get back at Locke, and when his obsession with Claire led to his getting hung by Ethan, and his subsequent vengeful murder of Ethan.⌀

Hurley's obsession is with food, and like Charlie's heroin obsession, it came from someplace more personal, covering a deeper issue having to do with his accident. In a flashback, Hurley's mom indicated that he had always been a big guy, and while at the Santa Rosa Mental Institute, his therapist recounted the events surrounding "the accident": At a party, Hurley walked out onto an already over-crowded deck; the deck collapsed, and two people died. Hurley was shattered. Although the deck was only engineered to hold eight people, 23 were already on it by the time Hurley arrived.✢ After the accident, Hurley was catatonic for a while, and when in the Santa Rosa Mental Institute, he began "hanging out" with Dave, a manifestation of his imagination who

---

⌀But Charlie certainly had more right to shoot Ethan than he did to attack Sun or Locke.

✢And there are two of the numbers again, 8 and 23; 23 is also 15 more than the recommended 8, and 15 is the third number in the sequence; add Hurley, and you get 16 over the limit, and the fourth number. This sort of thing happens more often than you might think: At a June 29, 2003 college party in Chicago, party-goers had spilled out onto the second and third story deck, with as many as 50 on the upper deck. The deck collapsed onto the second story deck, both then hit the ground, 12 people died, and 57 were injured. Hey, be safe out there!

coaxed Hurley into continuing to overeat, against his doctor's orders. Once on the island, Hurley seems to have confronted his obsession much more directly than other survivors; he admits to his obsession, asks for help, and actively works at overcoming it. He even managed the distribution of food on the island – twice. Sure, food's not exactly heroin, but then again Charlie didn't have an imaginary demonic buddy feeding him his scag.

Both Michael and Rousseau became obsessed with getting their children back from the Others. Rousseau's obsession has driven her to become a kind of jungle guerilla, complete with traps, weapons, snares and torture devices for use when she catches one of the Others. Michael seemed to be heading down the same road; he learned how to fire a rifle and then went commando into the jungle, determined to get Walt back. Indeed, if Walt hadn't been returned to Michael at the end of season two, it would be easy to imagine Michael becoming a kind of parent-twin to Rousseau, as they both roamed the island, waging their respective insurgencies against the Others.

In the first 48 days on the island, Kate was obsessed with hiding her criminal past. She was willing to lie, steal a dead passenger's identity papers, and use fellow survivors in an effort to erase her history. Jack was the first person to recognize her concerns. He told Kate that everyone on the island deserved a fresh start. Kate spent time with Jack, but she felt a kind of kinship to Sawyer, a fellow criminal. Sawyer's obsession isn't so much with hiding his past – he openly steals from and takes advantage of others on the island – but his criminality is driven by the man who conned and effectively killed both of his parents. His own complex history at times got in the way of his cons, and even left him open to being taken advantage of by one of his partners –

which is why he was in Australia in the first place: He believed he was killing the original Sawyer, but the colleague (Hibbs) who had tipped him off had in fact lied to him, and the victim of Sawyer's lifelong vendetta turned out to be a stranger who owed Hibbs money. Kate and Sawyer aren't alone in having criminal pasts: Jin's obsession with bettering his social status and taking care of Sun led him into a brutal life as a kind of corporate enforcer for Sun's father, Mr. Paik. Jin's inability to break out of this violent mode led to his abuse of Sun when they first arrived on the island (before he knew she could speak English) and his violent encounters with Michael on the island when he thought Michael had stolen the Rolex he planned to deliver to an associate of Mr. Paik in L.A.

The Tailies had their criminals as well. Ana-Lucia was obsessed with exacting revenge from the man who shot her and caused her miscarriage. This obsession led to her putting her job, her relationship with her mother, and her life all at risk. Mr. Eko, on the other hand, seemed to at first relish his criminal warlord lifestyle (his reputation was so fearsome, he was rumored to have no soul), but he was obviously obsessed with being his brother's brother. If it weren't for his willingness to take his brother's place with the soldiers when he and Yemi were children, Eko never would have become the criminal he did. Eko's obsession continued after Yemi died trying to save Eko, and he re-organized his entire life to live as his brother. As far as obsessions go, Mr. Eko's may be one of the healthier ones among the survivors.

The two soldiers on the island, Sayid and Desmond, are both obsessed with the great loves of their lives. Sayid was in Australia as part of a plan to reunite with Nadia. Sayid had helped Nadia escape from the Iraqi Republican Guard, and the

CIA had information on her location in the United States. (In fact, in a flashback Locke inspected the home that Nadia bought in California.) Sayid agreed to help the intelligence authorities break up a terrorist cell in Sydney by exploiting his connection with a college friend, and in exchange he would be able to return to Nadia after more than a decade apart. Like Sayid, Desmond longs to reunite with his lost love, Penelope. Desmond constantly wrote to Penelope while he was in prison, but her father kept all his letters from her. Penelope eventually assumed Desmond had moved on; she became engaged to another man, but her feelings for Desmond hadn't changed. When Desmond was finally released from prison, he learned the truth about the letters, and became determined to earn back his honor (and Penelope) by winning the round-the-world solo sailboat race her father sponsored, during which he ran aground on the island. His obsession led him to the island, but he has no way of knowing that Penelope may still be looking for him. (Season Two, "Live Together, Die Alone.")

The final obsession is that of the audience themselves. If you're reading this book, you're probably looking for some keys to understanding the show and are willing to take time out of your day to devote toward trying to crack the enigmas of the narrative. You may already have visited online forums, you may have listened to one of the ever-growing number of podcasts discussing the show. You're clever enough to have turned to some of the books spotted within the show looking for some kind of Rosetta stone revealing what the whole thing is about. Perhaps you've posited your own theories about what's going on to your friends or online or even in your own blog dedicated to *Lost*. And of course you were thrilled when you caught the writers acknowledging your obsession with theories about the island in the second season finale, when Sawyer said of the Others, "My theory, they're aliens. That's why they use the fake beards." (Season Two, "Live Together, Die Alone.") Face it, you're hooked. Just remember to feed the dog and take showers regularly.

Literary References: There are some 22 writers working on the show, and most episodes are developed by two writers working together. When the show was conceived and the pilot was outlined by J.J. Abrams, he only had a week to work it out. The subsequent writing, casting and shooting schedule was on such an accelerated pace that prime time television's conventional wisdom was pushed aside. In effect, *Lost* became a writer's playground. And for English majors who grew up with a healthy dose of pop cultural literacy (especially those who were born in the 1970s), and don't discriminate much between literature, fantasy and sci-fi, *Lost* became a way to recast their vocabulary and references into a kind of mythology.

• Until Flann O'Brien's *The Third Policeman* appeared on the show, O'Brien had been a fairly obscure Irish modernist (verging on post-modernist) writer, known primarily to those living near Howth Castle and Environs, and those lucky enough to come across *At Swim-Two-Birds* on a syllabus. O'Brien's books are published in the United States by a small press affiliated with Illinois State University and the Center for Book Culture, the Dalkey Archive Press (named after another O'Brien book). Within two days of O'Brien's *The Third Policeman* being flashed on the screen, the Dalkey press sold 8,000 copies of the book. That's absurdly amazing – those are nearly Oprah numbers for an independent publisher. Real literature that has been kicked around in dusty academic departments and shelved far away from the popular mindset suddenly became like the movie of the week. (OK, maybe an independent film). What's more, the books that are chosen by the writers are generally challenging, multi-layered, and have a rich history of criticism attempting to explain their intricacies. Not every reference will yield all there is to know about the narrative of *Lost*, but every reference is there for a purpose. What follows isn't an exhaustive list, and to be sure there are more in the pipeline, but these references seem to carry a lot of weight:

• The Bible makes appearances in all sorts of ways. It has appeared in the names of episodes ("Numbers," "Exodus," "Psalm 23"), in many of the names of characters (Nathan, Aaron, Christian Shephard, all the Toms), and in the Catholicism of Mr. Eko and Charlie. In the online community, Psalm 4, Psalm 8, Psalm 15, Psalm 16 and Psalm 42 have been kicked around as thematic touchstones since Psalm 23 made its appearance. The Old Testament Book of Numbers, incidentally, is about the census Moses takes of the Israelites when they are lost in the Sinai Desert. Mr. Eko carves scripture into his club and tells tales that relate various survivors' situations to biblical stories. Eko's club recalls the staff of Moses, but as noted above, his scripture carvings also mirror twin him with Cormac McCarthy's character Judge Holden from existentialist western *Blood Meridian*; the Judge was a large man like Eko, and also a cold-blooded killer (although unreformed), but he was albino-white, hairless, and whereas many cowboys gave their guns names, the Judge inscribed the Latin memento mori "Et en Arcadia Ego" into his rifle – "I am also in Arcadia/paradise." The greater theme of *Blood Meridian* is man's warlike nature, even going so far as to claim that war and god are one and the same. (As seen in the Alvar Hanso Sri

Lanka video, the entire existence of the Dharma Initiative began as a response to the warlike nature of man that led to the Cuban Missile Crisis.) Finally, Mr. Eko found another section of the orientation film inside a hollowed-out Bible that was in the abandoned station the Tailies stayed in. When Eko gave the film to Locke, he first told him the Old Testament story of Josiah and how the temple was rebuilt with a book, and then he handed Locke the Bible. Locke seems to be just playing along, until he discovered the secret film inside. The symbolism here makes the Bible less of a book of stories and more a tool with utilitarian purposes. (Season Two, "What Kate Did.")

• Homer's *Odyssey* provides the archetypal model for Desmond and Penelope's story, complete with the voyage around the world, getting caught on an island for years, and Penelope waiting for her lost love. Odysseus was punished by Poseidon when he put out the Cyclops Polyphemus's eye; Poseidon exacted revenged by wrecking Odysseus's boat in a storm, much as Desmond's boat was wrecked in a storm, and both Odysseus and Desmond ended up on phantom islands. The moment when Odysseus had to navigate his ship between the whirlpool of Charybdis and the rock of Scylla was re-articulated by James Joyce in *Ulysses* when he had his Odysseus figure of the chapter, Stephen Dedalus, navigate an argument between the whirlpool of mysticism and the rock of practical empiricism. That model of argument was revisited time and again between Locke and Jack.

• *The Epic of Gilgamesh* was quickly noted when Locke was trying to work on a crossword puzzle at the Swan's computer. (Season Two, "Collision.") *The Epic of Gilgamesh* is an ancient Babylonian poem, possibly the oldest known piece of literature in the world. It tells of two man-gods: Gilgamesh is the god-king of

Uruk, and the wild man Enkidu is created by the goddess Aururu to be an adversary to Gilgamesh. Enkidu is tamed by a priestess, and then challenges Gilgamesh. They fight to a stand-off (some of the story is missing, and it looks like Gilgamesh just had enough), and decide to go off to the cedar forest to kill Humbaba, the demon guardian of the forest. They later kill the bull of heaven when it's sent to avenge a rejected Ishtar (she wanted to sleep with Gilgamesh but he rejected her – don't hate the player, Ishtar, hate the game). The gods become angry after this and kill Enkidu. The crossword clue was a 9-letter word for "Enkidu's friend," which seemed to indicate "Gilgamesh," but that answer makes all the crosses incorrect.[69] Some in the community have speculated that since Locke first met Mr. Eko just after working on this crossword, that Locke and Eko will be the Gilgamesh and Enkidu of the island. If so, who will Locke reject? (With Eko being a priest, it leaves him out of the running for sleeping with anyone, unless he's real progressive.)

• Charles Dickens's *Our Mutual Friend* (1864) was his last novel, and displays one of his more sweeping and complex plots. It focuses on the son of a wealthy man who cannot collect his inheritance unless he marries a woman he has not met, an arranged marriage on the basis of his wealth, so he fakes his own drowning in the Thames. His inheritance then is given to others and reaches far across London. But the protagonist returns under an assumed identity, becomes a self-made man, and then marries the same woman – this time based on who he is and what he has done, not on his given wealth. He then reveals his true identity and reclaims his inheritance. Desmond saved this book to read just

---

[69]The clue was also number 42 down – another instance of the numbers.

before he died – he wanted it to be the last book he would ever read. His story also seemed to parallel the protagonist's story somewhat; he could not marry the woman he wanted to until he could prove himself, and is presumed drowned. In a May 25, 2006 New York Times interview, Damon Lindelof and Carlton Cuse admitted to getting the idea of Desmond saving the book for his last from an interview with John Irving, who claimed to be doing the same thing. They also wanted to incorporate Dickens because of the episodic nature of his narrative; like writers for television, Dickens's work was serialized (in newspapers), so he was required to turn in chapters week after week. It wasn't always clear if Dickens had the plan for the entire narrative before he wrote, or if he was building off the previous installment and just let the narrative lead him. Desmond's copy of the book held a letter Penelope wrote to him years before as he left for prison, but he had never seen the letter (since he hadn't read the book). At around the survivors' 40th day on the island, Desmond still did not know about them. His despair had gotten the best of him, and he was preparing to take his own life, which meant it was time for *Our Mutual Friend*. When he opened the book Penny's letter fell out, and as he read it, he heard Locke banging on the hatch from above. This was enough to keep him going a little while longer. (Season Two, "Live Together, Die Alone.")

• Jules Verne's *Mysterious Island* (1874) is obliquely referenced in a few ways. First, the island in the book is found by five Civil War POWs from the Union States who escape by stealing a hot air balloon and crash on an island in the South Pacific. *Lost*'s island has its own hot air balloon wreckage, which Ben appropriates as part of his alias and alibi. Second, *Mysterious Island*'s escapees find an intelligent orangutan on the island and call it

Jupiter, but they nickname it Jupe; *The Lost Experience*'s Joop is also an orangutan, and is the subject of The Hanso Foundation's Life Extension Project, one of a number of projects The Hanso Foundation funds, including the Dharma Initiative. Third, the book's island is full of surprises: they find guns, ammunition, and tools, all seemingly placed there for them, and seem to have someone watching out for them, much the way the hatch works for the survivors of Oceanic 815. The POWs find out that the island was used as a harbor for Captain Nemo, who was also helping them when they weren't looking. Nemo was already noted in reference to the French lyrics for a song from the cartoon *Finding Nemo* on Rousseau's map. *Mysterious Island*'s Nemo is a mysterious Hanso-like presence on the island, especially in the 1961 Cy Endfield and Ray Harryhausen film adaptation, where he performs genetic experiments with animals and tries to invent ways to end war.

• Ambrose Bierce's *An Occurrence at Owl Creek Bridge* (1886) is a short story that utilizes the narrative technique of the flash back to great degree. The story concerns a confederate planter who is about to be hung from Owl Creek Bridge by Union soldiers for trying to burn the bridge so the Union couldn't get across. As he's pushed from the bridge, the rope breaks. He escapes through the river below, then walks all day and into the night through the woods back to his home. Pangs of pain let him know how the rope injured him as he fell, and by the time he made it home, his neck was swollen in excruciating pain. In fact, the pain was because the rope never broke; he imagined the entire escape in the moment between being pushed off the bridge and when the noose broke his neck. The story is a classic example of the unreliable narrator, and expands a minute into nearly a day's time. It's a technique used in every episode of *Lost* and across the narrative as a whole; for the audience, over two years have passed, but on the island, only 65 days have gone by. This story was made into a famous episode of *The Twilight Zone*, which is another influence on *Lost*.[◁]

• Fyodor Dostoevsky's *The Brothers Karamazov* (1880) is, appropriately enough, prison reading for Ben. The book follows four brothers who conspire to murder their terrible father. The theme of the novel is reflected in the way characters like Locke and Jack have difficulty with their fathers (in fact, fathers in general have it rough in *Lost*). Beyond the level of the plot, however, the book also explores conflicts of faith, reason and free will, all of which are seen in *Lost*. When Ben talks literature with Locke, he quotes from the book: "Men reject their prophets and slay them. But they love their martyrs and honor those whom they have slain." (Season Two, "Maternity Leave.") If you want to get a broader understanding of the underlying drives of the characters in *Lost*, you could do a lot worse than to read *The Brothers Karamazov*. It's brutal, but worth it.

• Henry James's *The Turn of the Screw* (1898) is sitting on the shelf of the Swan hatch in front of the orientation film. The book is about a governess who comes to discover her charges are haunted by the ghosts of their prior governess and her lover, the estate's valet. The governess tries to protect the children from what she deems to be a growing threat, but it's hardly clear whether the governess is actually seeing ghosts, or is mad, or if the narrator is actively misleading the reader. The fact that the orientation film is behind this particular book – Kelvin told Desmond to make sure

◁J.J. Abrams, interview with David Bianculli, *Fresh Air*, National Public Radio, October 14, 2004.

he put the film back behind *Turn of the Screw* – suggests that maybe there is something untrustworthy about the film. The narrator of the film, Dr. Marvin Candle, also appears in the Pearl's orientation film, but this time under the name Dr. Mark Wickmund. Furthermore, Dr. Candle appears to have a false arm, while Dr. Wickmund has two perfectly functional arms.

• Joseph Conrad's *Heart of Darkness* (1899) is an early modernist novel about a seeming pillar of the Belgian Empire, Mr. Kurtz, and how he – or anyone – can slip into tyrannical savagery when free of the bonds of civilization. Kurtz was the chief of a Belgian ivory company's Inner Station in the deepest Congo. While there, the station's ivory shipments ceased, and soon Kurtz's communications ended as well. He had shirked the mores of European society and set himself up like a god in the jungle. The book is not directly mentioned, but Charlie makes brief nod to the story when he calls Hurley "Colonel bloody Kurtz," a reference to the Francis Ford Coppola cinematic adaptation of the story, *Apocalypse Now*.☆ (Season One, "Numbers.")

• Frank L. Baum's *The Wonderful Wizard of Oz* (1900) is another literary reference where hot air balloons figure heavily. Aside from the larger general sense of someone we can't see behind the curtain pulling levers and making the place seem very scary (Ben? "Him"?), the wizard was in a hot air balloon in Omaha and got caught in a gust that carried him to Oz. Henry Gale is the name of Dorothy's uncle; Henry Gale is the name of the Minnesotan whose hot air balloon crashed on the island (and whose identity Ben assumed to infiltrate the Lostaways' camp via

---

☆Incidentally, Kurtz was played by Marlon Brando, who would only wear black clothes because of his weight, and Hurley's weight is an issue for him and some of his fellow survivors on the island.

Rousseau's net). In Baum's third book, *Ozma of Oz*, Henry's Kansas farm is in financial trouble and he is ordered by his doctor to take a vacation in order to relieve his stress. So he goes to – where else? – Australia.

• William Golding's *The Lord of the Flies* (1954) is almost too obvious a connection to *Lost*; indeed the book hasn't been seen on the show, but the story is so common that both Sawyer and Charlie mention it in passing. The Cold War-era story follows a group of British schoolboys who are being evacuated from an area under attack when their plane is shot down over a tropical island. They elect one of the boys, Ralph, as their leader, but another boy named Jack starts agitating for power. They believe there is a beast in the forest, and when they investigate, they find a pilot who parachuted down to the island but was dead before he ever landed. Much like Locke's discovery that the Swan was a behavioral experiment, the god from the machine was dead. Jack breaks off to form his own tribe that will war with Ralph's, and the boys slip deeper into savagery. They are only saved when Jack's tribe starts a forest fire, and a passing battleship sees the smoke and saves them. The book draws much of its thematic tone from *Heart of Darkness*, another book that's alluded to but not seen.

• Madeleine L'Engle's *A Wrinkle in Time* (1962) is a young reader's fantasy novel that follows children who are looking for their father, a scientist who disappeared into another dimension that is inhabited by strange creatures (centaurs who get pretty religious). They are led to this other dimension by a strange old lady named Mrs. Whatsit, who tells them tesseracts, or 4-dimensional cubes, exist, and proceeds to take them there to find their father. The idea of alternative dimensions at least gave *Lost*'s audience food for thought regarding where the island really might be located.

• Flann O'Brien's *The Third Policeman* (1967) is one of the more enigmatic books to make an appearance in *Lost*. Briefly, it concerns an unnamed narrator who was orphaned while young and raised in a boarding school, where he became obsessed with the work of a philosopher named de Selby.꜡ De Selby has a number of interesting theories about how the world works, and O'Brien's text abounds in these theories – often in asides and footnotes that go on and on, including a four-page footnote describing how night is actually just an accumulation of black air (something which makes many in the *Lost* audience think of the stomping smoke on the island).⌾ The narrator needs funding for his scholarly endeavor, and goes in on a plan to kill a wealthy man in his Irish parish and steal his black box of cash. However, his accomplice immediately hides the box, and the narrator has to outwait him; during that time he never lets the man out of his sight. His accomplice eventually decides it's safe enough to tell him where to find the box. As soon as the narrator touches it, the box disappears and things around his parish start to change and become increasingly odd; it becomes colder, the light of the morning becomes dim, and he forgets his own name. The narrator then finds a police station, and asks two policemen to help him find the black box. The policemen tell him strange things, like how the people in that parish and their bicycles tend to become one another after years of riding; the molecules of the bicycle transfer into the rider and the molecules of the rider transfer

꜡De Selby is most likely not a real philosopher, but he does make appearances in various books every now and again.

⌾Before there was David Foster Wallace, there was Flann O'Brien, taking the piss out of academic ad nauseum.

into the bicycle until some are half bicycle and half person. They show him a contraption that captures sound and turns it into light, and another that divides scents the way a prism divides light. They also introduce him to an underground bunker called Eternity, where they work a contraption with levers and dials and take regular readings – all reminiscent of the hatch for the *Lost* audience. He learns that the third policeman, who resides in his own station away from the other two policemen, has his black box, and the box has something inside it. The substance is called omnium, and it's basically the kernel of everything and can be anything. This third policeman uses it to clean his leggings, make eggs just right, and he also used it to tweak the readings of the bunker to danger levels just to watch the other two policeman run rampant trying to reset everything. A final alignment with *Lost* is the map of the parish that the narrator discovers on the ceiling of one of the policeman's room; what first looks like cracks clearly becomes a detailed map of his town. And he's told the map wasn't made, but was always there, and they're quite sure it was there before that. By the end of the novel we learn that the narrator is actually being punished for murdering the man, and will be forced to live in this frustrating ever-changing parish for eternity. There seems to be quite a bit in *The Third Policeman* to suggest it's some sort of key to... something. But O'Brien was also interested in the places where narrative and audience broke down. In *At Swim-Two-Birds*, a novel about writing a novel, the characters who are being written don't like the trajectory of their narrative and work to drug their author – if he's asleep, he can't control their world. The characters become a kind of audience and the narrator a character, which is echoed in the way the audience of *Lost* has become part of the fabric of the narrative, not only through the alternate reality game and the scrutiny with which the writers follow the online response to the show, but in the way that audience tends to re-enact the characters' moves by searching for answers to the enigmas, forming and cultivating a cooperative community, and performing repeated activities which are themselves watched as closely as they are watching the show.

• Hergé's Tintin comic book adventure *Flight 715* (1968) follows the scrappy little Belgian adventurer to Djakarta, Indonesia, where he takes a flight to Sydney, Australia in a millionaire's private prototype jet. But when the flight is hijacked and taken down on an unknown island, they're forced off the plane and Tintin's dog Snowy runs off into the jungle, *a la* Walt's dog Vincent. The hijackers then hold Tintin and his entourage hostage in underground bunkers. When they escape, they meet a strange man on the island who can control their minds. The structural similarities exist, but whether they're deliberate or not is anyone's guess. Damon Lindelof has written comic books (he wrote the 2006 Marvel series *Ultimate Wolverine vs. Hulk*), and Tintin was one of the more internationally famous comic books during its long span.

• Richard Adams's *Watership Down* (1972) is, according to Sawyer, "about bunnies." It chronicles a group of rabbits in search of a place to make a home. One of the rabbits, Fiver, has the ability to see into the future, and sees that the warren they lived in would be destroyed by men, so a group of rabbits split off and go in search of a place to establish another warren. They then have the problem of populating that warren – they have no does. So they infiltrate another neighboring warren that's overcrowded and run as a totalitarian state and entice away some of the does. Aside from the natural association of a group looking to re-establish a home, Fiver's supernatural sight may also recall Walt's special abilities.

• Stephen King's *The Stand* (1978) is about two groups of people trying to re-establish civilization in North America after a super flu virus called Captain Trips wipes out nearly everyone. One group of survivors is average, everyday people who are brought together by shared dreams leading them toward one place and one person, Mother Abigail. The other survivors are organized around a personification of evil named Randall Flagg. Damon Lindelof has noted *The Stand* as an influence on the wide-ranging narrative and cast of *Lost*, but the island's good/bad distinctions are hardly as pat as they are in King's novel.

• Gary Troup's *Bad Twin* makes an appearance on the island, and has a number of character and thematic parallels with the *Lost* narrative.❂ The Widmores, Mr. Paik, Alvar Hanso, and Thomas Mittelwerk all make appearances in the book, and are name-dropped as if they were real figures who headed industries as common as Dow and IBM. The major function of *Bad Twin*, however, seems to be to lead readers down blind paths toward what seem like revealing clues about the *Lost* mythology, but actually yield very little. Troup's book, as its title suggests, is a bad twin for the *Lost* narrative.

Electromagnetism: After entering the hatch, none of the Lostaways were quite sure what the Swan station's purpose was. Jack and Sayid discovered a room sealed shut with about 10 feet of concrete, but despite this, a magnetic force could be felt

❂See "Appendix: The Manifest's Destiny (The Lost Experience)."

whenever anyone walked by it: Jack noticed the key on his neck lifted up, and Desmond said, "But the film says this is an electro-magnetic station. And I don't know about you, brother, but every time I walk past that concrete wall out there, my fillings hurt." (Season Two, "Orientation.") Kelvin told Desmond that the experiments on the island were due to "geologically unique electromagnetism." (Season Two, "Live Together, Die Alone.") The blast door map also contained a note about the geological composition of a part of the island "likely to cause magnetic interference with weather project," and two equations on the map calculated a magnetic flux density and the strength of a magnet-ic field – although these were just symbolic equations, useless without variables to calculate solutions. The Hanso Foundation and the Dharma Initiative have done research into electromag-netism, and indeed it was Hans Christian Ørsted (Hans Ø) from Denmark who discovered electromagnetism in the 19th century. An incident prior to 1980 (the date of the Swan's orientation film) necessitated the sealing off of part of the station, and led to the 108 minute button-pushing protocol. This protocol required at least one person present to enter the code and ensure that the electromagnetic build-up was properly discharged. If the numbers were not entered in time to reset the timer, hieroglyphs appeared in the place of the timer's numbers, and things began to fly around the room.

The question is to what purpose is this geologically unique electromagnetism being put? As seen in the Sri Lanka video from *The Lost Experience*, Alvar Hanso first funded the Dharma Initiative in response to the Cuban Missile Crisis and in an effort to solve the Valenzetti Equation, an equation that attempts to predict the extinction of humanity. We also learned from this video that Dharma is actually an acronym for Department of Heuristics and Research on Material Applications – a name which meant they could create models of something and study the models to learn about the thing itself. If Alvar Hanso's goal was to stop something like a world-ending war, one step toward that end would be discovering a renewable, non-polluting energy source. Perhaps the Dharma Initiative created a model that harnessed the geologically unique electromagnetism for a new kind of power plant – after all, the stations must be getting their electricity from somewhere.

But what makes this island geologically unique? There are more than a few questions to be answered here, including how a 19th century slave ship came to rest on a hill in the middle of the island, and why a Nigerian puddle jumper that could barely make it out of Africa landed in the island's jungle canopy. There's a theory of geologically unique places on the planet called the "vile vortices" – think Bermuda Triangle, but there are twelve of them. The vor-

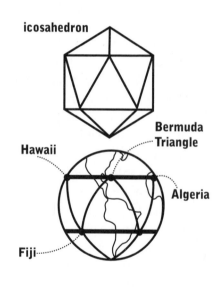

tices were first called so by Scottish naturalist Ivan Sanderson in his 1970 book *Invisible Residents.*❂ Sanderson was interested in

---

❂Sanderson began his career as an orthodox scientist, but later became very interested in cryptozoology, UFO's, and the general strangeness of our world.

how ancient sailors mapped the earth, and in his research kept coming places on the earth where strange things would happen – airplane instruments would go haywire and get lost for hours, but when they came back no time had passed; ships disappeared; the basic sorts of things that are so common from Bermuda Triangle lore. He noted that these places appear in regular frequency around the earth: five in regular intervals along the Tropic of Cancer, five along the Tropic of Capricorn, and one at each pole. Polyhedral grids are often used in cartography to map coordinates and locations around the earth, and Sanderson noted that if you plot an icosahedron around the earth (a 20-faced shape made up of equilateral triangles), the points where the triangle corners met marked the vortices around the globe.[*] One of these vortices stretches across Algeria, one is located in the South Pacific around Fiji, and still another is around the vicinity of Hawaii.

Three Russian scientists picked up on Sanderson's work. Nikolai Goncharov, Vyacheslav Morozov, and Valery Makarov were interested in seismic fault lines, migration patterns, weather patterns and the like, and found commonalities in these patterns that led them to build on Sanderson's map by adding a dodecahedron (a 12-faced shape made up of pentagons). The two shapes, icosahedron and dodecahedron, were two of what Plato described as the regular solids that made up the earth.[†] However, in 1983 anthropologist Bethe Hagens and industrial design professor William Becker re-adjusted the two maps to have their

---

[*]Image based on illustration from *Paradox* by Nicholas R. Nelson (Dorrance & Co., Ardmore, PA, 1980).

[†]The other three are the tetrahedron (pyramid), hexahedron (cube), and octahedron (diamond); for Plato, these represented fire, earth and air respectively, while the icosahedron represented water and the dodecahedron represented aether.

coordinates match up, and doing so they were able to fit all of the other Platonic regular solids into their planetary grid map.⌒ There are 62 points on this grid where the lines of the shapes converge. In an April 14, 2006 post on *Entertainment Weekly's* Popwatch web page, it was pointed out that those points of convergence on the grid are supposed to have stronger magnetic fields, and a few of those points – 15, 16, 23, and 42 among them – are prime candidates for where Oceanic 815 may have gone down (and are of course the values of the Valenzetti Equation).

Consider the bagua shape mentioned above (in "Twins & Twinning"). The bagua is octagonal, and the octahedron (an 8-

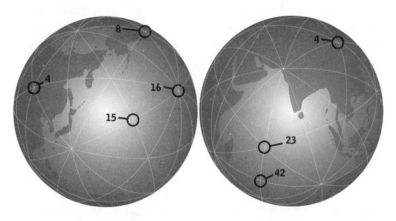

faced shape) can be mapped onto this grid. As it happens, the points of convergence in an octahedral grid match up with the points of convergence in the icosahedron map that marks the 12 vile vortices. It is also the only polyhedral shape that, when

⌒The map is widely available, but under the Gnu public license can only be reproduced and distributed without charge. Hagens has also released a free Google Earth plugin that reproduces all of the grids over the map in a maneuverable three-dimensional virtual globe.

mapped onto the planetary grid, hits every one of the points from the string of numbers; the octahedral lines converge at 4, 8, 15, 16, 23 and 42. None of the other polyhedral shapes on the planetary grid hit all six of these points. The Dharma Initiative symbolism just may be closely linked to the numbers.

Since we really don't have any good (public) knowledge about what goes on in these places, but the lore suggests that things like ships and planes just disappear, we can start with the possibility that both the Caribbean slave ship and the Nigerian drug smugglers' plane hit their respective vortices and ended up at the island, which is in yet another vortex. And just maybe these vortices display geologically unique electromagnetic qualities – they at least could in fiction. One of these vortices overlays one of the points on the Becker-Hagens planetary grid, point 16; this is out in the middle of the Pacific Ocean, and also contains Hawaii, where *Lost* is filmed.

The strange electromagnetic properties of the island also explain why the survivors' compasses don't work, why the tides rise unusually quickly, and why Michael had to follow a bearing of 325 degrees if he wanted to leave the island – any other bearing would lead him back to the island, as happened with Desmond. They may help explain why some people on the island were rapidly healed of chronic ailments.[♥] Electromagnetic energy makes up the full spectrum of light, and if some sort of engine existed that discharged a large amount of energy at once, like in the season two finale, it might explain the strange light seen flooding over the island. And if the machine was harnessing such

---

[♥]Any insomniac has seen the late-night infomercials on magnetic bracelets that are supposed to increase a person's health and well-being. If that were true, imagine that property increased from refrigerator-magnet strength to tide-shifting strength.

a large quantity of electromagnetic energy – that also makes up light – perhaps this machine can bend light around the island, effectively rendering the island invisible. As Ben said to Locke, "God doesn't know how long we've been here, John. He can't see this island any better than the rest of the world can." (Season Two, "Dave.")

And if you really want to get out there and consider why polar bears and horses and dead dads appear on imaginary command, you could ask if electromagnetism has something to do with parapsychological abilities. Consider: the Dharma Initiative was studying parapsychology on the island; every electrical charge also creates a magnetic field, and a magnetic field is a part of an electrical field; every thought we have is an electrical impulse that jets across the neural networks of our brains; if there is electrical activity in the brain, there may be some kind of magnetic field working along those neural networks; if you could properly apply some kind of electromagnetic force to that neural network, altering or enhancing the quality of neural electrical impulse, could you alter the quality and effects of your thoughts? Who's to say, but it's well within the realm of the possible in fiction. (Then again, it could just end up being New Age shock treatment.)

Cold: The cold is a regular theme *Lost*'s narrative returns to now and again. First we saw the polar bears, which would seem to have no business anywhere near a beach.✿ Then we met Kelvin; his was not exactly a common name, and was evocative of the temperature scale that descends to absolute zero, the temperature where all kinetic energy ceases – everything freezes. A low Kelvin temperature is necessary for superconductivity, which you

---

✿Although, with the polar ice cap melting like it is, polar bears may have to get used to warmer conditions.

need if you want to make a really powerful electromagnet. When Kelvin first met Desmond, his first question was, "What did one snowman say to the other?" again bringing up an image of the cold. (Answer: "Smells like carrots.") Desmond repeated this question to Locke, and when Desmond ended up back on the island after 23* days at sea, his response was that the world had become a "bloody snow globe." If you needed any more cold imagery to drive this theme home, the final scene of the second season finale showed an observation station in what appeared to be an arctic location, complete with Portuguese-speaking chess players. (Season Two, "Live Together, Die Alone.")

Body Parts: Body parts – especially missing body parts – were a constant refrain the narrative visually returned to. In many episodes and scenes, from the pilot on, shots opened with a close up of an eye. It was all about what we saw and what we thought we saw. There was a glass eye seen in the abandoned Arrow station, where the Tailies initially set up camp. Locke had real eye issues: He has a scar over one eye; he appeared to have one black eye and one white eye in Claire's attack dream. (Season One, "Raised by Another.") And when he was pinned under the Swan's blast door, we saw the map reflected in his eye. (Season Two, "Lockdown.") Damon Lindelof has suggested a few times that we've seen the monster more than we realized, we just don't know it yet. Beyond eyes, missing body parts seem to recur (conspicuous through their absence): in the Swan's orientation film, Dr. Marvin Candle seems to have a prosthetic left arm. Ray Mullen, the Australian farmer that employed Kate before delivering her to Mars was missing his right arm. Montand, a mem-

---

*And 23 is the fifth number in the code.

ber of Rousseau's team, lost his arm while in the dark territory. When Hurley went to Australia to meet Martha Toomey, the wife of one of the listening station operatives who heard the numbers, she was missing a leg. The unnamed narrator in *The Third Policeman* was also missing a leg – he had a wooden left leg. And Jack nearly cut off Boone's leg in an attempt to save him. Locke gave up his kidney. Nathan nearly had to give up his finger (and ended up losing much more).

The statue Sayid, Jin and Sun spotted on the other side of the island was a foot missing an entire body, not to mention a fifth toe it never seemed to have – the model naturally had only four toes. The size of the statue recalls the Colossus of Rhodes, which was about the same size as the Statue of Liberty. It collapsed in an earthquake in 224 B.C.E., and only the legs below the knees were left standing. The Colossus depicted the Greek god of the sun, Helios, who was also known as Hyperion, and became conflated with Apollo; Elio is a character in *Bad Twin*, which was published by Hyperion Press, and the candy bars found in the hatch are called Apollo bars. Another giant statue cut off at the knees is Ozymandias, the colossus of Ramesses II immortalized by Percy Byshe Shelley in a sonnet called *Ozymandias*. And for the comic book-inclined, Ozymandias is the name of a hero from Alan Moore's graphic novel *Watchmen*; he hatches a plan to make the world think it's under attack by an alien threat in order to make warring countries unite and thus avert a real nuclear threat, which sounds rather Alvar Hanso-ish. Yet there's still the question of the toes: Humans display a number of vestigial structures, physical elements that exist but are nearly useless, and only remain because we haven't evolved past them. Wisdom teeth, the appendix, some ear muscles, and the tail bone are all examples of vestigial structures, and some argue that the little toe belongs in that category. It plays next to no role in balance or locomotion, is pretty fragile, and who can actually cut that nail? We could easily imagine an evolved human species where tail bone cracks, appendicitis, wisdom teeth surgery, and broken little toes are a thing of the past because the body parts don't develop in the first place.

Let's see if Walt only has four toes on each foot.

Red Herrings & Overdeterminedness (the Numbers): One thing the creators of the narrative decided to do is throw plenty of decoys out to the ravenous fans ready to eat everything tossed their way. Certain hints, Easter eggs, clues and elements from *The Lost Experience* seem to make *just about* everything fall into place, but not quite. And then, when you think you've locked onto something good – like the idea of purgatory, or watching the numbers – they start to appear everywhere, and even coincidence seems determined. This tactic seems to become more prevalent as the narrative grows, occurring at both the plot level and at the level of audience reception. At the plot level it happens with the cons, with the Pearl station workers watching the Swan station but being the experiment itself, and again with the Others: Even their tent town and facial hair ended up being red herrings for the Lostaways.

But for the audience, it's another story. The way the narrative is structured – constantly posing questions, but only providing partial answers – invites a steady stream of theorizing. The writers and actors have generally stayed away from addressing such theories. The actors don't receive their scripts until a few days before shooting, so they aren't privy to the writers' plans for the season or the motives of the characters they interact with. In a kind of Kubrickian manner, the actors are put in positions that elicit similar responses to the characters' own. At the 2005 Hawaii International Film Festival, Harold Perrineau (Michael) said the actors "never know what's going on with your own or others' characters, so it keeps things fresh and tense. Plus the actors are stuck out on the island, so they're necessarily losing work, which can add to the tensions the actors can bring to the characters."📚 The actors live in a situation just a step removed from the immediacy of reality, and have to deliver the lines with that immediacy intact. In a strange way, they're almost in the position many of us dream about: being able to say what we think we should have (or wish we would have) said, rather than what we actually said. They get the good lines *and* the ability to react with a measure of spontaneity and authenticity because they're constantly being misdirected about characters' motives, just as the audience is.

As noted above, the writing staff is paying attention to the audience responses on an episode-by-episode basis, and working ideas into the narrative that play with those responses. We've already seen the examples of how the writers are watching the audience response to the washer and dryer looking too new and to the Hurley Bird. Another such example occurred just before the third season began, with Rachel Blake's final video. Over the summer those involved with *The Lost Experience* began speculating on who Rachel Blake was. She shared the same first name as Tom

---

📚Stanley Kubrick was downright cruel to Shelley Duvall when directing *The Shining*, nothing she could do was right or good enough, and he let her know in no uncertain terms. It wasn't until later that Duvall realized Kubrick was making her tense, angry, frightened and reactive, because that's what they needed to get for the character on film.

Brennan's wife, so that was a possibility. But many began speculating that her obsession with The Hanso Foundation was because she was related to Alvar Hanso. Maybe some *Lost* fans had just seen *The Empire Strikes Back* too many times, but this was a going theory, and in Rachel's final video, she finds Alvar and he claims to be her father. This almost has to be a joke. And shortly after the third season began, another online community theory was toyed with in "A Tale of Two Cities," and summarily debunked. Some people online speculated that Jack's wife Sarah was actually having an affair with his father, Christian Shephard. As icky and soap-opera-ish as that sounds, people were kicking the idea around. And the episode plays into this theory as Jack finds out Sarah had been calling his dad. But when Jack tracks his dad down, he finds Christian had actually been going to AA meetings, and was not after his wife.☑

For some time, one of the sure-shot theories was that the survivors were all in purgatory, and that the major characters needed to atone for something before they could die (like Boone and Shannon had). *The Third Policeman* seemed to point in this general direction, since the protagonist was already dead and didn't know it. *Bad Twin* also suggested purgatory connections: "Gary Troup" is an anagram for purgatory, and the detective Paul Artisan at one point compares a morgue to purgatory. Despite the writers denying this theory, the idea stuck for some time. So did the notion that the rest of the world had died, and the island's inhabitants are the only people left on the planet; Desmond suggests as much in the second season finale: "This is all

---

☑Incidentally, Jack attacking his father at the AA meeting may have been the end of Christian Shephard being on the wagon

there is left, this ocean, and this place here. We are stuck in a bloody snow globe. There's no outside world; there's no escape." (Season Two, "Live Together, Die Alone.") It wasn't until the final scene in that second season finale, when we finally saw a cut to two places outside the island where the action was occurring in simultaneous time with the action on the island – the arctic station and Penelope Widmore's bedroom. In the same May 25, 2006 New York Times article noted above, Damon Lindelof said, "It's time to actually blow up several theories of the show."

As Eko advises, "don't mistake coincidence with fate;" neither should viewers risk being like *Bad Twin*'s Detective Artisan: "He dreaded the possibility that he might have to rip apart all the logical connections he'd painstakingly put together, and be forced to reassemble them from scratch."⬤ Locke's crossword problem was similar – Gilgamesh should be the answer, it just makes his other answers wrong. In fact, Gary Troup's book is one of those large, overblown, overdetermined red herrings that seems to feed the best and the worst of the theory community. As literature, or even as a hard boiled detective story, the book is questionable at best. Many in the various online forums and in some of the podcasts considered the book a kind of challenge to *Lost* fans to see if they would actually put up with it. There were the mirror twins Cliff and Zander Widmore, the American side of the Widmore line, overly-suggestive names like Artisan, Moth, and a wise man named Weissman, literary references (especially Homeric and classical) pouring out of Weissman's mouth like a librarian starved for attention, an island community of "others," and a secret in Australia. Add to that a couple of cameo appearances by

⬤Gary Troup, *Bad Twin* (New York: Hyperion, 2006), p. 197.

The Hanso Foundation and Thomas Mittelwerk, and the fact that the book is dedicated to the flight attendant who was with the Tailies, Cindy Chandler, and you have yourself a smorgasbord of possible keys that leave you nearly... where you started. *Bad Twin* can be an entertaining diversion, seeing how much you've soaked up from *Lost* and how much of it you see elsewhere, but it's not necessarily as revealing or insightful as, say, the forums at www.thefuselage.com or www.4815162342.com.

And then there are those numbers again. They are everywhere. They seem almost mystical. They're not part of any known mathematical sequence (mathematician fans have checked). Where did they come from? They're first heard by Leonard Simms and Sam Toomey while working a naval listening station. And there may be something very real about what Leonard and Sam encountered – it comes from the Cold War era, and it's still occurring today. If you know how to work a shortwave radio and can find the right frequency, you can tune in anonymous broadcasts somewhere out in the ether that repeat strings of numbers, over and over and over again. No one is sure where this comes from, but there are an untold number of such recorded strings to be found and heard. One theory is they were codes used to pass messages to spies during the Cold War (and perhaps still today). The voices are usually female (but sometimes male, or even a child's), usually European; different recordings are in different languages, some have strange, repetitive melodic tones, and many recordings begin with NATO phonetic alphabet codes (like "Delta - Foxtrot – Delta").⇨ These recordings can be found online through The Conet Project: Recordings of Shortwave Numbers

⇨Which is where the band Wilco got the name for their album of the same name, *Yankee Hotel Foxtrot.*

Stations, which has also released a four-CD set of the recordings.★

The *Lost* numbers add up to 108, which is the number of minutes that pass between each code protocol cycle; 108 is also a sacred number in Buddhism. The 16th point on the Becker-Hagens planetary grid is overlapped by a vile vortex. The fateful flight was Oceanic 815. Season one covered the first 48 days on the island, and season two covered – you guessed it – 23. There were 48 original survivors from the middle section, and by the end of season one, there were 42. Hurley won the lottery playing the numbers, which he learned from fellow Santa Rosa patient Leonard Simms. The numbers appeared on the hatch door as a kind of serial number, and they appeared again in the name of the vaccine. They appeared on the blast door map, as did the squares of the first three numbers under square root symbols. There were 48 original survivors from the middle section (4 and 8). The safe deposit box Kate robbed was labeled #815. The Tailies met the Lostaways 4 days into the second season, the number 7418880 (the product of the numbers) appeared on a screen at the arctic station at the end of season two, and the numbers are all values in the Valenzetti Equation.⊠

Pretty soon the numbers appeared just about any and everywhere; in fact, with enough imagination, you could add and subtract and manipulate them in order to see them everywhere. There's a reason for this. No doubt the writers are including them intentionally, but do they mean as much as we think they do? Ever had the experience where you hear a strange word that

★See www.irdial.com/conet.htm. The recordings have also been collected in the Internet Archive at www.archive.org/details/ird059.

⊠According Douglas Adams's book *The Hitchhiker's Guide to the Galaxy*, the answer to life, the universe and everything is also 42.

you normally don't encounter, and then you hear it twice more in the same week? You might come across a song someplace that you hadn't heard in years, but then you hear it at the grocery store and on the radio and in a commercial. Or maybe you email an old friend and mention another old friend in the message, and as you're sending the message that other old friend is sending you a message. Here's a test: In recent years, journalists have taken to using the term "toney" when they want to find a new adjective for "elite" or "swank." A restaurant is the toniest restaurant on the east side, a few square blocks are the toney neighborhood in town, and reporters will be vulturing outside the tonier Academy Awards parties to get reviews. Tony is the guy who sat next to you in geography or fixed your transmission; toney's not an adjective, at least not a commonly used one. But if you come across something and for whatever reason you pay extra attention to it, you just may start to see it with greater frequency, whether it's coincidence or fate.↗

In severe cases, like with conspiracy theories, a person can run the risk of seeing the trigger for their paranoia absolutely everywhere: in the dollar bill, in architecture, in movies and in advertising. Lately in the United States it's all about illegal immigrants and terrorists, and as the 2006 midterm elections approached, those two groups started to become confused. More on this in the following section but suffice it to say that Americans' unchecked distress over terrorism is manifesting in normally level-headed citizens seeing terrorists everywhere.

↗I recently had the experience of coming across no less than five .38 Special songs while channel surfing the radio on the way from my home to Washington D.C.; it was an hour and a half drive ("Caught Up In You" three times and "Hold On Loosely" twice). This may say more about bad radio management than anything else, but for the next month .38 Special seemed to be staging their comeback tour.

Again, we can look to *Bad Twin* and the detective's professor friend Manny Weissman for a nugget that tells us less about the narrative than it does about how we experience the narrative:

> You're hurtling toward the solution – and you realize you've still got half the book to go. You think, wait a second, this can't be. Turns out that, halfway through the book, the thing is solved with airtight reasoning – but the solution just happens to be wrong. You see? The clues are all in place. The logic is fine. The deductions are sound – they just don't happen to match reality. Turns out there are *other* inferences, other deductions that are equally correct. So the second half of the book *undoes* the first half, puts the pieces back together, and solves the crime even more brilliantly. It's a masterpiece. (p. 130)◀

But there's one example of this kind of finding-too-much-all-over that is too cool to be ignored, and it has to do with what the island actually is. Many are kicking around the Atlantis idea; the problem is that Atlantis is supposed to be in the Atlantic, and our island is almost certainly in the South Pacific. Enter Lemuria: Lemuria, sometimes called Mu, is the Pacific version of Atlantis, and possibly older. Lemuria was posited by seers like Madame Blavatsky in the late 19th century and Edgar Cayce in the early 20th, but it was also believed to have existed by many different peoples along the Indian and southern Pacific Oceans, as well as by some Tamil people of southern India and Sri Lanka. And the discovery of the underwater temples off Japan at Yonaguni proves that there was once some civilization there before the waters were too high. Geologist Philip Sclater first called this proposed lost continent "Lemuria" when he was trying to explain why lemurs are only found on Madagascar, but their fossils are found up through China and Pakistan; his notion was that a land mass must have sunk, and with it the fossil record. Fair enough, but what could be done with this theory? Enter ASCII code: if you hold down the alt key while entering a string of numbers in Microsoft Windows notepad – and you have to use the actual numerical keypad, no laptop numbers allowed – enter 4 8 15 16 23 42 then release the alt key, you get "μ," which is the Greek symbol for Mu (a micron). This seemed too obscure to be coincidence. And it gets better: On the Hanso Careers website, there was a hidden anagram code in the letters of the descriptions. In each description, a few letters appeared a little grayer than the rest. (If you checked the source code of the page, they were indeed lightened.) Those letters, **n s l u t m i e m a y** and **a**, are an anagram for *asylum inmate*, which is a password for part of *The Lost Experience*. However, the letters also unscramble to spell glyphs explains that they described coming from the lost continent of Mu. The Mayan sacred calendars, the Tzolk'in and Haab', also predicted the end of humanity at the end of the current Long Count (December, 2012), just as the Valenzetti Equation was supposed to do.

So Mu was being confirmed all over the place. And it gets better: As noted above, the narrative is structured like a Möbius strip, where the audience believes it was on one side and the characters were on the other side of the narrative, but as we followed it along, we found we were all on the same side. Mu is a cornerstone in the Möbius equation which yields the Möbius strip – μ(*n*). Mu is furthermore the denotation for the muon, a subatomic fundamental particle used in quantum mechanics. At the Brookhaven National Laboratory, an interesting experiment with muons has been ongoing, the Muon g-2 Experiment. At one point, physicists thought that a vacuum was devoid of matter. Then the new quantum mechanics, superstring theories, supersymmetry, and other theories came along and suggested that a vacuum may in fact hold a sea of virtual particles that blink in and out of existence in our dimension. Brookhaven's experiment shot muon particles through a strong magnetic field inside a round vacuum chamber and watched their spin; they wobbled in a manner that's inconsistent with what's called the Standard Model, meaning that something was disrupting or otherwise affecting their wobble. That would suggest they weren't alone in that vacuum, and that virtual particles and supersymmetric counterparts quite possibly existed, and if so, we were all living alongside an invisible world made up of supersymmetric particles.❖

An invisible counterpart to our world made up of supersymmetric particles, the whole thing being based on Mu, the island not being able to be seen nor escaped and seeming to exist outside of our time and space – it all seemed too perfect. Because it was. The ASCII trick was a fluke; it worked with just 15162342, and even that much was a complete coincidence. The numbers, like many of the other clues in the show, were overdetermined and became everything and nothing – they're only what *we* make of them. The Mu thing was an amazing coincidence, though, and it took a dedicated participant right down the rabbit hole of what *Lost* could offer. The writers,

---

❖For a relatively clear breakdown of this experiment, see James Glanz, "Studies Suggest Unknown Form of Matter Exists," *New York Times*, July 31, 2002: A12.

producers and actors have created something that they can basically wind up and let go, and we'll do the rest. It's proof positive that *Lost* is a show that can grab the imagination, turn people to literature, scientific and esoteric research, and engage them in a broader dialog exercising the same critical faculties that television is often blamed for shutting down.

LIVING LOST

TRIANGULATING THE SIGNAL

...a good metaphor implies an intuitive perception of the similarity in dissimilarities.
-*Aristotle*❖

Sayid gave me this so he can triangulate the distress signal we heard — find the source.
-*Kate*✶

❖Aristotle, *Poetics*, trans. Ingram Bywater (New York: The Modern Library, 1984), 255.
✶Season One, "Walkabout."

It started with a plane crash.

The survivors collected themselves after the disaster, only to find they were under some kind of attack. Who was attacking them? They couldn't be seen, and appeared to be some strange beasts. Members of the group began to accuse each other of causing the disaster, but these accusations were based on half-truths, partial information and prejudicial assumptions. They began collecting themselves, but soon found that not everyone in the group could be trusted – some lied, some kept secrets, and some took advantage of the dire circumstances for personal gain. This lack of trust caused others in the group to overreact. The attacks by the beasts gave way to a larger threat: attacks by others who were believed to be part of the group. The survivors discovered they were under surveillance by these others without knowing it; there were lists of names, descriptions, backgrounds. There was also a threat of some exotic infectious disease, and although the group seemed generally healthy, some thought they had reason to be scared, and their fear spread amongst the group. Beasts, mistrust of those in the group, attacks from people who seemed to be part of the group but weren't, and the threat of disease all led to a destabilized state of being. All the while a secret was being exposed, but what to do with the secret became a point of contention within the group, since the secret also seemed to offer them protection and aid. Attempts to safeguard the group began to seem more damaging than the potential threats – the remedy was worse than the disease – and members of the group died in the ensuing confusion. Some found their religion in the experience, seeing the entire endeavor as an entry into some larger spiritual awakening, while others found such reactions to be unreasonable, even offensive. The others managed to sow discord among the group and capitalized on that discord, which led to the deaths of group members. The trust of some of the faithful was shaken when expected answers weren't forthcoming, while the faith of others was deepened. Those who lost faith attacked the secret, which nearly destroyed the group.

If this abstract of the *Lost* narrative sounds familiar, it might be because it could easily be read as an abstract of what has happened in the Western world since the attacks of September 11, 2001. Since the first attacks – and the subsequent attacks in Madrid, London, Bali, Jakarta, and all over the hot spots in the Middle East – we have been caught up in the psychodynamics of terror. Ordinary citizens have been largely helpless in dealing with those dynamics; we can only wait for news of more threats, victories, horrors, and other elements over which we have almost no control. Internally, political opponents accused each other of capitalizing on fear and capitulation with the enemy. These are the kind of dynamics that lead to the sense of estrangement that fuels *Lost*. In comparing the characters' experiences to the real world experiences of the audience, we can triangulate where the sense of estrangement comes from, and it's cultural and political.

Are the Others terrorists? Not exactly, not in the popular sense: Terrorists need to be dehumanized in the rhetoric used to describe them in order to reinforce their difference from us. This often comes in the form of turning them into animals and monsters.* The Others don't use the same tactics we've come to

---

*As if this needs examples, but anyway… The point is not to debate whether or not terrorist tactics are animalistic or monstrous, but to point out the use of the rhetoric: After the Madrid bombing in 2004, Christiane Amanpour reported on CNN, "What we can say is that people are really, really eager to know who did this. When we asked them would it make a difference if it was al Qaeda or ETA they said no. Whatever it is, whoever they are, they're

associate with terrorism, like beheadings and suicide bombings. The Others' drives are quite different from the drives of terrorists; the Others are trying to manipulate the Valenzetti Equation in order to keep humanity from extinguishing itself, while terrorism's goals range from political sovereignty to ethnic cleansing. And the Others seem too similar to Westerners; in fact they *are* Westerners, and even the (non-Western) Iraqi soldier seems familiar enough with his perfect English. But that's the point: the "threat" has begun to look increasingly, even uncomfortably, familiar to us. At the 2005 Hawaii International Film Festival director Jack Bender claimed that *Lost* was the right show at the right time because it "speaks to those issues" that we're dealing with in a post-9/11 world, "which means it's right on the pulse of people's concerns and desires." Some of those concerns have to do with the people

just monsters and animals, the people that did this to us, but we need to know who it was and why." (Transcript, "CNN Newsnight with Aaron Brown," CNN, March 12, 2004.) In a May 10, 2006 blog post, a conservative Washington, D.C. columnist responded to a report of Indonesian terrorists beheading Christian students with one word: "Animals" (michellemalkin.com/index.htm). In the responses to liberal columnist David Corn's online article about Senator Dick Durbin condemning torture at Guantanamo Bay, one person wrote, "We are fighting this war against a bunch of animals that will kill as many of us as they possibly can," and another responded, "You don't get it. Yes, terrorists are monsters, but how does that justify us stooping to their level?" (David Corn, "An Apology *for* Durbin? But Don't Wait for Rove," The Huffington Post, June 24, 2005 [www.huffin gtonpost.com/david-corn/an-apology-for-dur_b_3148.html].) In the June 8, 2006 ABC News blog article on Abu Musab al-Zaraqawi's death, one respondent wrote, "Terrorists are warped, rabid animals - with apologies to the SPCA - that need killing to protect the rest of society." (Brian Ross, "No Thought Given to Taking Zarqawi Alive," ABC News: The Blotter, June 8,2006 [blogs.abcnews.com/theblotter/2006/06/no_thought_give.html].) And in President George W. Bush's January, 2002 State of the Union address (the famous "Axis of Evil" speech), he referred to terrorists as "parasites." The rhetoric goes both ways, of course: writer Martin Amis wrote of how Sayyid Qutb, the founder of the Islamist group the Muslim Brotherhood, called Americans "arrogant animals" who were "unworthy of life." Amis's suggestion in his article was that Qutb's point of view had become the dominant one in Islam, which is quite arguable, but serves to set up a dynamic where the accuser (Qutb, Islamists, and according to Amis, all of Islam) is worthy of similar denigration. (Martin Amis, "The Age of Horrorism," *The Observer,* September 10, 2006. Review.)

we find ourselves living and working amongst. As noted earlier, just such concerns were stoked by programs like Operation TIPS, a Justice Department program set up so citizens could report the "suspicious activity" of their neighbors.□ Writer/ producer J.J. Abrams put it this way to *The Guardian*: "OK, I'd say the show raises questions we all have – especially in the current climate – about who that person is that's sitting next to you on the plane that you wouldn't think twice about but who suddenly has your life in their hands. On the surface it's how do you survive on a desert island, but I think the show's about a lot more than that."✚

We know the writers and producers are watching the online audience and responding to them in the narrative, and they've been paying attention to current events as well – Ben even tells Jack that the Red Sox won the World Series,◁ and that Bush was re-elected President in November, 2004. (Season Three, "The Glass Ballerina.) A "who's who" allegory correlating the *Lost* characters with the real-world players defeats the purpose; the *Lost* narrative is more complex than such a literal approach, and there are no direct one-to-one correspondences. The Others may *seem* like the logical corollaries for terrorists, but as seen above, the beasts on the island fit this cultural category a little better. The survivors may *seem* to be a stand-in for an audience living in an age of war and terrorism, but their circumstances are far more

---

□Editorial, "What is Operation TIPS?" *The Washington Post*, July 14, 2002: B06.

✚Tony Horkins, "Survival of the Fittest," *The Guardian*, Aug. 6, 2005: The Guide, 4.

◁The reference to the Red Sox has extra meaning for Jack: It recalls Christian Shephard's habit of saying, "And that's why the Red Sox will never win the World Series." Christian uses this phrase when he encounters Sawyer in Australia; when Jack says the same thing on the island, Sawyer recognizes the statement and makes the connection between Jack and the alcoholic man he left at the bar.

immediate and intertwined than the general audience's.▲ Furthermore, the writers don't necessarily need to think allegorically for events on the island to share characteristics with the audience's own real-life circumstances. Any cultural work is, by definition, informed by its historical context; neither a creator nor an audience can just turn off contemporary consciousness when dealing with a work. And unless you were actually near the World Trade Center, the Pentagon, or more recently on the London Underground or on a certain Madrid train, your experience of what being terrorized in the Western world means has already been mediated by at least two degrees: reporter and medium (be it radio, electronic, television, or print). The *Lost* audience is following the narrative the same way we witnessed the events of 9/11 – on TV, with repeated viewings, and more in-depth analysis later in the press and on the Internet.

An important aspect of the *Lost* narrative is the partial and misleading information the survivors have to work with; they don't know enough about each other, the hatch, the Others, or the purpose of the island to fully trust their assumptions. This fractional understanding is refracted through *The Lost Experience*, where the audience is consciously led down blind alleys and given partial clues that frustrate any transparent understanding. And the management of this misinformation is all handled, Oz-like, behind the scenes by people who are literally scripting and directing the lives of others. The difference between this and the audience's everyday experience, as noted above, is that *Lost* gives up some truth about itself at times, keeping the audience mystified by hanging on. In a way, the puzzling manner of the *Lost* narrative

▲Perhaps the redshirts on the island are more representative of the general audience; if you're not sure what a redshirt is, ask the nearest Trekkie.

can be seen as a kind of model of our own generally puzzled experience with the real or phantom threats in the War on Terror(ism). But the quality of our understanding of any possible threat is in direct proportion to the quality of information we get from media and officials, and it's hard for us to continue to operate on vague information without becoming numb and turning away when the truth of the information is constantly in question.

If the *Lost* narrative can be seen as a model of our own puzzled experience with the information received during wartime, the way *Lost* manages information in a way to frustrate understanding also has its cognates in the real world. Consider the February 7, 2003 terrorist alert. Attorney General John Ashcroft and Homeland Security Director Tom Ridge raised our dandy color-coded terror alert scale on that day to Orange Alert, "High Risk of Terrorist Attack," the second highest level. This was the first time it had been done since the 9/11 anniversary in 2002 (which was the first Orange Alert).* Why the alert? We weren't exactly told. The corresponding 9-page, 3600+ word press release remains on the White House web site, and it's just as confusing today as it was in 2003.✹ Ridge claimed that near the end of the Hajj,✣ Al Qaeda might attack either in the U.S. or abroad; Ashcroft rejoined that Al Qaeda was planning to attack apartment buildings, hotels and other soft targets (such as schools – going after the children, like the Others). They might use a chemical, biological, or radiological weapon. They may attack economic targets, transportation systems, or something symbolic. "This one's

---

*.The level has never gone below yellow (elevated) since its inception in the continental U.S.; it remained at blue (guarded) in Hawaii during February, 2003. ("Hawaii Stays at General Risk for Terrorism," *Honolulu Star Bulletin*, February 8, 2003.)

✹www.whitehouse.gov/news/releases/2003/02/20030207-6.html

✣A Muslim religious pilgrimage to Mecca, which in 2003 ended in mid-February.

for real," claimed GlobalOptions crisis management chair Neil Livingstone on the *USA Today* front page. "Al Qaeda's been licking its wounds for a long time now, and they want to hit us where we live."❂ But, at the same time they presented the American public with a lengthy and non-specific list of threats, they told us not to panic. "We are not recommending that events be canceled or travel or other plans be changed." Sure: anything could happen any place any time, but don't change your plans. Just do everything exactly as you would have before, but you might want to work out an emergency contact plan with your family.△

There was just one problem with that threat – it was bunk. One week later, on February 14, ABC News reported that the intelligence Ashcroft and Ridge used to jack up the fear had been fabricated.✳ The CIA informant who relayed the information did not pass the FBI's lie detector test, and was found to be lying. When asked why the informant wasn't vetted before the terror alert was raised, ABC's Brian Ross said that the informant's report seemed to coincide with other information, and "they just believed it." What's more, Ridge announced that although the terror alert would someday be lowered, for the time being, it would remain at orange, even though the threat was false.✫ So we'd just be at the second-highest terror color until ... we weren't.

But such management of (mis)information went far beyond press briefings. Shortly before James Risen and Eric Lichtblau of *The New York Times* revealed in a December, 2005 article that the

❂Mimi Hall and Jack Kelly, "Terror Threat is 'Significant,'" USA Today, Feb. 11, 2003: 1A.

△This was also around the time Tom Ridge was telling people to seal themselves into their homes with plastic sheets and duct tape.

✳Brian Ross, "Good Morning America," *ABC News*, Feb. 14, 2003.

✫Ronald Powers, "Ridge: Terror Alert Likely to be Lowered," *Associated Press*, Feb. 16, 2003. Note the title of the article; the headline suggests the terror alert was to be lowered, while the article stated the alert would stay at orange.

administration had secretly authorized the NSA to spy on U.S. citizens,* the President himself spoke with executive editor Bill Keller and publisher Arthur Sulzberger, requesting the story not be run.○ In fact, the story revealed that the *Times* sat on the story for over a year; the story was vetted and prepared for publication before the November, 2004 presidential election, but was withheld for over a year in discussions that "included talks with the Bush administration."❏ In other words, the public's experience of the war was being managed through the prior management of the public's media. One might think of Locke's assertion to Eko when he tried to destroy the computer: "We're only puppets – puppets on strings." (Season Two, "Live Together, Die Alone.")

Such media management jumped a lane into entertainment media when ABC ran its 2006 miniseries *The Path to 9/11.*⊗ The miniseries purported to lay out the history of U.S. policies toward terrorism from the 1990s up to 9/11, but included fabricated scenes that changed what's already on the public record. Such scenes directly contradicted findings of *The 9/11 Commission Report* about who had authorized which CIA actions, and when and where forces were located in Afghanistan,* inaccurately depicted former Secretary of State Madeleine Albright and

*James Risen and Eric Lichtblau, "Bush Lets U.S. Spy on Callers Without Courts," *The New York Times*, December 16, 2005: 1.

○Jonathan Alter, "Bush's Snoopgate," *Newsweek* web exclusive, December 19, 2005 (www.msnbc.msn.com/id/10536559/site/newsweek/).

❏Byron Calame, "Behind the Eavesdropping Story, a Loud Silence," *The New York Times*, January 1, 1006: Section 4, p. 8; Byron Calame, "Eavesdropping and the Election: A Question of Timing," *The New York Times*, August 13, 2006: Section 4, p. 10.

⊗Tom Shales, "ABC's Twisted 'Path to 9/11,'" *The Washington Post*, September 9, 2001: C01.

*One 9/11 Commission member, Jamie S. Gorelick, wrote to ABC's Bob Iger, "I do have a problem if you make claims that the program is based upon the findings of the 9/11 Commission Report when the actors, scenes and statements in the series are not found in - and, indeed, are contradicted by - our findings." (Howard Kurtz, "ABC to Alter Show on Pre-9/11 Run-Up," *The Washington Post*, September 8, 2006: A2.)

National Security Advisor Sandy Berger contradicting Clinton-era policies to pursue Al Qaeda,❉ and recast recent history by excising the month-long vacation the President took after receiving an August 6, 2001 Presidential Daily Briefing from National Security Advisor Condoleezza Rice entitled "Bin Laden Determined to Strike in US," a document whichannounced in its first paragraph that Bin Laden's followers "would follow the example of World Trade Center bomber Ramzi Yousef."✧ Again the public's media (this time entertainment as opposed to news) was being pre-managed and used to alter perception of recent history. In fact, ABC partnered with Scholastic, Inc. to produce lesson plans about the miniseries that were sent to 25,000 high school teachers around the nation; after the show's criticism arose, Scholastic, Inc. eventually removed the lesson plans from their website, but the original aim was to teach *The Path to 9/11* to high school students as if it were verified history.★ Comedian Stephen Colbert calls this *truthiness* – if it *feels* true, then it somehow *becomes* truth, facts, evidence and logic be damned. Indeed, the miniseries was roundly criticized for these problems before airing. But the example serves to remind us that the narrative we have of the War on Terror(ism) is one that is being manipulated and altered before our eyes, and then presented to us as fact – which is just what *The Lost Experience* did when it injected fiction into reality with its Hanso Foundation commercials, websites and the publication of *Bad Twin.*

❉Shales, "ABC's Twisted Path to 9/11."

✧Transcript of August 1, 2001 Presidential Daily Briefing, "Bin Laden Determined to Strike in U.S.," CNN.com, April 10, 2004 (www.cnn.com/2004/ALLPOLITICS /04/10/august6.memo/).

★Kurtz, "ABC to Alter Show on Pre-9/11 Run-Up."

It's also what *Lost* accomplishes with the figure of Walt, who can unconsciously make elements of his imagination appear in reality. Walt's ability is presented as innocuous enough at this point, but potentially powerful or dangerous. But it also reflects something more dangerous in our current political culture. Ron Suskind was one of the few reporters outside of the Fox News staff that had ready access to the White House between 2000-2004 (at least he did for a while). In his 2004 article "Without a Doubt,"□ Suskind dug into the idea of faith-based policymaking – not faith in some god, but faith in policy despite countervailing facts. Suskind reports that in the summer of 2002, he was dressed down by a senior White House adviser after writing a critical article about former communications director Karen Hughes. As Suskind put it:

> The aide said that guys like me were "in what we call the reality-based community," which he defined as people who "believe that solutions emerge from your judicious study of discernible reality." I nodded and murmured something about enlightenment principles and empiricism. He cut me off. "That's not the way the world really works anymore," he continued. "We're an empire now, and when we act, we create our own reality. And while you're studying that reality – judiciously, as you will – we'll act again, creating other new realities, which you can study too, and that's how things will sort out. We're history's actors ... and you, all of you, will be left to just study what we do.

□ *The New York Times Magazine*, October 17, 2004: 44. List," *The Guardian*, July 13, 2006: 23.

Creating their own reality, willing things into existence and acting on them – this is what Walt does, only Walt does it unconsciously, not with forethought and planning. Fiction being manipulated into fact makes for fantastic television, but questionable public policy; facts are stubborn things, and don't just appear, change or disappear on impulse alone. For the *Lost* narrative, reality consistently asserts itself over willing something into being. The Dharma Initiative is precisely located in the reality-based community, gathering evidence to try to alter the facts of the Valenzetti Equation, but the Others soon look for a way to get Walt off their hands because his presence interferes with their projects. Locke believes he's found a spiritual purpose on the island, until the cold reality of the hatch rips his willed world apart. And the facts of the war in Iraq – no weapons of mass destruction found, troops not greeted as liberators, a prolonged engagement with no real post-invasion plan to successfully sustain a military presence – have all trumped the willed realities that the war was a complete success before it ever began. Reality-based communities don't seem to mix well with faith-based communities.

So how are ordinary people going on about their daily business supposed to respond to such twisted info and non/threats? The evidence from such events as the February 7, 2003 terrorist alert, the NSA civilian spying program, and the altered history presented in *The Path to 9/11* was vague and broad enough to invite all kinds of horrid scenarios, yet we are to live our lives as normal. In a very real way, it's like that old psych-out game, *don't think of a white bear.* As soon as you're told not to think about something, and then you stop trying *not* to think about it, that thing will flood your thoughts.* (Now we're back to white bears; maybe *Lost's* writers chose polar bears for a reason.) Walking around with the thought in your subconscious that you may be attacked at any given moment at an airport, a bank, on the road, at school, at your apartment, or even if you're traveling abroad, starts to play hell with your attitude; you either become paranoid or numb, or struggle for some space between those poles. We were effectively living with the fear that the Others were close and something terrible lurked nearby to get us.

That kind of distress is probably more vivid for people living in target areas, like New York City, Washington, D.C., and other Eastern Seaboard megalopolis cities, the Upper Midwestern industrial hulks like Chicago, Milwaukee, and Detroit, and Hollywood and Silicone Valley to the west. Yet more homeland security money was being spent per capita in places like Indiana, Wyoming and South Dakota than in places that have been attacked or where attacks have at least been attempted, New York or California. As of 2006, New York received $2.78 a person, while Wyoming got a whopping $14.83.※ In July, 2006, Indiana beat out every other state, claiming the longest list of terror targets; among the 8,591 targets identified by the Department of Homeland Security are a petting zoo, a flea market, a popcorn factory, and a roller rink.* It took *The Daily Show*

---

*Samuel Carter III, David Schneider, David Wegner and Teri White, "Paradoxical Effects of Thought Suppression," *Journal of Personality and Social Psychology*, 53.1 (1987): 5-13.

※Eric Lipton, "Security Cuts for New York and Washington," *New York Times*, June 1, 2006: A1. Of course, New York and California are famous for being Democratic "blue states," while Wyoming is not only a Republican "red state," it's the home of Vice President Dick Cheney.

*Eric Lipton, "Come One, Come All, Join the Terror Target List," *New York Times*, July 11, 2006: A1; Oliver Burkeman, "Petting Zoo and Flea Market Make Nonsense of US Terror Target to present this with just the right touch of absurdity, when Dan Bakkedahl went to some of the sites and asked how many terrorist attacks they'd sustained that month.[●] Homeland Security claimed Indiana legitimately had 3,000 more targets than New York, and more than twice as many as California. Indianans can't even explain this one. A small town of 15,000 people in Wisconsin received $8,000 in Homeland Security funds for – and you couldn't make this up – clown and puppet shows, to be put on by the fire department.[❀] Des Moines got $69,000 (again, for clown and puppet shows).[✰]

When you're conditioned to stay afraid, when outlets for proactive measures are few to none and your government is spending security funds on puppet shows and petting zoos, you've gone through the looking glass. But there is a payoff: it does the job of sustaining fear. Even people living in very low-risk areas are being sent the message that they're really in more danger than they think they should be in. And as long as the wars continue, there's no real arc to this distress, no projected ending in sight; it just persists. This kind of unbounded distress is mirrored in the Lostaways' fear of the Others and their smoky security system (as Rousseau calls it),[♦] as well as in the way the Tailies and the Lostaways differently perceived the threat.

Such amorphous distress, when it lacks definition, limit and contour, can easily twist into other kinds of fear-based reactionary behavior. It's the imagination at work; as Hurley says, "It's,

[●]Dan Bakkedahl, "War on Terra Haute," *The Daily Show*, Comedy Central, August 10, 2006.
[❀]Onalaska, Wisconsin.
[✰]Audrey Hudson, "Homeland Security Grants Spent on Clowns and Gyms," *Washington Times*, April 21, 2006: A04.
[♦]"Its purpose is that of any security system - to protect something." (Season One, "Exodus.")

like, transference." (Season Two, "What Kate Did.") Take immigration. Isn't it really a case of the "others" coming over to our side of the island? Aside from the wars and the fat price of gas, illegal Mexican immigration became the bogey man of many a southwestern U.S. politician and their Minute Men picket-fence protectors, and the increasing focus of Labor Day and May Day marches in California and the heavily industrialized areas of the Northeast and Midwest. The government got on top of the dialogue with House bill 4437 (The Border Protection, Anti-Terrorism and Illegal Immigration Control Act of 2005), which declared illegal immigrants, and anyone who helped them, to be felons. Thus the "other" was criminalized, and the criminal in Western culture is always a safe whipping boy and figure of fear.

Some politicians and media politicos have made the most of the cosmic alignment of immigration and terrorism fears; in his 2006 re-election bid, Arizona incumbent Republican Rep. J.D. Hayworth told constituents:

> The director of the FBI [Robert Mueller] testified in front of a congressional subcommittee that we are now apprehending illegals from nation states exporting Islamo-fascism, and among those picked up are several who change their names to Hispanic aliases, and who attempt to acquire a working knowledge of Spanish so to blend in with the masses coming northward from Mexico.*

*Mike Pesca, "Fiery Rep. Hayworth in Hot Arizona Race," *Day to Day*, National Public Radio, Aug. 15, 2006.

This is the same Rep. Hayworth who voted no on H.R. 4437, which passed despite his efforts. If the bill hadn't passed, there would have been a steadier stream of immigrants for him to demonize. In fact Mueller testified that only one person had made it across the border, not several, and he didn't use the term Islamo-fascism.❖ Stretching the facts has helped spread the fear into the blogosphere that swaths of criminal/immigrant/terrorist /others are flooding over our borders (as if some immigrant levees broke), and once it's in print, truthiness takes over. But it's not the reality of the situation that's important, it's feeding the overall sense of distress. By capitalizing on that distress and conflating terrorism with immigration, we see fiction entering reality as if terrorism were another alternate reality game. So goes unchecked fear, and like the *Lost* narrative, fiction and reality openly bleed across each other's boundaries.

This general sense of unchecked fear could be reined in were some sort of framework put to the fear. For example, our popular media could make an effort to distinguish between Persians, Arabs, and Kurds, terrorists and insurgents, political terrorism and fundamentalist extremism. Or maybe if we saw Homeland Security actively protecting ports instead of Midwestern petting zoos; a General Accounting Office report of March, 2006 showed that the Customs and Border Protection's Automated Targeting System, a system designed to predict and

---

❖The case Mueller discussed is about Mahmoud Youssef Kourani; he bought his way across the border in 2001 by hiding in the trunk of a car, was arrested in Dearborn, Michigan in 2003 and charged with giving material support to Hezbollah. See David Goodman, "Federal Judge Sentences Lebanese Man to 4.5 Years for Aiding Hezbollah," Associated Press, June 15, 2005; Testimony of Robert S. Mueller, III, Director of Federal Bureau of Investigation Before the Senate Committee on Intelligence of the United Sates Senate, February 16, 2005(www.fbi.gov/congress/congress05/mueller021605.htm)

target incoming port containers for inspection by Homeland Security, "has not yet put key controls in place to provide reasonable assurance that ATS is effective at targeting oceangoing cargo containers with the highest risk of containing smuggled weapons of mass destruction."✿ Maybe we would feel better if we saw more sincere efforts to end the wars we're embroiled in, rather than half-measures which prolong and engender conflict. Never mind all that; what's important is this overwhelming, amorphous sense of unchecked distress. That distress is what *Lost* taps into.

Again, it's not as if *Lost*'s writers and producers actively set out to create some sort of allegory of the times. When you're steeped in the culture (as an artist or a consumer), some kind of reaction to events and circumstances will exercise itself through a work, whether directly, obliquely, or by actively ignoring those circumstances. Producer Jean Higgins noted at the 2005 Hawaii International Film Festival that the number one show at the height of the Vietnam War was *Laugh-In*, an escapist comedy show that had next to nothing to do with the war (but may have been so popular because it provided some release in an era when non-embedded journalists reported from the front lines on the 6 o'clock news, bringing the war "into our living rooms" for the first time). *Lost* doesn't take our current circumstances head-on like *24* or *Rescue Me* or any of the other law and protection shows that have sprung up with a September 11th backdrop.⊗ But this makes

---

✿Richard M. Stana, "Cargo Container Inspections: Preliminary Observations on the Status of Efforts to Improve the Automated Targeting System," United Stated Government Accountability Office, March 30, 2006 (www.gao.gov/new.items/d06591t.pdf).

⊗Albeit there is an Iraqi Republican Guard communications officer on the island, and references to terrorism and the Patriot Act; but after the first two seasons, for the survivors, it's still 2004.

sense; if we are stuck in a state of unconscious distress because we don't have any clear grasp on what it is we're supposed to be afraid of, we can't really confront that distress directly because we just don't know enough about it.

But we know the *sense* of it. It's the reason the weekly scare-dates✚ about bird flu gave rise to popular hysteria until they culminated in a made-for-TV movie that suggested shaking hands could kill you. We haven't yet seen any bird flu on this continent, and we know you almost have to eat a sick bird or share your living quarters with a sick bird to catch it, but that's not the general sense being portrayed to us.◁ The sense is that there are phantom diseases that could twist us into quivering husks of people, and we have no idea if a vaccine will be available, let alone if it will work. This sense is quite likely fueled by the real and exaggerated fears of disease that stem from AIDS. This specter of disease is of course seen in the way Claire, Rousseau, Desmond, and the Others fear the suggestion of infection on the island; yet it's just that, a suggestion. As of the end of season two, no one seems to have been infected. Does the vaccine in the hatch and the Staff station even do anything? How would they or we know? If not, why was Ethan so dead set on kidnapping Claire to inoculate her unborn child? But finding out the truth about the vaccine is really secondary to understanding why that part of the

✚Scary updates.

◁Creutzfeldt-Jakob disease, a neurological disorder that develops in livestock whose feed contains ground bits of their own species' spine and brain, got similar treatment in the 1990's when a variant developed called bovine spongiform encephalopathy, or mad cow disease. The original idea was to give the livestock a protein boost, but it led to holes in the brain's nerves cells. The first cases were discovered in Britain in 1986, and hit a high water mark in the 1990's; The X-Files captured the fear in an episode called "Our Town" (1995), where a chicken factory was putting ground human remains in the chicken feed, leading to Creutzfeldt-Jakob disease in townspeople. Those who caught it had seizures and acted erratically from induced dementia.

narrative grabbed our attention. Our own distress about bird flu, anthrax, mad cow disease, super strains of AIDS, or what have you, is shifted into a related kind of stress that's played out in the narrative of the show. The narrative contained a representation of an unidentified infectious disease. This easily tapped into our own unconscious social fear of infectious diseases; we were hearing about them almost daily. And then the narrative responded to our connection by containing the emotions we associated with the threat of the disease in our own world. None of this has to operate at a conscious level, but by containing and giving shape and context to these forms of fear, the show provides a kind of release from our own stress. And in functioning this way, the show utilizes another form of mirror twinning, this time between the audience and the characters of the narrative, but on a less immediate, more unconscious (and, most importantly, a *safer*) level for the audience. While it's not likely that anyone in the audience was happy about the threat of disease on the island, it was nice to know that there might be an answer, even if we didn't know what it was yet. And even if Claire, Aaron, or Desmond were infected with a mysterious disease, at least it's one disease we don't have to worry about catching. As with the sense of terror(ism), the amorphous fear of strange diseases is enclosed in the mental frame of the narrative and the physical frame of the actual television, making it a kind of container for the audience's own fears.

By 2004, when *Lost* first aired, and especially during the same months when viewers were watching season two (October 2005 through May 2006), things were happening in the real-world news that called some previously-untouchable institutions into question. Oil companies reported record profit after record profit while consumers paid up to three times what they'd paid the year before for gasoline. (And the companies got tax cuts on top of these profits.) The oil companies were capitalizing on the raised value of a scarce resource at the general group's expense, and we had almost no choice but to continue to buy from them. The survivors don't have oil on the island, but they do still have medicine and guns, both of which they desperately need to survive. And, like us, they have someone who is hoarding those goods; Sawyer scavenged necessary items from the plane and bodies and used them – and the fear of their absence – as leve age over the other survivors. Even when he didn't have something, like Shannon's asthma medicine, he refused to let anyone know, thereby maintaining his power position as keeper of a scarce resource. (Season One, "Confidence Man.") And when he could, he took a necessary resource (the guns) and hoarded it for his own benefit. (Season Two, "The Long Con.") It's another example where a more democratic approach was trumped by selfish capitalism, supported through violence and fear. When ExxonMobile CEO Rex Tillerson was asked about price gouging on NBC – ExxonMobile reported a 300% gain in profits between 2002 and 2005 – he responded that "the profit we earn is what the market gives us."⇨ Couple this with the fact that political instability, and the fear of instability, drives prices erratically up,✳ and that we're embroiled in destabilizing oil states like Iraq and Iran and their adjacent regions, and we can see why that market gives so generously to oil companies charging so much for gasoline, and why the U.S. Congress

---

⇨Michael McAuliff, "No Remorse from Oil Exec: 'We're In the Biz to Make Money,'" *The Daily News (New York)*, May 4, 2006: 12.

✳Steven Mufson, "A Price Inflamed by Fear," *The Washington Post*, July 14, 2006: D01.

is interested in hearings on price gouging.⊐ Sawyers all around.

Around the time we in the audience met the Tailies and learned that Goodwin, an Other, had infiltrated the group, Sawyer and Charlie were busy turning on their own group for their own purposes. At this point, Ben was captured (perhaps on purpose) and began to work his way into Locke's head. These episodes aired in February and March of 2006, and more than at any point in the course of the show, questions were being raised on the island about who could be trusted, and how far individuals or groups of individuals would go to achieve their own goals at the expense of the group. At this same time, Americans learned that their lives and privacy had been infiltrated by their own National Security Agency (as noted above). The NSA had embarked on a wide program of surveillance collecting data on U.S. citizens, even though its mandate is strictly for gathering foreign intelligence. If you had friends or family abroad and contacted them, and it looked like their Internet or telephone communication might be deemed related to some network of terrorist activity,○ whole mechanized systems went into play that started to record your data and dump it into a massive government database without your ever knowing. In short, we were being watched and data was being collected. If the NSA had gone through the Federal Intelligence Surveillance Act, which the courts had set up in 1978 for just such purposes, the surveillance would have been legal, but the administration chose to ignore that proviso and effectively sidestepped both Congress and the courts.

○Which was loosely defined as Al Qaeda and its affiliates. This *could* mean that if a corn-fed farm kid from Kansas called a friend from college who attended a mosque, and that mosque once had an individual who attended a Taliban-run madrasah in northern Pakistan, that Kansas kid's information could end up in the database as a subject of interest.

So much for checks and balances. Just as the Others had been keeping tabs on the survivors, a surreptitious infiltrator literally had lists of us, and thanks to the Patriot Act of 2001, we had no way of knowing (and no right to know) if someone we knew was under investigation or being detained. It seems like rule more in the mode of Hobbes, rather than Locke, Rousseau or Hume.

This brings us back to the Others. We've encountered them on several occasions, but we still don't know who they are or just what drives them. They may have completely noble goals (as Ben, Ethan, Nathan, and Tom have all stated). They may be there to work out ways of manipulating the Valenzetti Equation. Or their efforts could just as easily be ruthlessly pragmatic and self-interested. At the 2006 San Diego International Comic Con, Carlton Cuse responded to a question about the Others' use of the term *namaste*; it's a traditional Buddhist and Hindu salutation that acknowledges the divinity within another person, but the Others appeared to be the bad guys. Cuse responded that the Dharma Initiative initially *had* good motives; they wanted to better society and make it safer without adding to the military industrial complex, but we don't know enough about them yet to know just what they believe now. What we're left with, though, is a group that purports to project positive goals and may in fact have had positive intentions at one point, but from our point of view (and from the standpoint of the survivors), they appeared as everything from menacing to dangerously aggressive. Again, we're dealing with a pattern that echoes the same psychodynamics at play in our own contemporary national and internationalcircumstances. No person or group sees itself as *bad*; it's not unusual, however, for that same group to identify another entity that contradicts its own goals as bad, and begin working to counter the perceived efforts of that person or group, perhaps by attacking them, for the good of the original group. The attacked entity then has real reason to feel negatively toward the attacking group. This can lead into a "You started it!" "No you started it!" situation, but as Cuse suggested, we need to get more information before we make our decision about the Others (and the survivors, for that matter). The methods of those with good intentions can often seem as destructive as the problem they attempt to solve – the remedy can be worse than the disease. Aspartame is supposed to cut out the nasty effects of too much sugar without losing the flavor, except it apparently can cause brain lesions and lymphoma.⊗ The Inquisition attempted to create a peaceful Christian world by torturing people into conversion. Chemotherapy can be as damaging as the cancer it's used to destroy. The Iraq invasion was supposed to stop terrorism, but a National Intelligence Estimate leaked in September, 2006 claimed the war is a "primary recruitment vehicle for violent Islamic extremists" and their numbers are increasing faster than the U.S can reduce the threat.♦ Sam Donaldson gave a good example of the good intentions/problematic methods problem when asked in 2004 for a criticism of former President Ronald Reagan: "If you were down on your luck, Reagan would literally give you the shirt off his back, and then he'd sit down in his undershirt and he'd sign legislation throwing your kids off the school lunch program, maybe your parents off Social Security, and of course the Welfare

---

⊗Morando Soffritti, Fiorella Belpoggi, Davide Degli Esposti, Luca Lamertini, "Aspartame Induces Lymphomas and Leukemias in Rats," *European Journal of Oncology*, vol. 10.2, 2005: pp. 107-116.

♦Karen DeYoung, "Spy Agencies Say Iraq War Hurting U.S. Terror Fight," *The Washington Post*, September 24, 2006: A01.

Queen off of welfare."❈ Like Thomas Mittelwerk suggests in the Sri Lanka video, sometimes the perceived greater good (which is almost always subjective) necessitates harming others. Just try explaining that to those getting harmed.

We've seen the same kind of moral ambiguity at play with the Others, and in another mirror-twinned way we've seen it in our own recent history. At the most obvious level, plenty of people in the U.S. and around the world fervently and justifiably believe that the U.S. had no business invading Iraq, but there are others who continue to believe America was justified in attacking Iraq because of September 11th – even though Iraq was not involved in that attack. The confusion stemmed partly from the mixed information we received, again from our own officials; for instance, we couldn't get a straight answer on whether Iraq was involved with September 11th or not. In 2003, 69% of the public believed Iraq was involved in the attacks, despite the 9/11 commission's findings that Saddam Hussein saw Al Qaeda as an enemy and a threat to his power.✳ Why would people think this? It's called enthymatic argumentation – a sort of guilt-by-association rhetorical strategy. The idea is to put Iraq and 9/11 near each other in enough sentences, and the association gets made in the mind of the audience without ever having really been made. Except when they outright say it: Vice President Dick Cheney told Tim Russert on *Meet the Press* that it had been "pretty well confirmed" that 9/11 hijacker Mohammed Atta met with an Iraqi official in Prague, making the direct link between the Iraqi regime and the 9/11 attacks.❐ When asked by

❈Sam Donaldson, *Good Morning America*, ABC News, June 11, 2004.

✳Dana Milbank and Claudia Deane, "Hussein Link to 9/11 Lingers in Many Minds," The Washington Post, September 6, 2003; A01.

❐Tim Russert, interview with Vice President Dick Cheney, *Meet the Press*, NBC News, December 9, 2001.

Russert a year and a half later why 69% of the public thought there was a link between Iraq and 9/11, Cheney responded he didn't think it was surprising people made that connection, but that they just didn't know.♣ But when Cheney's claim on Atta was shown to be false, Cheney denied to CNBC reporter Gloria Borger that he ever said it.✩ If he wants to rewrite history, he might want to take down the transcript of the original Russert interview from the White House website.♦ We were also told that Iraq had weapons of mass destruction they could hand off to Al Qaeda; Secretary of Defense Donald Rumsfeld stated on *ABC This Week* in 2003, "We know where they are. They're in the area around Tikrit and Baghdad and east, west, south and north somewhat."⊠ Except, of course, they weren't there, and when the intelligence was published, it became clear that we never really knew what was claimed. When President Bush addressed soldiers at Fort Bragg, North Carolina on June 28, 2005, he enthymatically told them, "The war reached our shores on September 11, 2001," and that "Iraq is the latest battlefield in this war." September 11th was mentioned six times, but weapons of mass destruction were not.▽ Four months later, CBS News reported that marines at Parris Island, South Carolina claimed they were training to go to Iraq because of

♣Cheney reiterated in this interview that they had established a relationship between Iraq and Al Qaeda; Road Runner and Wile E. Coyote had a relationship too, but relationship doesn't necessarily mean cooperation. (Tim Russert, interview with Vice President Dick Cheney, *Meet the Press*, NBC News, September 14, 2003.)

✩Gloria Borger, interview with Vice President Dick Cheney, *Capital Report*, CNBC, June 17, 2004.

♦Let's hear it for freedom of information: www.whitehouse.gov/vicepresident/news-speeches/speeches/vp20011209.html.

⊠George Stephanopoulos, interviw with Secretary of Defense Donald Rumsfeld, *ABC This Week*, March 30, 2003.

▽President George W. Bush, "President Addresses Nation, Discusses Iraq, War on Terror," June 28, 2006 (www.whitehouse.gov/news/releases/2005/06/20050628-7.html).

"what they did to us on September 11th."> But in a moment of candor, President Bush was asked in an August, 2006 press briefing what Iraq had to do with 9/11; he responded, "Nothing, except for it's part of − and nobody has ever suggested in this administration that Saddam Hussein ordered the attack." What about the weapons of mass destruction? "Now, look, part of the reason we went into Iraq was − the main reason we went into Iraq at the time was we thought he had weapons of mass destruction. It turns out he didn't, but he had the capacity to make weapons of mass destruction," but of course even that capacity is in question.♦ So was Iraq involved in 9/11 or not, and if not, why would the public continue to know something that just isn't so? Maybe it comes from moments like Donald Rumsfeld in a May 7, 2006 Fox News special report called "Why He Fights." As he entered his office, he picked up a chunk of the plane that crashed into the Pentagon on 9/11, a piece he had mounted, and said that it was a "wonderful reminder to people of what happened." Why he fights? September 11th.* Where does he fight? Iraq. The cost of fighting? Priceless. Managing misinformation is a full time job.

But if Iraq is not the cause of the War on Terror(ism), there are some from the CIA and other government agencies who believe we sowed the seeds of blowback✦ when we built up and

▷Sharyn Alfonsi, "Volunteering for War," *CBS Evening News*, October 10, 2005.

♦President George W. Bush, press conference, August 21, 2006 (www.whitehouse.gov /news/releases/2006/08/20060821.html).

✳The wreckage is just wonderful.

✦A CIA term describing unintended consequences of secret operations; it's a shorthand way of saying something was set in motion because it seemed beneficial at the time, but turned out to be harmful. To use a non-CIA example, take DDT; it was thought to be useful when it killed malaria-spreading mosquitoes, but the blowback was it became a toxin that biomagnified up the food chain, becoming concentrated in large mammals like people. May 1, 2001 (abcnews.go.com).

funded the fundamentalist-extremist Mujahideen to fight the Soviet Union in Afghanistan during the 1980s.✪ The Mujahideen was a loosely-formed group of fighters assembled from Afghanistan and Pakistan, and funded and trained by the U.S. (just watch *Rambo III* to get an idea of how the U.S. thought of the Mujahideen back then). After the Soviets were driven out, the U.S. left, the Mujahideen had its own internal struggle, and the religious fundamentalists broke off, forming the Taliban in Afghanistan, the same group that harbored Osama Bin Laden. This is one illustration where the methods of those with good intentions (Americans fighting communism) yielded very destructive ends. But this example seems almost innocent when compared to one of Defense Secretary Donald Rumsfeld's programs. As noted above, in 2002, defense analyst William Arkin mentioned a program that Secretary Rumsfeld had initiated, the Proactive Preemptive Operations Group (P2OG). This black-ops group was established for "stimulating reactions" from terrorists, "prodding terrorist cells into action and exposing themselves to 'quick-response' attacks by US forces."❖ The program was not covered widely in the U.S., but *The Asia Times, The Hobart Mercury* (Australia), *The Herald* (Glasgow), *The Moscow Times,* and *The New Statesman* in Britain all published articles asking just how P2OG would be able to prod terrorist cells into action, and why a group that was outwardly in a war with terrorists try to stimulate terrorist attacks.★ The methods

---

✪Andrew Marshall, "Terror 'blowback' burns CIA," *The Independent* (London), Nov. 1, 1998: 17.

❖William Arkin, "The Secret War," *Los Angeles Times,* Oct. 27, 2002: M1. This program echoes the now-declassified Operation Northwoods of 1962, a black-ops group that was to stage an attack in Florida and make it look like the Cubans did it, then use that attack as a pretext for a Cuban invasion. The program was declassified in 1997, and was called off by President Kennedy. See David Ruppe, "U.S. Military Wanted to Provoke War with Cuba," ABC News, May 1, 2001 (http://abcnews.go.com).

of the group can belie its motives, just as with the Others. And it should be noted that *Lost* is aired all around the world, including places that receive news that may raise questions about the methods used in the War on Terror(ism). Such questions and ambiguity, and the lack of forthcoming information and answers in such circumstances, can make it easy for people to shut off their critical faculties.

But this may be part of why *Lost* grips so many imaginations; it sets up psychological circumstances which are mirror twins of circumstances we have been suffused in for five years. Like our own world, the show chooses to withhold information as it sees fit. But unlike our own real-lives, we are actually rewarded for questioning and seeking answers, and encouraged to continue doing so. In the contemporary political and social climate, journalists are threatened with jail for protecting their sources, and citizens who choose to speak against the war are vilified and labeled un-American.⊛ Having the opportunity to wonder and to question can charge up our critical faculties further; pushing our thinking, constantly asking questions, testing assumptions, and developing new theories of the narrative also exercises a critical ability that too

★David Isenberg, "'P2OG' Allows Pentagon to Fight Dirty," Asia Times Online, November 5, 2002 (www.atimes.com/atimes/Middle_East/DK05Ak02.html); Tim Thorne, "Facts Fail to Ease War Fears," *Hobart Mercury (Australia)*, February 26, 2003 (web.lexisnexis.com); Ian Bruce, "U.S. Anti-Terror Force Planned," *The Herald (Glasgow)*, November 15, 2002: 14; Chris Floyd, "Global Eye Into the Dark," *The Moscow Times*, November 1, 2002 (www.moscowtimes.ru/stories/2002/11/01/120.html); John Pilger, "John Pilger reveals the American plan; two years ago a project set up by the men who now surround George W. Bush said what America needed was 'a new Pearl Harbor.' Its published aims have come alarmingly true, writes John Pilger," *The New Statesman*, December 16, 2002: 13.

⊛Which, of course, happened with the Valerie Plame Affair; Deputy Secretary of State Richard Armitage outed Plame as a deep cover CIA agent working on weapons of mass destruction in Iran to conservative columnist Robert Novak, putting her life and her work in danger; White House Chief of Staff Karl Rove and Scooter Libby passed it on to a number of other reporters, but only Novak wrote the story. Many reporters were threatened with jail if they refused to give up their sources; Judith Miller of *The New York* often lies dormant (especially when watching television). And just as the real psychodynamics are reflected in the narrative, *Lost* has re-warped them in the alternate reality game *The Lost Experience*, taking reality into fiction and then pulling that fiction back out into reality. It's the Möbius effect; we think we're on the other side of the divide, but we've been on the same side all along – because, in fact, there *is* only one side. It also recalls the mirror twin idea entailed in the yin/yang symbol: a dark circle from yin is always part of the wave of yang, and a light circle of yang is always part of the wave of yin.

What's more, as we watch the show and see those psychodynamics played out on the screen, it's limited in its hour-long scope, its immediate narrative arc, and by the physical boundaries of the screen. As we watch and intuit the same psychodynamics of terrorism in the narrative, we know that those dynamics are occurring in a confined, limited space that will be done at a set time. Through the well-wrought mythology of the narrative, we are given the opportunity to experience the dynamics that usually have no bounds being played out in the limited physical space of our homes and controlled to an extent by the constrictions of the form. By inviting us to engage critically with the narrative and actually find answers, *Lost* has engaged its audience in a way that has transcended the immediate function of television as entertainment, and approached the social function of art.

It could even help us get a grip on a column of smoke.

Times actually went. And after *The New York Times* ran the NSA wiretapping story (a year late), the Justice Department began issuing subpoenas, claiming that these reporters can be tried as spies under the Espionage Act of 1917. (Daniel Schorr, "Can Journalists be Prosecuted as Spies?" *The Christian Science Monitor,* March 10, 2006: 9; Geoffrey Stone, "Scared of Scoops," *The New York Times,* May 8, 2006: A21; Scott Shane, "Leak of Classified Information Prompts Inquiry," *The New York Times,* July 29, 2006: A10.)

LIVING LOST

APPENDIX: THE MANIFEST'S DESTINY

A QUICK INDEX OF THE CHARACTERS, IN NO PARTICULAR ORDER:

LIVING LOST

THE LOSTAWAYS

Jack Shephard
James "Sawyer" Ford
John Locke
Kate Austen
Sayid Jarrah
Hugo "Hurley" Reyes
Michael Dawson
Walt Lloyd
Charlie Pace
Claire Littleton
Jin-Soo Kwon
Sun Kwon
Rose Nadler
Boone Carlyle
Shannon Rutherford

THE TAILIES

Ana-Lucia Cortez
Mr. Eko
Cindy Chandler
Bernard Nadler
Libby

THOSE ALREADY ON THE ISLAND (WHO AREN'T THE OTHERS)

Danielle Rousseau
Desmond Hume

THE OTHERS

Ethan Rom
Goodwin
Tom
Alex Rousseau
Pickett
Ms. Klugh
Ben
Juliet
Colleen
Karl

THOSE OFF THE ISLAND

Penelope Widmore
Charles Widmore
Mathias and Henrik
Leonard Simms and Sam Toomey

THE LOST EXPERIENCE

Gary Troup
Rachel Blake
DJ Dan
Alvar Hanso
Enzo Valenzetti
Thomas Mittelwerk
Kelvin Joe Inman

Despite being located on one remote island, the world of *Lost* presents a wide-reaching narrative with a huge cast of characters. It's important to note that the cast, like the audience, is left in the dark about the mysteries of the island. Cast members don't receive scripts until shortly before shooting, and they are not privy to other characters' motivations or storylines that might be in those other characters' scripts.○ This sets up a situation that turns the execution of the show into something closer to real life interaction, where people don't know one another's motivations, no one is sure how anyone else will respond, and there certainly aren't scripts they can consult. Adewale Akinnuoye-Agbaje, the actor who plays Mr. Eko, has said, "To be on *Lost* is to dance with its writers."☆ Our own uncertainties are reflected in a rather authentic way in the actors' (and their characters') interactions.

It would be understandable for the survivors of a plane crash on a remote island to assume they were on their own. Not so on *Lost*. Oceanic Flight 815 did not "crash" into the island in the traditional sense of the word; it was actually ripped apart mid-air, with two large sections of the plane landing on different parts of the island. It is odd enough that the plane was torn in half, but stranger still, that there are a relatively large number of survivors. There are the original survivors from the middle part of the plane (the focus of the show's first season), whom we'll call the Lostaways. The Lostaways believed themselves to be the sole survivors of the crash; they were not initially aware that the back of the plane landed in the ocean on another part of the island, leaving a number of additional survivors of Oceanic 815 (referred to

○In an *Entertainment Weekly* interview, Daniel Dae Kim (Jin) said that they received their scripts for the season two finale a day after they began shooting. (Interview with Doc Jensen, www.ew.com, May 17, 2006.)

☆*Entertainment Weekly*, interview with Doc Jensen, www.ew.com, April 11, 2006.

as the Tailies). The survivors of flight 815 are not alone on the island. Aside from polar bears and the smoke monster, there are other human residents of the island who appear every now and then in unnerving and menacing ways. Some are part of a group called "the Others," who seem to be hostile, and then there those *other* than the Others. Across all of these groups, certain narrative ties bind the characters and their back-stories together. The following character run-downs provide an overview of what we know of the characters after 69 days (or two television seasons) on the island.❖ These descriptions untangle some of their back-stories and lay out the characters' narratives in a more regular timeline to help illustrate how the characters fit into the overall *Lost* narrative. Of course, since many of the events significant to the narrative involve more than one character, and have different ramifications for each character (even in their back-stories), some repetition is necessary. For the casual viewer this overview will help make sense of the sprawling and intentionally unbalancing narrative; for the devoted *Lost* addict, some of this material may be familiar, but this breakdown demonstrates some of the broader structures in the overall narrative. The way the narrative works, each character also provides more information about the other original survivors. As for those original survivors, the focus of the first season, we have:

The Lostaways: Fuselage/Middle Section of Oceanic Flight 815

❖In the third season episode "The Glass Ballerina," Ben tells Jack, "Your flight crashed on September 22, 2004. Today is November 29; that means you've been on this island for 69 days." This was a nice narrative trick to help situate the audience in the timeline of the story.

Jack Shephard is a super-surgeon who went to Australia at his mother's bidding to find his father and bring him home. His father drank himself to death in Sydney, and Jack was returning to Los Angeles with his father's remains on Oceanic 815 when it went down. Jack is a hyper-competitive, hyper-responsible, sometimes hyper-tense enigma of a person; he comes off as a kind of reluctant hero, a by-product of his hyper-responsibility, and he rarely betrays personal feelings beyond superficial gut reactions. Jack holds his secrets closer than most of the survivors: he is the refugee of a failed marriage, he has a complex and competitive relationship with this father, and at some point in his past, he ducked out of American society and traveled in Southeast Asia. Jack has become the de facto leader of the Lostaways due to the other survivors' constant appeals for his medical help and guidance after the crash, and as such, Jack has lived up to his name as a kind of shepherd on the island – names are important in *Lost*. (See "Narratives and Nodes: Names.")

Much of Jack's back-story involves his issues with his father, Dr. Christian Shephard. Christian presented a conflicted model for his son; he pushed Jack beyond reasonable expectations, while at the same time reminding Jack of his limits. In a flashback of Jack as a boy (which opens with a close-up of young Jack's eye, much like the opening shot in *Lost*'s pilot episode), Jack stood up for a friend at school, and was rewarded for his efforts by being beaten alongside the boy. Rather than commending his son for his efforts on behalf of a friend in need, Dr. Shephard echoed the words of the playground bully, who told Jack he "shoulda stayed down." Dr. Shephard advised his son: "I have what it takes. You don't want to be a hero, you don't want to try to save everyone, because when you fail, you just don't have what it takes." (Season One, "White Rabbit.") Christian was a functioning alcoholic whose drinking ended up costing him his career and his life; as such, his platitudes rang hollow when he refused to live up to the standards he set for Jack (and hardly lived up to his own name). His father clearly influenced Jack's decision to go into medicine, and Jack did so perhaps to out-do his father; yet by following in Christian's footsteps he also invited his continued criticism. As Jack grew older, he began to resent this double standard, and was driven in part by a desire to divest himself from his father, a desire evident when Jack occasionally yells, "Don't tell me what I can do."

Jack surgically removed Christian from his life after an incident at the hospital where they both worked (and where his father was Chief of Surgery). Jack witnessed his father cause the death of a patient and her unborn child by performing surgery while drunk; despite his father's pleas, Jack outed Christian to a review board that revoked Christian's license, effectively ending Christian's career. Christian then left for Australia, where he drank himself to death. This was not the first time Dr. Shephard had abandoned Jack and his mother; in fact, in a flashback from when Christian was in Sydney (with Tailie Ana-Lucia as his bodyguard) it became clear that Christian had an illegitimate daughter there, whom Jack doesn't seem to be aware of. (Season Two, "Two for the Road.") But even his father's death was not sufficient to settle their relationship; Jack argued with the ticket agent at the Sydney airport about getting his father's remains on Oceanic 815. "I need it to be done. I need it to be over. I need to bury my father." (Season One, "White Rabbit.") Arguably, had Jack not reported his father's conduct, Christian would not have been fired, would not have run off to Australia; Jack would never have ended up on Oceanic 815, and he would not have been on the island.

Jack's back-story is also dominated by a risky surgery he performed on a spinal-injury patient named Sarah. (Season Two, "Man of Science, Man of Faith.") Sarah and another patient had been injured in a car wreck, and both victims were brought into Jack's emergency room. Jack chose to work on Sarah, even though the patient from the other car stood a better chance of survival. (We later learn this other patient was Adam Rutherford, the father of Shannon Rutherford, another Lostaway – another seemingly random back-story connection among the passengers of flight 815.) Jack's father chastised him for choosing to attend the more damaged victim; if Jack had operated on Adam Rutherford, as his father told him he should, Mr. Rutherford probably would have survived, and Shannon most likely would not have been in Australia, and neither of them would have been on Oceanic 815. Against all reason, and to the shock of his colleagues in the operating room, Jack promised Sarah that she would not only walk again, but that she would dance at her upcoming wedding. After the surgery, all indications were that Jack had not fulfilled his promise to Sarah; when he informed her fiancé that Sarah would not walk again, the fiancé balked at the thought of caring for a paraplegic and left her. In fact, the surgery proved a success, and Jack was able to keep his promise; Sarah *could* dance at her wedding – only now she would be marrying Jack. Sarah's miracle surgery may have further fueled Jack's sense of accomplishment and his professional ambition, which drove him to obsess over his work, and helped ruin their marriage.

The miracle of Sarah's surgery likely affects Jack's inflated belief in his ability to save a person against all odds, which manifests in his strong stubborn streak of practical idealism. That stubbornness also pushed him on when Charlie was hung by Ethan; Jack revived him by continuing to pound on his chest when Charlie appeared to be dead. (Season One, "All the Best Cowboys Have Daddy Issues.") Jack's idealism at turns brings him into conflict with, among others, Locke and Sawyer; Locke has a more blind-faith-based idealistic approach to how things should operate on the island, while Sawyer's selfish pragmatism is in conflict with Jack's more social pragmatism. The fact that Jack also appears to be competing with Sawyer for Kate's attention makes Jack a special nemesis to Sawyer – at least in Sawyer's eyes.

Jack spends most of his time on the island trying to keep the Lostaways together and alive, and he reacts angrily, even violently, toward anything that threatens the group. But this obsessive protection wears on Jack; in the first season episode "White Rabbit," he works himself into exhaustion and thinks he's hallucinating when he sees his father walking around the island. Jack follows this apparition into the jungle, where he finds Christian's coffin outside some caves. The coffin was empty, but the caves where Christian's coffin came to rest prove to be a source of much-needed fresh water and shelter for the survivors. If it weren't for Jack's unresolved issues with his father, he arguably would not have found the caves.

Jack's style brushes up against others besides Sawyer and Locke. In the first season episode "The Moth," after about a week on the island, Jack manages to convince some of the group to move to the caves for shelter. While moving supplies up to the caves, Jack asks Charlie to get his guitar out of the way; Charlie was already edgy from heroin withdrawal, and the request sets him off. Charlie yells at Jack, causing a cave-in that traps them both and dislocates Jack's shoulder. When Charlie and Jack finally emerge, the other survivors can see that Charlie looks rough, but Jack covers for him, saying he just "has the flu." (Season One, "The Moth.") Jack shows similar compassion toward Kate when he tells her he doesn't want to know about her criminal past, and toward Ana-Lucia after she accidentally kills Shannon. (Season One, "Tabula Rasa;" Season Two, "Abandoned.") But Jack's approach is more or less pragmatic; he is more concerned with the survivors' conduct on the island than with their respective histories, and isn't worried about moral judgments unless the group is put into danger. This pragmatism is seen in the early episode "Walkabout," when he announces that the bodies in the fuselage need to be burned and "we don't have time to sort out everybody's god." In the subsequent episode "White Rabbit," when he tries to convince people to move to the caves, he tells them, "It's time to start organizing. We need to figure out how we're gonna survive here... Last week most of us were strangers. But we're all here now. And God knows how long we're gonna be here. But if we can't live together, we're gonna die alone."

Jack's exaggerated sense of responsibility for the survivors' health and safety tests him in a number of ways. In the first season episode "All the Best Cowboys Have Daddy Issues," Charlie and Claire are abducted by Ethan Rom, an Other who had been posing as a Lostaway, and Jack forms a search party to follow their trail into the jungle. He is soon caught and badly beaten by Ethan; Ethan then warns Jack, "If you do not stop following me, I will kill one of them." Heedless of the warning, Jack and Kate keep after Ethan, only to find Charlie hanging from a tree by a vine. Kate believes Charlie is dead, but Jack stubbornly refuses to stop CPR and is just able to resuscitate him. Jack's need to save people literally costs him much of his own blood when Boone is fatally injured in the first season episode "Do No Harm." Locke doesn't tell Jack the truth about the cause of the injury, so Jack can't treat Boone correctly. In a last-ditch effort to save him, Jack transfuses his own blood to Boone until Sun makes him stop.

Locke's contribution to Boone's death carves out a deep divide between Jack and Locke, and the rivalry puts them at odds as to how they should use the hatch. Just before blowing open the hatch in the first season finale, Jack tells Kate, "If we survive this, if we survive tonight, we're gonna have a Locke problem." (Season One, "Exodus.") Locke initially feels the hatch is kind of test of faith, and regularly ensures the code is entered into the computer, whereas Jack is more interested in the hatch's practical uses for the group. This leads to an ongoing debate in the second season as to what exactly their purposes are on the island; Locke argues for destiny, believing they are on the island for a purpose, while Jack argues for survival.

The seeming security of the hatch and the guns from the

hatch's armory only deepen Jack and Locke's paranoia. When the Tailies arrive at the Lostaways' camp in the second season episode "Collision," Shannon is accidentally killed by Tailie Ana-Lucia in the jungle. Jack's first reaction is to round up the guns and go out into the jungle (before he knew it was Ana-Lucia's fault), but Locke tries to talk Jack out of it. But after the Tailies' arrival, Locke breaks protocol and takes it upon himself to change the combination of the armory without consulting Jack as they'd agreed to do. In the second season episode "The Hunting Party," the Others catch Kate trailing Jack, Sawyer and Locke in the jungle and use her as a hostage to get the three other survivors to give up their guns. Jack responds to this affront by attempting to build an army with Ana-Lucia's help, and in the process learns that Locke changed the armory's combination behind his back. (Season Two, "Fire + Water.") When Jack asks Locke for the new combination, Locke shows his wariness to share the combination, and makes a deal that if either of them wants the guns, one will first consult the other. (Season Two, "The Long Con.")

The stormy rapport between Jack and Locke is recognized by the other Lostaways and is exploited by Sawyer when he works out a plan to steal the guns from the hatch. Shortly after Jack and Locke settle their armory deal, Sawyer instructs Charlie to sneak-attack Sun in her garden. Sawyer correctly assumed Jack would blame the Others for the attack (as he had with Shannon's death) and go for the guns; Sawyer warned Locke about Jack's plan, knowing that Locke would move the guns to keep them from Jack. Sawyer tells Charlie to follow Locke and report the guns' new hiding place, which Sawyer then easily took for himself. Sawyer's con illustrates how Jack and Locke's mutual mistrust can make them easy targets to distract;

as Ana-Lucia later observes, "Jack and Locke are a little too busy worrying about Locke and Jack." (Season Two, "The Whole Truth.") Even the prisoner, the fake Henry Gale (Ben Linus) picks up on this simmering rivalry, and exploits it for his own purposes.* (Season Two, "One of Them.")

Jack and Locke's rivalry is crystallized in their dealings with the Swan hatch's computer; Jack doesn't believe that entering the code means anything, while Locke believes it means everything. Sayid brings the newly-captured "Henry" to the hatch and locks himself in the armory with him, where he proceeds to interrogate and beat him. Jack hears the ruckus and tries to get into the armory, but can't enter because Locke changed the combination yet again. As Jack and Locke argue, the computer's timer runs down and the alarm goes off; Jack grabs Locke and prevents him from entering the code until after Locke opens the armory door; the code is important enough to Locke to give in to Jack's demands.

Jack has an unlikely connection to the hatch – or, more specifically, to its keeper. Long before he ended up on the island, Jack was burning off stress running the stairs at a stadium after Sarah's surgery. While running, Jack twisted his ankle, and another runner named Desmond came to his aid. When Jack enters the hatch in the second season episode "Man of Science, Man of Faith," he and Desmond recognize each other, but they don't advertise their prior meeting; the coincidence would seem too fantastic. Besides, just a day before finding Desmond, Locke told Jack that they were all on the island for a purpose, but Jack stated he doesn't believe in destiny; admitting that he knew Desmond would shake Jack's epistemological approach to the

---

*The fake Henry Gale got the nickname "Fenry" with the online *Lost* community in the second season; it was revealed in the third season premiere that his name was actually Ben.

island and force him to admit that maybe Locke was on to something. (Season One, "Exodus.")

But much of Jack's stay on the island is a struggle between what he knows as fact and what challenges those facts. Jack also struggles with what he knows is best for the group and what challenges his best judgment. In the second season finale, Michael leads Jack, Sawyer, Kate and Hurley to the north side of the island, ostensibly to rescue Walt from the Others. Before they leave, Sayid warns Jack that something is wrong with Michael's plan, and that he believes Michael had been "compromised." Jack and Sayid work out their own counter-plan: Sayid and Jin would follow along the coast and set a signal fire when they arrived, alerting Jack that they are there to help if the need arises. When the signal is sent, Jack realizes Michael isn't taking them to the other side of the island and confronts Michael. Hurley, Sawyer and Kate are surprised by Jack's secret, but he reassures them, "You have to know that I would never bring you out here if I didn't have a plan." (Season Two, "Live Together, Die Alone.") The plan doesn't work, though, and when the Others ambush the group with tranquilizer darts, Jack, true to his hyper-competitive nature, is the last to go down as he stumbles up a hill carrying Kate.

Jack carries forth his defiance when he's held captive by the Others after Michael's betrayal. He is kept prisoner in an underwater station called the Hydra, and politely questioned by an Other named Juliet, but he refuses to cooperate or eat, and tries to escape when they open his door to feed him. Juliet asks Jack questions about his past, even though she has a large file documenting his entire life; how she got this information isn't clear. In the third season episode "The Glass Ballerina," Ben tells Jack the survivors had been on the island for 69 days up to that point, and since then George Bush was re-elected and the Boston Red Sox won the World Series; Jack believes Ben is lying, until Ben has a TV wheeled into the room and shows him the 2004 World Series celebration. But just because Ben *says* it's only been 69 days doesn't necessarily mean that's the truth.

James "Sawyer" Ford is a con man who was in Australia tracking the man who led to his parents' death. Sawyer represents rampant capitalism on the island; he scavenges items from the plane's fuselage and dead bodies following the crash, and then sets up a kind of barter system where he controls the capital. This results in his isolation from the other Lostaways, and on occasion Sawyer proves willing to put the group at risk for his own benefit.✤ Sawyer also has problems with animals: he is hassled in turn by a

---

✤His ability to get money out of people, admission that he's never voted democrat (Season One, "Whatever the Case May Be,") and tendency to give the people around him snappy nicknames liken him to a certain U.S. president from Texas.

boar, a polar bear, and a tree frog.

Sawyer often seeks to exploit the personal weaknesses of other survivors, but on occasion protects those same weaknesses. This tendency could be seen in Sawyer's life before arriving on the island; through flashbacks, we see that he once planned to pull the same con that was pulled on his own parents, until he learned his mark had a little boy, and called the deal off. (Season One, "Confidence Man.") Another time, Sawyer fell in love with the woman he was working in a long con, and again called it off. (Season Two, "The Long Con.") Both times, Sawyer put himself at risk of bodily harm; his associates weren't interested in Sawyer's emotional state of mind, just the money he could get.

James Ford adopted the name "Sawyer" because that's the name of the man he is hunting. When James was eight years old, a con man named Sawyer seduced his mother and stole his parents' money; when James's father found out what happened, he raged, and as James hid under his bed, his father shot his mother, then sat on the bed James was hiding under and shot himself. James wrote a letter to the man who ruined his family, a letter he always keeps with him. When James grew up, he adopted Sawyer's name, became a con man himself, and searched for the original Sawyer so he could kill him – in a real way, Sawyer becomes the very thing he's trying to kill. (Season One, "Confidence Man.")

Because of his shifty demeanor, Sawyer tends to be the automatic suspect whenever someone from the group commits an offense, whether that suspicion is justified or not, and especially when Jack is pointing the finger. He seems to accept (and even relish) being the scapegoat of the group, and also seems unnerved when things get too comfortable for him. This personality trait veers toward the masochistic: In the first season episode

"Confidence Man," Boone believes Sawyer scavenged Shannon's asthma medicine; when Boone confronts him, Sawyer refuses to admit he doesn't have the medicine, and attacks Boone for rooting through his possessions. Sayid and Jack eventually tie Sawyer to a tree and Sayid tortures him, but Sawyer still refuses to say anything. When Kate stops the torture, Sawyer still won't talk until he gets a kiss from her, at which point he admits he never had the medicine.

Sawyer eventually earns a more respected place among the group after a little more than a month, and joins Michael's rescue raft. But in the first season finale, they meet the Others in the ocean shortly after launch; the Others destroy the raft and shoot Sawyer as he attempts to keep them from abducting Walt. He eventually returns from the other side of the island with the Tailies, only to discover the Lostaways divided his belongings among themselves. Sawyer had to wait to settle the score; he was still recovering from the septic bullet wound and needed Jack's medical help (but receiving Jack's care doesn't make Sawyer appreciate him any more). In the second season episode "The Long Con," Sawyer plots an elaborate scheme with Charlie's help to exploit the tensions between Jack and Locke in order to steal the guns in the hatch. Charlie first attacks Sun and makes it look like the work of the Others. Sawyer knows the attack will infuriate Jack, who will go for the guns and then after the Others. Sawyer warns Locke that Jack is coming for the guns, knowing Locke will move them, and has Charlie trail Locke to the guns' hiding spot. Sawyer takes the guns, which he uses as capital to regain a power position on the island. Jack is undaunted by Sawyer's ruse; he spends the next few days coolly letting Sawyer know that if he wants the guns he'll get them, and hints at his ability to best Sawyer by beating him handily at poker. Jack had picked up some gambling tricks in Thailand, a fact which leads Sawyer to reassess his opinion of Jack, whom he'd written off as a Dudley Do-Right. (Season Two, "Lockdown.")

Jack and Sawyer have more in common than just their alpha-male personalities and gambling abilities. Sawyer was one of the last people to see Jack's father Christian Shephard alive; he bought Christian drinks in an Australian bar. By the end of the first season, Sawyer figures out that the man he drank with is the same man Jack had gone to Australia to collect, and in a rare moment of compassion tells Jack that his father told Sawyer how proud he was of his son, even though Jack had cost Christian his career. (Season One, "Exodus.") Whether Sawyer does this out of his deep-felt sense of child-parent justice or a real feeling of empathy, it shows that Sawyer has more to him than he lets on. The Others recognize this quality in Sawyer, especially after he takes a bullet trying to save Walt, and this may be one reason Sawyer is on the list of people they tell Michael bring to their side of the island in exchange for Walt.

But something the Others didn't count on is Sawyer's calculating manner. A con man professes in deception, and although Sawyer comes off as hotheaded and rash, he's often thinking a few steps ahead (as when he scammed Locke and Jack out of the guns). In the third season episode "The Glass Ballerina," Sawyer and Kate are put to hard labor by the Others after being abducted in the second season finale. Kate is forced to break rocks (while wearing a sun dress, not exactly work-wear), and Sawyer has to haul the rocks away. If they talk or do anything out of line, they get shocked by a tazer. Midway through the day, Sawyer stares at Kate, drops his work, grabs her and starts to kiss her; he is immediately attacked by some of the Others, and he of course fights back, until one of the Others puts a pistol to Kate and Sawyer ends up shocked and subdued. This all seems like Sawyer acting up, and he doesn't pretend it's anything else, until Kate pushes him later that night:

> Two of those guards got some real fight in them. The rest of them, I ain't that much worried about. The heavy-set guy packs a hell of a punch. The shaggy-haired kid's got some sort of martial arts training, but I think I could take him if I had to. Oh, and F.Y.I., those zapper things got a safety on them. [...] I'm guessing most of these boys never seen any real action. But that blonde who had the gun pointed at you – she would have shot you, no problem.

Sawyer planned the whole thing as a way to test the physical limits of the Others, and he took careful measure of what he encountered, yet he never betrayed his purpose (and managed to get another kiss from Kate in the process).

John Locke is the island shaman of sorts, a man the Lostaways first perceive as a kind of weird, militant cross between MacGyver and Yoda. In fact, Locke was actually unable to walk and confined to a wheelchair before he arrived on the island. Locke's strange presence is established in the pilot episodes, where he grins at Kate with a wedge of orange in his teeth, cryptically tells Walt about backgammon and his "secret," and smiles open-armed up at a storm as the rain falls on the beach. Locke had traveled to Australia for an adventure/vacation in the

Outback (a "walka-bout"), but when the organizers learned he was wheelchair-bound, they sent the angry and bitter Locke home on Oceanic flight 815.

Locke was abandoned as a child, and was raised in foster homes: in a flashback, we learned that as an adult he was found first by his birth mother, then by his estranged father, Anthony Cooper. But Cooper only arranged to meet Locke because he needed a kidney transplant; his relation-ship with Locke was a ruse to con Locke out of a good kidney. (Season One, "Deus Ex Machina.") After getting what he needed, Cooper cut off all contact with his son, but Locke couldn't let it go, and took to spending nights parked outside Cooper's home, staring at the fence which kept him from his father. (Season Two, "Orientation.") Some time after losing his kidney, Locke lost the use of his legs and was confined to a wheelchair. Locke's frustration with the limits in his life and his shame at his experience with his father can be heard in his frequent cries of "Don't tell me what I can't do!" (as opposed to

Jack's "Don't tell me what I can do!").

Locke was also not a lucky romantic. He met his great love, Helen, in the anger management group he joined after his father's betrayal. Two people in need of anger management might not seem to be the best love match, but they got along well until Locke's obsession with his father got in the way: Locke would leave Helen in the middle of the night to stake out Cooper's home. Helen eventually forced Locke to choose either life with her or a life spent angry with a father who didn't care for him. Locke chose Helen, and seemed to have moved past his feelings for his father when Helen noticed Cooper's obituary in the newspaper. Locke soon discovered that Cooper's death was in fact a ruse to help him escape with swindled money. Cooper enlisted Locke's help in recovering the money, offering to give him a portion. When Helen caught Locke with his undead dad, she left him for good. Locke didn't get over the relationship easily, and took to regularly calling a phone sex line and talking to a woman he called Helen.

On the island, Locke's new mobility allows him to reinvent himself. He becomes a kind of guru to various survivors – especially Boone, Walt, and Charlie. He finds a kind of kindred spirit in Mr. Eko, and even has a dream where he *is* Mr. Eko. (Season Two, "?") He takes great interest in Claire and her baby, and becomes protective of them when he suspects Charlie of backsliding into heroin addiction and threatening their safety.

Locke's spiritual understanding for being on the island takes shape when he discovers the Swan station hatch with Boone. At first Locke seems to believe that the island itself is communing with him, and becomes obsessed with opening the hatch. He even has prophetic dreams about the hatch; he first dreams of the

Nigerians' plane crashing into the jungle canopy, and then sees a bloody Boone standing in the jungle, repeating, "Theresa falls up the stairs, Theresa falls down the stairs." (Season One, "Deus Ex Machina.") Locke had no way of knowing about the plane or who "Theresa" is; they had not yet found the Nigerians' plane, and Theresa was Boone's nanny who fell down the stairs and broke her neck. Such events lead Locke to believe that it was his "destiny" to enter the hatch. (Season One, "Exodus.") Once inside the hatch, Locke literally gets deeper into the island, only to find an enigma.

Locke's obsession with the hatch is indirectly responsible for Boone's death. In the first season episode "Deus Ex Machina," Locke's legs begin to fail him after long, physically-taxing days with Boone trying to open the hatch, and his legs continue to fail when they find the Nigerian drug smugglers' plane in the jungle canopy. With Locke unable to climb, Boone goes up into the plane alone, tries the radio and makes brief contact with someone (Bernard and the Tailies on the other side of the island, as we later learn), but is fatally injured when his weight causes the plane to fall from the canopy. Locke chooses not to tell Jack the whole story of Boone's injury, which keeps Jack from properly treating Boone and leads to Boone's death. (Season One, "Do No Harm.") When Jack discovers the truth the next day, he beats Locke savagely; Locke's later claim that Boone was a sacrifice the island demanded doesn't help bridge their differences. This beating parallels the beating Locke gives Charlie when he believes Charlie is back on heroin and endangering Claire's baby.

After delivering Boone's broken body to Jack, Locke returned to the hatch and desperately banged on the window, yelling "I've done everything you wanted me to do. So why did you do this? Why?" when suddenly a light shines through the window. At that same moment, Desmond, who was manning the Swan station, was at his own lowest point, believing he would never leave the island, would never see his girlfriend again, and contemplating suicide. When he hears Locke banging on the hatch, Desmond finds the hope he needs to continue; in turn, Desmond's light confirms to Locke that his own search for meaning isn't in vain. When Locke finally enters the hatch, Desmond initially believes Locke is his replacement in the Swan station (Desmond's predecessor Kelvin Inman had led him to believe a replacement would eventually come), but when Desmond figures out Locke is not the replacement, he turns his gun on Locke and forces him to enter a code into an old green-screen computer. Desmond's assignment, initially intended for a pair of operators according to the hatch's orientation film, is to input the numerical code 4 8 15 16 23 42 every 108 minutes, the same code at the heart of the narrative.⌘ Once successfully entered, a timer resets and begins a new countdown. Failure to enter the code, the film explains, will result in an "incident," some ominous, unexplained disaster, possibly having to do with an electromagnetic pulse unique to this part of the island. Locke comes to believe entering the code is his destiny, and Jack eventually and reluctantly comes to agree with him and joins Locke on computer detail.

Locke's faith is tested after a man claiming to be Henry Gale (Ben), the victim of a balloon crash, enters the survivors' camp. (Season Two, "One of Them.") Sayid finds Ben caught in one of Rousseau's jungle traps, and moves him to the hatch's armory. Rousseau immediately suspects Ben of being an Other, and Sayid proceeds to interrogate him to find out if Ben really is who he

---

⌘The sum of the numbers also happens to equal 108.

claims to be. During the interrogation, Jack enters the hatch, hears Ben's screams and demands to know what is going on. Both Locke and Jack were supposed to know the armory's combination, but Locke had changed it without telling Jack, keeping Jack from reaching Ben and Sayid. Locke's refusal to open the door forces Jack's hand: when the computer's timer goes off, he grabs Locke and won't let him go enter the code until he opens the armory lock. The stalemate continues until, for the first time since the Lostaways entered the hatch, the timer runs completely down. The digital readout flips from black and white numbers to black and red hieroglyphs. Locke quickly enters the code and resets the timer, but the appearance of the hieroglyphs confirms that the code is something more than a game.

In the second season episode "Lockdown," Locke's faith is tested when the hatch reveals another secret. As Locke is guarding Ben, a voice comes over the hatch's loudspeaker and gives a kind of countdown, after which blast doors drop around the hatch.◁ Afraid of being trapped, Locke manages to slide a crowbar under one of the blast doors before it seals. Locke then tells Ben he won't allow anyone to hurt him if he helps Locke open the door. Ben agrees, Locke lets him out of the armory, and together they manage to pry the door up with a toolbox. But as Locke attempts to slide under the door, the toolbox gives and the door pins Locke down, breaking his leg.

Caught under the door and knowing he couldn't enter the code into the computer, Locke asks Ben to crawl through the air vent and enter the code in Locke's place. As Ben makes his way to the computer, the lights shut off in the room where Locke is

◁After this incident, the other survivors find a palette of food airdropped into the jungle; the lockdown seems to be designed to keep whoever was in the hatch oblivious to the airdrop.

pinned, and black lights come on in their place. Locke then sees the black lights illuminating a hidden map on the blast wall, a map depicting the different stations on the island and cryptic phrases in English and Latin; at this point, Locke is literally and figuratively caught under the image of the island.• While Locke studies the map, the computer is reset, the doors raise, and Ben returns to Locke's side.

When it comes to the hatch, Ben provides Locke with more uncertainty than answers. Locke asks Ben if he was captured on purpose in order to locate the hatch for the Others, but Ben tells Locke that the Swan station is "a joke," and that in fact he had *not* entered the code while Locke was pinned under the blast door. Ben claims that when the timer ran down, he saw hieroglyphs (as Locke himself had seen), but that the computer simply reset itself without the entry of the code. (Season Two, "Dave.") On hearing this, Locke begins to question his purpose on the island, and in the following episode, is found sulking on the beach by Rose. (Season Two, "S.O.S.") Rose is the only person who knows that Locke was wheelchair-bound before the plane crashed into the island; she had seen Locke in the Sydney airport when he handed her a bottle of medication she had dropped. When Locke tells Rose that Jack predicted his broken leg would be in a splint for at least four weeks, she replies, "But honey, you and I both know it's not going to take that long." (Season Two, "S.O.S.") And sure enough, about four days later, Locke drops his crutches and splint and walks again. (Season Two, "Three Minutes.")

As Locke was healing, Mr. Eko has a dream where his brother

◆An old college trick: If you paint something on a wall in liquid laundry detergent, it will dry clear, but glow under a black light. Dorm walls are probably safer to try this on than your home's painted drywall.

Yemi tells him, "You must help John. He has lost his way. You must make him take you to the question mark." (Season Two, "?") Michael had just shot Ana-Lucia and Libby and blamed it on Ben, and Eko gets Locke to go with him into the jungle by claiming they were tracking Ben. But once in the jungle, Eko forces Locke to take him to the question mark. After hiking all day, they camp, and Locke has another prophetic vision: He dreams he is Mr. Eko, and he sees Eko's brother Yemi beckoning him up a cliff. At the top of that cliff he finds Yemi sitting in Locke's old wheelchair. When Locke tells Mr. Eko about the dream, Eko climbs the cliff, and from the height sees the giant question mark etched into the earth, and finds the Pearl station under it. (Season Two, "?")

Inside the Pearl station, Locke and Eko find evidence indicating that the Swan station is simply part of a behavioral experiment that is being monitored from the Pearl station, and that all of Locke's button pushing has been pointless. They find logs from a dot matrix printer that show all of the computer entries made at the Swan station, and Locke begins to think he was made a fool of. But while the Pearl revelation delivers a fatal blow to Locke's faith, the same evidence convinces Mr. Eko that entering the code is more necessary than ever.

After Locke's wall of faith is knocked down by the Pearl station orientation film, Locke vengefully wants to test the hatch by not entering the code. But Eko's faith in the hatch has been strengthened, and Locke couldn't keep Eko from entering the code. In the second season finale, Locke and Mr. Eko physically struggle over the computer and Eko easily takes Locke down. As Eko throws Locke out of the computer room, Locke yells, "No, it's not real! We're only puppets – puppets on strings! As long as we push it, we'll never be free!" (Season Two, "Live Together, Die

Alone.") When Desmond ends up back on the island after failing to escape on his sailboat, Locke tells Desmond about the Pearl station logs, and solicits his help to get Eko out of the Swan. Desmond trips the blast door mechanism and locks Eko out of the hatch. But in the process, Desmond sees the Pearl station printouts; Des realizes that the last time the code wasn't properly entered was when he was outside the hatch with Kelvin Inman on September 22, 2004 – the same date Oceanic 815 was ripped apart in mid-air and landed on the island. When Desmond tries to convince Locke that the code needs to be entered, Locke becomes angry and smashes the computer, rendering it useless.[□] The electromagnetic charge builds up and begins to tear the hatch apart, and as Locke realizes what he's done, he simply states, "I was wrong." (Season Two, "Live Together, Die Alone.")

Kate Austen is a tomboy and fugitive from Iowa who is wanted for, among other offenses, the murder of her father Wayne. She was in Australia hiding from Edward Mars, the federal marshal who eventually captured her. Kate and Mars were returning to America via flight 815 when... well, you know the story by now.

By killing her father, Kate intended to free her mother (and herself) from an untenable situation, but in fact it only led to other increasingly difficult situations and desperate behavior. Kate proves fairly worthy of handling these difficult and desperate situations, echoing the previous J.J. Abrams TV heroines, *Alias's* Sydney Bristow and the title character from *Felicity*.[*]

[□] Apparently his anger management sessions didn't take.

[*] J.J. Abrams and Joss Whedon are two television writers who have moved decisively in the direction of kick-ass female leads who can perform heroic acts normally reserved for the hyper-masculine, without losing a foothold in everyday reality. Sydney Bristow's strained relationship with her father Jack is also a predecessor to the parent/child issues that the narrative of *Lost* explores.

Kate was raised to believe Wayne was her stepfather, but it wasn't true – Wayne was in fact her biological father, and her "father" Sam Austen was actually her stepfather. Wayne's drunken physical and sexual cruelty led Kate to take drastic measures; she burned his house down when he was passed out inside. Kate tried to explain to her mother Diane that she had only meant to make life better for her by killing Wayne (and buying insurance for the house before burning it down), but Diane turned Kate over to the authorities. (Season Two, "What Kate Did.") Kate is an unlikely fugitive, although she can handle herself as a criminal just fine. She tries to care for those she may be trying to take advantage of (not unlike Sawyer's compassion for the victims of his cons).

Mars took an interest in Kate when she started calling him, and they began a cat-and-mouse chase across the globe, usually to Mars's detriment. Mars arrested her at a bus stop as she was buying a ticket to Tallahassee, but as he drove Kate back to the arraignment through a heavy thunderstorm, a horse walked across the road, causing Mars to whip the steering wheel and crash the car; this appeared to be the same horse Kate and Sawyer later saw on the island. (Season Two, "What Kate Did.") Kate took this opportunity to kick Mars out of the car and escape, and between that escape and the crash of Oceanic 815, she committed robberies and other crimes to keep going. (Season Two, "What Kate Did.")

Mars pursued every angle he could find, and even set a trap for Kate that exploited her responsibility for the accidental death of her high school sweetheart, Tom Brennan. In 2001, when Kate was on the run, she learned that her mother Diane was dying of cancer, and Tom surreptitiously arranged for Kate to see Diane at the hospital. Before seeing her mother, Kate and Tom retrieved a time capsule from their days together and Kate took a toy airplane from the capsule. When Kate later saw her mother, Diane began shrieking, the police were alerted, and Kate and Tom fled in Tom's car. Tom died in the car as Kate rammed through a police barricade.✿ After Tom's death, Kate fled, leaving the toy plane on the back seat. (Season One, "Born to Run.") Mars took the plane and used its sentimental value to trap Kate; he understood her devotion to her loved ones, and planted it in a safe deposit box in a New Mexico bank to draw her out. Kate planned an elaborate bank heist to retrieve the toy – robbing the bank was the only way she could get to Tom's plane, since she wasn't on the safe deposit box signatory card. She faked her name and even seduced one of the other robbers she fell in with

---

✿He may have been shot, or he may have died from the impact.

to make him think the whole plan was just another stick-up. But once inside, she shot the man she seduced in the leg, got her plane, and got away. (Season One, "Whatever the Case May Be.")* It's this sort of experience that helps Kate speak Sawyer's language, and demonstrates her loyalty to those she cares for.

Mars finally captured Kate (with her plane) in Australia. Kate had taken refuge as a farm hand for a one-armed widower named Ray Mullen who desperately needed the help. She was saving her money and planning her next move; when Mullen found her packing to leave, he offered to give her a ride to town. Kate had no idea the farmer had seen her wanted poster and the $23,000 reward offer at the post office, and was in fact driving her to meet Mars.▼ When Kate saw Mars in another car on the road, Mullen apologized, explaining that he needed the reward money for his mortgage. Kate caused Mullen to crash his truck, but rather than run, she dragged the unconscious farmer to safety; after all, Mullen had helped her when she needed it, and Kate helps those who help her. But this act also gave Mars just enough time to capture her. She showed a similar concern toward Mars during the crash of Oceanic 815; in the turbulence, a hard case fell out of the overhead compartment, hitting Mars on the head and knocking him out. Kate made sure Mars's oxygen mask was fitted on him and he was okay before she fitted her own mask, lifted his handcuff keys, and freed herself. (Season One, "Tabula Rasa.")

In the pilot episode, Mars caught a piece of shrapnel in his chest from the crash and was slowly and painfully dying on the island. When Kate inquires about Mars's condition, Jack asks her

---

*It's not clear just why she didn't take any money, but in the flashback where she received the letter that her mother was sick, she also received cash. (Season One, "Born to Run.")
▼$23,000 is also another instance of one of the numbers in the code.

if she knows him, but she lies and tells Jack that he was just the man sitting next to her on the plane. As Jack attends to him, Mars mumbles that Kate is dangerous, and steers Jack to Kate's mug shot in his jacket, letting Jack (and later Hurley) know that Kate was the fugitive on the plane, but neither Jack nor Hurley choose to make anything of it. In the second episode, "Tabula Rasa," Kate checks on Mars as he is dying, and he grabs her. Just before the crash, Kate was about to ask Mars for a favor, and he wanted to know what it was. Kate explains that she wanted to make sure that the Australian farmer Mullen got his $23,000 reward, because he had "a hell of a mortgage" on his farm and desperately needed the money. Mars later regains consciousness just long enough to warn Jack not to trust Kate: "Listen to me: no matter what she does – no matter how she makes you feel – don't you trust a word that she says. She will do anything to get away." (Season One, "Tabula Rasa.") Later that day, Mars's screams of agony drove Sawyer to use the marshal's firearm to put Mars out of his misery, but he only succeeded in puncturing Mars's lung, putting him in even more pain. Kate again shows concern for Mars, asking Jack to finish the job Sawyer started. She then offers to tell Jack what she did, but Jack doesn't want to hear it, saying that after the crash they should all get to start over.

In the first season episode "Whatever the Case May Be," about a week after Mars's death, Kate and Sawyer are swimming in a small lake in the jungle when they find two Oceanic 815 passengers strapped in their seats at the bottom of the lake, and the marshal's Halliburton aluminum briefcase under one seat. Kate knows that the case holds four 9mm pistols, the toy plane, and her own arrest warrant, but the case is still locked and the keys are with the now-buried Mars. Kate convinces Jack to show her where

Mars's body is buried so she can get the key, but Jack, suspicious of her behavior, won't let her open the case alone. But when Jack learns what the case held, he keeps Kate's secret to himself.

Kate spends much of her early days on the island trying to hide her past. She is desperate for a new beginning, and when Michael begins building a raft she tries to join him. In the first season episode "Born to Run," she prepares to start over in the real world by doctoring the passport of a dead passenger to create a new identity for herself. She also works out a plan with Sun; Jin was planning to leave on the raft against Sun's wishes, and Sun was looking for a way to keep him on the island with her. Sun and Kate dose Jin's water with something to make him sick, but the plan is ruined when Michael accidentally drinks from Jin's water bottle and falls ill. Jack confronts Kate about the poisoning; Kate is insulted, asking Jack if he really thinks she is capable of such a thing, to which Jack responds, "I don't know what you're capable of." Little by little, Kate proves to be much more than she first appears to be, and capable of manipulating a situation to her own advantage if she wants to.

Kate proves to be resourceful on the island, but also a little precocious, sometimes getting herself and the group into trouble. In the second season episode "The Hunting Party," Michael goes off into the jungle alone looking for his son Walt. Jack forms a quick search party, but won't let Kate join them, despite her pleas. She follows them anyway, hanging behind, only to be caught by the Others in the jungle. That night, the Others confront Locke, Jack and Sawyer; their leader, "Mr. Friendly," asks the survivors to give up their guns.✧ When they refuse, Mr.

✧The Others don't get caught; they present themselves when they choose to.

Friendly calls for captured Kate, bound and gagged, and threatens to shoot her if they don't give up the weapons. Kate's drive in this case cost the survivors their weapons, and could have cost them more, but it stems from the same part of her that showed concern for both Ray Mullen and Edward Mars. Perhaps it is Kate's magnanimity that makes the Others put her on the wanted list they give to Michael at the end of the second season.

Kate appears to be the object of more than one man's affections. Time and again Sawyer tells Kate that they have more in common than superficial criminal backgrounds, which Kate coyly relates to Jack, possibly in an attempt to make Jack jealous. Sawyer may be referring to their shared capacity to care for those they take advantage of or are otherwise in conflict with. Sawyer uses this commonality to try to begin a romantic relationship with Kate (a fling, more or less, although he does manage to con a kiss out of her as they negotiate for Shannon's asthma medicine), whereas Kate expresses their connection by caring for him when he returns from the Tailies camp with the septic bullet wound in his shoulder. But Kate also definitely shows an interest in Jack; in the second season episode "What Kate Did," Kate was caring for the delirious Sawyer when he seemed to be channeling Kate's father Wayne, yelling, "Why did you kill me?" Jack later finds the shaken Kate in the jungle, and when Jack comforts her, she kisses him and runs off. Near the end of the second season, in "Three Minutes," Kate and Jack get caught in a net trap in the jungle; when Sawyer asks where Jack and Kate were all night, Jack tells him they were caught in a net, and Sawyer incredulously responds, "Is that what they're calling it these days?" Now that Mars is gone and she has achieved her goal of reclaiming a symbol of her more innocent past, Tom's plane, Kate is freer than she has been in some time.

Sayid Jarrah is a former Iraqi Republican Guard Communications Officer from the first Gulf War who specialized in gathering and using intelligence. In the second season episode "One of Them," we also learn Sayid is the son of a war hero, another of *Lost*'s complex father/son relationships.[※] He was in Sydney on his way to meet his lost love, Nadia, when he boarded Oceanic flight 815. Nadia was a dissident for whom Sayid put himself at great risk when he freed her from military custody in Iraq. His background as a torturer and tortured romantic would seem to make him one of the more schizophrenic survivors, but he proves to be one of the more stable, resourceful, and dependable people on the island.

The CIA knew that Sayid's roommate from Cairo University, Essam, had become a member of a terrorist cell in Sydney, and convinced Sayid to infiltrate the organization inexchange for a reunion with Nadia. Sayid arranged to "bump into" Essam at a Sydney mosque and joined his group, gaining their trust by "discovering" government bugs in their home. He remained with the cell as they prepared to carry out a suicide bomb attack. Just before the attack, Sayid confessed to Essam that he was working with the CIA, and gave him a chance to escape. Despondent at being betrayed by his friend, Essam instead committed suicide, shooting himself in front of Sayid. A distraught Sayid delayed his departure from Sydney (and his reunion with Nadia) and remain in Australia an extra day to prepare a proper Muslim funeral for Essam. (Season One, "The Greater Good.") If Sayid hadn't stayed

---

[※]Al Jarrah is also the name of an airbase in Northern Iraq.

to honor his friend, he wouldn't have been on Oceanic 815.

Early in the narrative, Sayid was the victim of racial profiling; in the pilot episode, Sawyer blames Sayid for the crash – "You're the terrorist" – and in a flashback we see him reported as a possible terrorist in the Sydney airport (by Shannon, no less, with whom he would later fall in love). As a former communications specialist, Sayid has the knowledge to

repair some of the plane's equipment, but couldn't work without being accused of making a bomb (again, by Sawyer). Early on, in the first season episode "Tabula Rasa," Sayid manages to use the plane's transceiver to pick up the faint distress signal set on a loop by Rousseau, and in "Walkabout," he is able to triangulate that signal to try to determine its origin. Sayid's knack for electronics consistently proves useful on the island. But later, after gaining the trust of the group, Sayid employs his skills as a torturer to force Sawyer to share the asthma medicine that Shannon desperately needs. (Season One, "Confidence Man.") Ashamed of his act,

Sayid leaves the group to trek across the island, and on his journey is captured by Danielle Rousseau.

Just as Sayid tortures Sawyer for something he doesn't have, in the first season episode "Solitary," Rousseau vainly tortures Sayid in search of information about her lost daughter, Alex. Rousseau assumes Sayid is an Other, and despite her partial madness, Sayid manages to convince Rousseau he has no knowledge of Alex, and even repairs a music box for Rousseau as an act of good faith. Because of this exchange, Sayid develops the best relationship with Rousseau of anyone on the island, and Sayid was able to escape with some of Rousseau's maps.

Shortly after returning to the Lostaways' camp, Sayid begins going over the maps, which are riddled with equations and French writing. Sayid can manage the mathematics, but cannot read the French, and approaches Shannon for help translating the text. Sayid knew Shannon had spent some time in France (she helped translate Rousseau's transmission), but Shannon didn't believe she could translate the material. Sayid convinces her that she is capable, and his confidence in her sparks a relationship between the two. (Season One, "Whatever the Case May Be.")

Early into the second season, Sayid and Shannon's relationship develops into a full-fledged romance. But before Walt left on the raft, he entrusted Shannon with his dog Vincent, which creates a strange tie between Walt and Shannon that gets between her and Sayid. She begins seeing the absent Walt in the jungle, dripping wet, and whispering to her. In the second season episode "Abandoned," Sayid and Shannon were spending the night together when Shannon sees Walt appear in their tent. She follows the phantom Walt into the jungle, and Sayid chases her. In the jungle rain, they stumble upon the Tailies with Sawyer, Jin and Michael making their way to the Lostaways' camp. Shannon surprises the group, and Ana-Lucia accidentally shoots Shannon, believing she was an Other. Sayid then tries to kill Ana-Lucia, but is tackled by Mr. Eko, who ties Sayid to a tree. While Eko and the rest of the group take the injured Sawyer back to the Lostaways' camp, Ana talks with the captured Sayid; they reach an understanding, and find they share the same dead feeling inside. Unfortunately for Sayid, his relationship with Shannon, like his relationship with Nadia, is left unfulfilled. (Season Two, "Collision.")

In the second season episode "One of Them," Rousseau captures an Other, Ben, in one of her jungle nets. Because she trusts Sayid, he is the first person she turns to, and Sayid takes Ben back to the hatch to interrogate him. In a flashback, we then learn how Sayid became a torturer with the help of U.S. military intelligence. Sayid once acted as an interpreter (for Kate's stepfather, Sergeant Major San Austen) during the Gulf War. Sayid also met Defense Intelligence Agency operative Kelvin Inman during that period; this is the same Kelvin that eventually manned the Swan station with Desmond prior to the crash of Oceanic 815. In Iraq, Kelvin tried to convince Sayid to torture his own commanding officer, in order to find out where a U.S. helicopter pilot was being held prisoner. To convince Sayid to turn on his superior, Kelvin showed Sayid a classified video of Sayid's village being hit with sarin gas by the Iraqi Army, and observes, "Loyalty is a virtue, but unquestioned loyalty – I don't think that's you." It isn't. Seeing the video convinces Sayid to help Kelvin, and this established Sayid's relationship with the U.S. intelligence agencies that would later approach him to get information about a terrorist cell in Sydney.

Sayid's military communications skills again prove their

worth when Locke finally gets inside the Swan hatch. In the second season episode "Orientation," Sayid is able to repair the computer after Desmond accidentally shoots it, which allows the Lostaways to continue to enter the code as instructed by Desmond and the orientation film. Later on, when Sayid and Jack investigate the hatch's inner areas in "Everybody Hates Hugo," Jack shows Sayid the eight-foot-thick concrete wall in the hatch that walls off a magnetic field that can be felt through it. As they explore the hatch's innards, they find the concrete barrier all over, and Sayid tells Jack, "The last time I heard of concrete being poured over everything in this was Chernobyl." Presumably, the statements on the orientation film about the island's unique electromagnetic properties are confirmed.

By the end of the second season, Sayid's military experience leads him to correctly suspect that Michael had been "compromised" during his time as a prisoner of the Others. (Season Two, "Three Minutes.") Michael tells Jack, Kate, Sawyer and Hurley that they need to join him in going after Walt; Sayid shares his suspicions with Jack, and the two of them work out a plan. In the second season finale "Live Together, Die Alone," Sayid sails to the north side of the island with Jin and Sun in Desmond's boat to help Jack. As they sail around the coast, they discover another disturbing mystery of the island: the remnants of a colossal statue. Only one foot remains, and it has only four toes; the fifth toe isn't destroyed, the complete foot just has four toes. As they continue around the coast, Sayid also recites *salat*, or the traditional Muslim prayer – another sign that Sayid may keep some religious traditions. When they find the Others' camp, Sayid reconnoiters the area, and finds it deserted; he also finds what appears to be another hatch, but when he opens the door, there is nothing but a rock wall, and yet another mystery. As with so much else in the *Lost* narrative, what initially appears to be a clear answer to a question ends up being a dead end that raises only more questions.

Hugo "Hurley" Reyes is the island's Mr. Howell turned inside-out. Hurley's net worth went from zero to over $150 million after he won the lottery (playing the numbers 4 8 15 16 23 42). Hurley's life had been ruled by these numbers following his lottery win, and he had gone to Australia to investigate the source of the numbers. Before winning the lottery, Hurley lived with his mother, worked at a fast food chicken joint, and spent time in the Santa Rosa Mental Institute; he wasn't exactly the stuff millionaires are made of (and may be the better for it). Hurley was institutionalized at Santa Rosa after a traumatic accident which left him catatonic. Hurley is a big guy; once at a party, he walked out onto an already over-crowded deck which then collapsed, killing two people. Hurley blamed his weight, and thus himself, for the accident (although the deck was already over-crowded), and his turn inward led to a mild schizophrenia that resulted in his time spent at Santa Rosa. Once at the hospital, Hurley met "Dave," an imaginary person that at once helped Hurley to cope yet limited his progress by encouraging him to continue overeating. In the second season episode "Dave," the imaginary man came back to Hurley on the island when Hurley was put in charge of distributing the Swan's food supply. Seeing Dave made Hurley believe the entire island existed only in his imagination, but Libby, a Tailie with psychological training, helped him get over the episode before he followed Dave over a cliff.

Hurley first became familiar with the numbers from another Santa Rosa patient, Leonard Simms. Leonard encountered the numbers while in the Navy working a listening station (possibly the Arctic listening station that picked up the electromagnetic discharge at the end of the second season); whatever experience Leonard had with the numbers, they left him a shell of a person who just repeated the numbers to himself.◻ Hurley played games of Connect Four with Leonard, heard Leonard constantly repeating the numbers to himself, and later used them to play and win the lottery. Hurley's big heart led him to try to help those around him with the money he won; he seems to have even helped his abusive former manager at the chicken joint after the place was destroyed by a meteorite.✐ But the ill fortune that befell those he helped led Hurley to believe the numbers were cursed. Hurley's grandpa died, his brother's wife left him for another woman, the house he bought his mother caught on fire (and his mother hurt her ankle when visiting the house), and things just generally didn't go well for him. He may have even indirectly irritated Locke, who worked at the box company Hurley bought and was continually harassed by Hurley's (possible) former manager.

On the island, Hurley provides a kind of release for the other survivors through his humor and is a focus of communal interaction; he salvages the trays of airplane food from the wreckage and

---

◻Strangely enough, there is an archive of odd short-wave signals that repeat numbers like the ones for the Swan's code. This archive has been collected by the Conet Project; no one really knows what they're for - one suggestion is that they are spy codes - and most of the voices repeating the sequences are female, but are sometimes children, male, or mechanical, and they speak in multiple languages. If you know where to look, you can pick them up on shortwave radio, and they're every bit as weird as they sound. You can listen to the archive at www.archive.org; search for "Conet Project."

✐Hurley bought a box company with some of his winnings, and gave his former manager a job at the company. Or it seems to be the case that the box company manager is the same as Hurley's old manager, but we may be dealing with a twin here; twins are a key element in *Lost*.

hands them out, builds a golf course, takes a census to account for the survivors, and is put in charge of the food in the Swan hatch.✤ Being in charge of the hatch food, however, triggers a deep fear in Hurley; after he won the lottery, he was afraid his relationships with his friends would change, and he held off on revealing he'd won for some time. He has a similar reaction when Jack asks him to manage the food in the hatch in the second season episode "Everybody Hates Hurley" – Rose stops him from trying to blow the hatch up. This is the first incident suggesting Hurley may be a bit unstable about some things, which is confirmed with the appearance of Dave. After Libby helps Hurley through his rough patch with the imaginary Dave, they soon develop a relationship which, like Sayid and Shannon's, is cut short when Libby is shot and killed by Michael. (Season Two, "Two for the Road.") However, it is revealed in a flashback that Libby was also a patient at the Santa Rosa Mental Institute when Hurley was there, and she used to watch him; she may have had other interests in Hurley, but she did help him. (Season Two, "Dave.")

Hurley is also a good and non-threatening listener with a helpful streak in him. Charlie often bends Hurley's ear, coming to him on occasion with confessions and questions. This may be because Charlie and Hurley are about the same age, and Charlie

---

✤Incidentally, Hurley's taking on the position of unofficial island deputy recalls another Hurley; in the early 1990's David Lynch television show *Twin Peaks*, Big Ed Hurley was also the unofficial deputy of the town of *Twin Peaks*. *Lost* and *Twin Peaks* share a few commonalities, like the strange mysteries that fascinate their respective audiences, supernatural occurrences blending with the everyday in a near magical-realist way, and an unorthodox presentation that rewards attentive viewing (and punishes passive viewing). There are more than a few commonalities between *Lost* and *Twin Peaks*. See what you can find out when you read footnotes? And they're right there for your convenience, not hiding in the back of the book like those shady endnotes.

feels he can confide in someone of his own generation. On the island, he does his best to help Jack work with the injured U.S. marshal, and helps Sawyer find the singing tree frog that is driving him mad, even though he doesn't do well with blood and doesn't do well with Sawyer. (Season One, "Pilot"; Season Two, "One of Them.") But when Sawyer teases Hurley during Hurley's semi-breakdown in "Dave," Hurley snaps and attacks Sawyer, indicting that his good nature does have limits. Hurley's goodness may be what draws the attention of the Others, who ask Michael to bring Hurley to their side of the island. The Others capture then release Hurley, charging him with the job of telling the rest of the survivors that they can never come to the Others' side of the island. (Season Two, "Live Together, Die Alone.")

No one on the island believes Hurley is a millionaire, but he owes Walt $83,000 in backgammon losses. (Season One, "...In Translation.")

Michael Dawson is a construction worker and artist who went to Australia to collect his son Walt after Walt's mother's death. Michael lost Walt in a custody battle when Walt was very young, and never had the chance to develop his fatherly skills; this becomes painfully apparent early in the narrative, as Michael becomes a figure of dominance and control rather than love and support. Michael tries to pack years of lost fatherly intentions and development into his short time on the island, and ends up doing as much harm as good.

Walt's mother Susan left the U.S. when she had the opportunity to join an international law firm; she took Walt with her, and moved across the world, eventually settling in Sydney, Australia for a time. Unfortunately for Michael, she also fell for and married Brian Porter, the lawyer that hired her. If this wasn't emas-

culating enough, Susan also paid for Michael's hospital expenses when he was hit by a car in New York after learning Susan was leaving him.★ Michael never really got back on track with his life after this; his art career stalled when he took construction work. Michael gave his son a stuffed polar bear and regularly sent letters to him, but didn't know that Susan had kept the letters from Walt (which parallels how Penelope Widmore's father kept Desmond's letters from her while Desmond was in prison).

When Michael went to Australia to get Walt, the father and son were seeing each other for the first time in nearly a decade, most of Walt's life. Walt knew next to nothing about Michael, and Michael became obsessed with being the father he didn't get the

★Susan told Michael she was leaving him while he was on a pay phone in New York; Michael hung up, stalked across the street, and was hit by a passing car. This car was a gold Pontiac Bonneville, a car that appears in multiple car crashes in the narrative. It's not clear yet if this is because the producers have a limited availability of crashable cars, or if there's something more to this particular car.

chance to be in the past. This led to his over-controlling Walt, and on the island, that control drives Walt toward Locke, who treats Walt with more respect. Walt's divided attentions soon drive a wedge between Michael and Locke, as Michael feels Locke threaten his role as father-figure. At one point Michael thinks he finds something he can share with Walt when Walt tells him he likes the pictures in the Spanish Green Lantern comic book; Michael tells Walt he used to trace comic books when he was a boy. "I taught myself about perspective. You know what that is – perspective?" (Season One, "Special.") But perspective is just what Michael lacks when it comes to Walt. In the same episode, when he finds Walt talking to Locke against his orders, Michael throws Walt's comic into the fire in anger, and Walt takes off into the jungle with his dog Vincent. Michael wrongly assumes Walt had returned to Locke, and confronts Locke. Instead of returning Michael's anger, Locke offers to help Michael find his boy, demonstrating the perspective Michael lacks. As they search the jungle, they hear Walt yelling as yet another polar bear corners Walt in a grove. Locke helps Michael save his son, and that act helps establish a trust between the two men.

Michael's relationship with Jin also begins negatively. In the first season episode "House of the Rising Sun," Michael finds a Rolex watch in the plane's wreckage and is wearing the watch when Jin notices it on his wrist. Jin was traveling to Los Angeles to deliver the watch for his father-in-law, Mr. Paik; he assumes Michael stole the watch, and attacks him. Michael assumes Jin attacked him because (in Michael's words), "Korean people don't like black people." The rift between Michael and Jin remains until Michael discovers that Jin's wife, Sun, speaks English, and she eventually explains to Michael why Jin attacked him. (Season

One, "...In Translation.") After this, Jin slowly comes to be loyal to and even protective of Michael.

Michael is on a mission to return Walt to the real world. When Jack tries to convince him to move to the caves for shelter, Michael does not go along: "I got one priority right now, and that's to get my kid off this island. If a boat passes, I'm not gonna miss it." (Season One, "House of the Rising Sun.") After about a month, Michael takes it upon himself to build a raft to get his son off the island. Jin helps Michael with the raft, partly as an act of good faith toward Michael, and partly because he is ashamed that he didn't his wife spoke English and wants to get away from her. Michael also receives help from Sawyer, who buys his way onto the boat with cable he scavenges from the wreckage. However, Michael's boat excursion faced some difficulties. Walt didn't want to leave the island, so he set the boat on fire. (Season One, "...In Translation.") And in "Born to Run," Kate shows how badly she wants a spot on the raft by helping Sun dose Jin's water with an herb to make him too sick to sail, at which point Kate would take his place. But Michael accidentally drinks from Jin's bottle and gets violently ill himself. As a result, Walt explains to Michael that he was the one who set the raft on fire because he didn't want to leave the island; Walt told him this because he didn't want Michael to learn from anyone else that he was the one who set the fire and then wrongly conclude Walt poisoned him. Walt sensed Locke was going open the hatch, and wanted to leave the island as soon as possible. This decision also shows a huge advance in Walt's trust of Michael.

Despite fire, poison and pressure to depart on time, and the raft still sails. Less than a day into their journey, however, the raft is ambushed by a tugboat manned by the Others; they kidnap

Walt, shoot Sawyer in the shoulder, and destroy the raft, leaving Michael, Sawyer and Jin for dead. (Season One, "Exodus.") The three eventually wash up on another shore of the island, where they are found by the Tailies. (Season Two, "Adrift.") At that point, Michael becomes obsessed with recovering Walt, and when he learns from Tailie Libby which direction the Others came from, and heads off into the jungle to find Walt. (Season Two, "...And Found.") Michael's rash action forces the Tailies to leave the protection of a hatch they discovered in the jungle, the Arrow, for fear of Michael drawing the attention of the Others, and once they track and catch up to Michael, they head to the Lostaways' side of the island.

When he returns to camp, Michael learns of the Swan hatch and starts taking shifts on the computer. On one of Michael's shifts, someone tries to communicate with him through the computer:

```
Hello?
>: Hello?
Who is this?
>: This is Michael. Who is this?
Dad?
```

It appears to be Walt.▣ (Season Two, "What Kate Did.") This encounter reinvigorates Michael's drive to rescue Walt into a kind of mad obsession. Michael asks Locke to teach him to shoot a rifle, and then turns on Locke, sealing him in the armory and taking a rifle with him when he leaves. With this act, Michael

▣It's not clear, though, just how Walt communicated with Michael over the computer. The terminal in the Swan station was supposed to be inoperable until four minutes before the 108-minute countdown ended.

shows he's willing to sacrifice the other survivors for his son. (Season Two, "The 23rd Psalm" and "The Hunting Party.")

Michael is eventually captured by the Others in the jungle and, as Sayid says, is "compromised." In the second season episode "Three Minutes," the Others take Michael to their odd, primitive camp on the north side of the island, draw blood from him and ask him questions about Walt. They finally let Michael see Walt, but soon take Walt away and offer Michael a deal: he is to return to the hatch, free Ben, and bring Hurley, Jack, Kate and Sawyer back to the Others' side of the island. In exchange the Others will return Walt to Michael and give them the tugboat to leave the island. It's clear from this scene that Michael is a broken man; as he sobs, he tells the Others he'll do anything to get Walt back: "Whatever you want."

Michael follows through on his part of the bargain. In the second season episode "Two for the Road," he returns to the Lostaways' camp exhausted and in rough shape, and recuperates in the hatch.△ When he awakens, he finds Ana-Lucia guarding Ben and cleaning the gun she lifted from Sawyer. She tells Michael that Ben tried to kill her that day and that she wants to take revenge, but can't do it, so Michael convinces her to let him kill Ben for her. As soon as Michael opens the armory door, he shoots Ana-Lucia instead, and then accidentally shoots Libby when she enters the hatch unexpectedly. As promised, Michael frees Ben, and then shoots himself in the arm to make it look like Ben managed his own escape. He couldn't tell the other survivors that he actually killed Ana-Lucia and Libby, but

---

△ This episode actually aired two episodes before "Three Minutes;" the material from "Three. Minutes" with Michael and the Others was actually an on-island flashback.

penitently cleans the blood off the hatch floor, and only says to Sun, "They were murdered."✦ (Season Two, "Three Minutes.") In the second season finale "Live Together, Die Alone," Michael leads Kate, Jack, Sawyer and Hurley into the Others' on the pretext that they are going to rescue Walt, and indeed gets Walt back. But before they leave on the tugboat, Michael asks Ben how he knows Michael won't tell anyone about the island, and Ben responds, "Maybe you will, maybe you won't. But it won't matter. Once you leave, you'll never be able to get back here. And my hunch is you won't say a word to anybody because if you do, people will find out what you did to get your son back." When Michael is assured that the Others won't hurt his friends, he then asks Ben, "Who are you people?" and Ben enigmatically says, "We're the good guys, Michael."

Walt Lloyd is Michael's son and one of the island's central enigmas. Walt was living in Australia with his mother Susan, and when she suddenly died from a blood disorder, he was turned over to Michael by his adoptive father Brian Porter. Michael went to Australia to get Walt, and they were returning to the states on Oceanic 815 when it went down. Walt at turns spooks and impresses people, as he seems to have some strange ability to unconsciously make his imagination manifest in reality. He also seems to have no conscious realization of this capacity. It may be this quality that causes the very bird he's reading about in a book

✦Cool soliloquy of the episode by Mr. Eko when he finds Michael cleaning the blood on the floor: "For a brief time I served in a small parish in England. Every Sunday after Mass, I would see a young boy waiting in the back of the church. And then one day the boy confessed to me that he had beaten his dog to death with a shovel. And he said that the dog had bitten his baby sister on the cheek, and he needed to protect her. And he wanted to know whether he would go to hell for this. I told him that God would understand, that he would be forgiven, as long as he was sorry. But the boy did not care about forgiveness. He was only afraid that if he did go to hell, that dog would be there waiting for him."

crash into his patio window in Sydney, brings on a polar bear attack in the jungle shortly after Walt reads a Green lantern comic with a polar bear in the story,* and makes him appear in the jungle to Shannon after the Others abduct him. When Walt's mother Susan died suddenly from a blood disorder, her husband Brian Porter did not want to retain custody of the boy, even though he had previously petitioned for legal custody, because of the strange things that happened when Walt was around. As he tells Michael, "There's just – there's something about him. [...] Sometimes when he's around, things happen. He's different somehow." (Season One, "Special.")

On the island, Locke's interactions with Walt help open his preternatural mind. Locke introduces Walt to backgammon (which is a much better game than... checkers), and he proves to be a fast learner, soon taking Hurley for $83,000. When Locke teaches Walt how to throw a knife, he also helps Walt access "his mind's eye," which sees a lot more than most eyes or minds, and may be tweaked by the island. (Season One, "Special.") Walt intuited that the island was a good place for him, so when Michael began building a raft to leave, Walt secretly set it on fire. (Season One, "...In Translation.") Locke knew Walt's secret and promised to keep it, but when Michael is later poisoned while building the replacement raft, Walt goes to Locke to tell him he didn't do it; when Locke touches Walt's arm, Walt steps away in fear, saying, "Don't open it Mr. Locke! Don't open that thing! Just don't open it!" Walt didn't know about the hatch, but sensed its danger, and then knew it was time for him to leave the island. (Season One, "Born to Run.")

---

*He was also given a stuffed polar bear by Michael when he was very young, and was just reunited with Michael, which may have brought back memories of the polar bear.

Walt spends much of his time with his yellow Labrador retriever, Vincent. In one flashback Walt is shown looking into Vincent's face as if he sees something others do not.❀ Before Walt leaves on the raft he entrusts Vincent to Shannon, who recently lost her stepbrother, Boone. Walt explains that talking to Vincent helped him feel better after his mom died, and maybe talking to Vincent will help her deal with Boone's death. Caring for Vincent helps Shannon develop a sense of responsibility, so Walt is indirectly responsible for helping Shannon to mature. But their connection grows deeper when Walt is taken by the Others and starts to appear to Shannon back on the island. On three separate occasions, Shannon sees Walt appear out of nowhere, and each time he is dripping wet, warning her that "the Others were coming" and not to "push the button." But each time he was speaking unintelligibly, very quietly, and backwards.❋ (Season Two, "Abandoned.") Shannon was chasing a phantom Walt into the jungle when she was shot by Ana-Lucia, so Walt is also indirectly responsible for her death.

The Others are very curious about Walt. When they abduct Michael, one Other, Ms. Klugh, asks him strange questions about Walt: Was Walt Michael's biological son? How young was he when he started talking? Did he ever get headaches? Did he

❀This also suggests that Vincent may be seeing something in Walt; *The Lost Experience* alternate reality game revealed an organization sponsored by The Hanso Foundation called Retrievers of Truth - a project working with clairvoyant yellow labs. However, if you can find the hidden forums, "sponsored by The Hanso Foundation" changes to "subjugated by The Hanso Foundation." (www.retrieversoftruth.com)

❋Walt's talking backwards may be another nod to *Twin Peaks* and the Man from Another Place. This person was a dwarf who, when he appeared, spoke in what was a looped backwards track that was re-recorded played backwards, and then re-looped forwards, creating a forward speech that had the cadence of a track being played backwards. This odd cadence marked the Man from Another Place as other-worldly and strange, which may be a sense the creators of *Lost* are recalling when Walt appears in places he's not supposed to be, speaking backwards.

ever appear someplace he wasn't supposed to be? (Season Two, "Three Minutes.") And when they return Walt to Michael, they tell him that they "got more than they bargained for" with Walt, echoing Brian's sentiments that Walt is "different somehow." Walt's abilities are still largely unexplored, but this much is clear: Walt has a knack for understanding and perhaps communicating with animals (Vincent), objects from his imagination seem to at times manifest in reality (the bird in Australia, the polar bears), he intuits the danger the hatch presented just by touching Locke, and he indeed appears in places he's "not supposed to be."

Walt's relationship with Michael is the most immediate of the strained son/estranged father relationships among the survivors – like Jack and his father Christian, Locke and Cooper, Sawyer and his dead father, and Jin and his fisherman father. Walt and Michael's relationship provides a model of reparation, but theirs is the only son/father relationship where the focus is on the father, rather than the son. Narratively, it also foregrounds the kind of development Michael goes through to forge a positive relationship with his son, and as such, Michael becomes a kind of surrogate model for the other sons who are distant or separated from their fathers – they can look to Michael and see the kind of care and devotion that they lack. Walt comes to recognize Michael's devotion when Michael and Locke save him from the polar bear, when Michael persists in building the raft to get Walt off the island, and in Michael's tireless efforts to rescue Walt from the Others. Walt leaves the island with Michael on the tugboat given to them by the Others.

Finally, Walt serves as a kind of crux between the two realms of the show, the fictional world of the narrative and the real world of the audience. Toward the end of the second season, elements of *Lost* began crossing from the fictional space of the show into reality beyond the show: The Hanso Foundation, which funds the Dharma Initiative's program on the island, began advertising during television commercial breaks; a Hanso Foundation representative appeared on the May 24, 2006 episode of *The Jimmy Kimmel Show* to distance the foundation from the TV show; a fictional author who died in the fictional crash of Oceanic 815 had his detective novel *Bad Twin* "posthumously" published by Hyperion Press; and in the summer of 2006, the Apollo candy bars found in the hatch began appearing in stores. This was all part of *The Lost Experience*, the alternate reality game initiated by the show's creators as a bridge to develop the mythology between seasons. This bleeding of fiction into reality mirrors one of the more significant aspects of the narrative concerning Walt: His ability to make the fiction of the imagination appear in reality mirrors the way the alternate reality game impresses fiction into reality, and bears out the Will Rogers saying that it isn't what we don't know that gives us trouble, it's what we know that just ain't so.

Charlie Pace is a British one-hit-wonder rock star with little going for him besides a sincere heroin habit. Charlie was in Australia trying to coax his older brother Liam to re-join their band, Driveshaft, and go on a short tour – the tour won't go on without Liam's participation. Liam originally helped Charlie get hooked on smack, but when his own habit threatened his marriage and baby girl, Liam took his family to Australia, cleaned himself up, and left Charlie and the band behind.

Charlie was once a devout Catholic, but in his addiction went headlong into the kind of life that led to long moments in the confessional. In flashbacks (as well as on the island), Charlie time and again shows that he is a liar, but of an immature, pathetic ilk who is more interested in protecting his fragile ego (and his addiction) than anything sinister. On the island he eventually manages to kick his habit with Locke's help, but kicking is a long process that brings out many of Charlie's demons. When Locke finds Charlie's stash, he takes the heroin, saying he'll let Charlie ask him for it three times, and on the third time he'll get it back. This marks Charlie's transformation.

Early on, Charlie feels useless on the island, especially around Jack. In the pilot episode, when Jack hikes through the jungle looking for the cockpit's transceiver, Charlie tags along hoping to find his drugs in the adjacent toilet. In "Walkabout," when boars charge from the plane's wreckage, Jin rushes to protect Sun, Sayid protects Claire, Sawyer protect Kate, Boone protect Shannon... and Jack protects Charlie. (Season One, "Walkabout.") When Charlie notices one of the survivors drowning in the surf in "White Rabbit," all he can do is call to Jack for help; Charlie doesn't swim. In "House of the Rising Sun," Jack finds food and shelter for everyone, while Charlie manages to find a beehive. Jack seems to have the survival skills and instincts that Charlie lacks, and Charlie's musician's skills are largely useless on the island, especially compared to a physician's skills.

In "The Moth," Charlie is mid-withdrawal when Jack begins moving supplies to the caves. Charlie tries to help Jack, but Jack sends Charlie away, telling him "We don't need you right now." Later, Jack finds Charlie's guitar in the way and asks him to move it; the combination of Charlie's already-fractured state Jack's slight was too much for him to take.♪ Charlie finds Jack in a cave and

---

♪Incidentally, Hurley was no fan of Charlie's band Driveshaft, calling them Suckshaft when he was still in California. (Season Two, "Everybody Hates Hurley.") Saying "suck" and "shaft" in the same sentence, let alone right next to each other, must have been a minor coup for prime time television, especially on a network owned by family-friendly Disney.

hollers at him, causing a cave-in that dislocates Jack's shoulder and traps them beneath the fallen rocks. The shock of the accident snaps Charlie back into sorts. He volunteers to crawl through the rocks, finds Jack, and helps put his shoulder back into socket (healing the physician). While the other survivors move the rocks from the mouth of the cave, Charlie finds a way out by following a moth to a crack on the other side of the cave, and helps Jack out of the cave. This event marks a symbolic rebirth for Charlie; when he returns to Locke and asks for his heroin back, it is only to destroy it.✿ Drug-free and armed with new confidence, Charlie becomes closer to Claire, and is able to help her prepare for the birth of her baby, Aaron.

But Charlie's sobriety is tested early and often. In the episode "Raised by Another," around the 20th day on the island, Charlie and Claire are kidnapped by Ethan Rom, an Other who has infiltrated the group by posing as a fellow survivor of Oceanic 815 to get to Claire's unborn baby. When Jack, Kate, Locke and Boone go after Charlie and Claire, Ethan catches Jack, beats him and warns, "If you do not stop following me, I will kill one of them." (Season One, "All the Best Cowboys Have Daddy Issues.") Of course Jack keeps going, and when he and Kate find Charlie, he's hanging by his neck from a tree vine. Jack is barely able to revive him, and the event leaves Charlie deeply shaken. After Claire escapes Ethan, he returns for her and once again delivers his violent message through Charlie, lifting him

---

✿Cool soliloquy of the episode by Locke when Charlie asks him for his heroin: "That's a moth cocoon… You see this little hole? This moth's just about to emerge. It's in there right now, struggling. It's digging its way through the thick hide of the cocoon. Now, I could help it, take my knife, gently widen the opening, and the moth would be free. But it would be too weak to survive. Struggle is nature's way of strengthening it. Now this is the second time you've asked me for your drugs back. Ask me again and it's yours."

by the throat and calmly saying, "You bring her here. If you don't, I'm going to kill one of them. And then if you don't bring her back before sundown tomorrow, I'll kill another, and another, and another, one everyday. And Charlie, I'll kill you last." (Season One, "Homecoming.") When Claire agrees to be used as bait, they finally catch Ethan, but before they can question him, Charlie fires six shots into the man, instantly killing him. It seems Charlie also has a violent, vengeful streak.

Charlie faces other dangers as he struggles to protect Claire and her baby Aaron. In the first season finale "Exodus," Rousseau takes Aaron, and Charlie and Sayid track her into the jungle.* Along the way they find the fallen Nigerian drug smuggler's plane that Boone died in. Sayid finds the heroin-stuffed Virgin Mary statues in the plane and tells Charlie the plane's inhabitants were drug smugglers, not knowing Charlie is a recovering addict. Charlie takes one of the statues and keeps it with him – a test of both his Catholic faith and his faith in himself. But Charlie has a difficult time with that test. After retrieving Aaron, Charlie begins imposing unwanted parenting advice, and Claire begins to wonder why Charlie carries a Virgin Mary statue with him everywhere – perhaps he was a religious nut. (Season Two, "Abandoned.")

In the second season episode "The 23rd Psalm," Mr. Eko learns from Claire about Charlie's statue, finds Charlie, and confirms it's one of the statues from his village in Nigeria. Charlie unwittingly confesses his habit to Mr. Eko and leads him to the plane, which still contains the bodies of one of Eko's associates and Eko's brother, Yemi. Eko gives Charlie a statue to

---

*Rousseau thought she was protecting the baby from the Others, but the survivors couldn't know this.

replace the one he broke, and then they burn the plane while Eko recites the 23rd Psalm; this experience gives Charlie and Mr. Eko an immediate spiritual connection, and Eko becomes the sage for Charlie that Locke once was.

While Charlie's statue experience earns him a new friend in Eko, it causes Claire and Locke to question his responsibility. Soon after being asked to stay away from Claire and Aaron, Charlie begins having vivid dreams that the baby is in danger. (Season Two, "Fire + Water.") At one point he even believes he sees Aaron in the water and rushes out to get him, only to find that while dreaming he actually ran into the surf with Aaron. When he asks Mr. Eko about the dreams, Eko suggests that they may actually mean something; Charlie takes this to mean he needs to baptize Aaron, and he makes this his life-and-death mission. Charlie's erratic behavior leads Locke to suspect Charlie of using again; he tracks Charlie to his stash of statues and takes them to the hatch's armory, which drives the first wedge between them. That night Charlie set a fire near the beach and took advantage of the chaos to carry Aaron out into the surf. Locke managed to convince Charlie to return Aaron to Claire, and then gave Charlie a humiliating beating in front of the group, driving another wedge between them.

As seen with Jack, Charlie does not respond well to feeling humiliated; and as with Ethan, Charlie proves vengeful. Charlie wasn't using again, and finds his opportunity to disgrace Locke by agreeing to help Sawyer in his con to get the guns. Charlie sets the con in motion by staging an attack on Sun as she works her garden, and receives a gun and a promise from Sawyer not to divulge what Charlie did.⊠ (Season Two, "The Long Con.")

Having settled his score with Locke, Charlie then has to earn his way back into the trust of the group, and in the episode "Dave" begins to help Eko build a church on the island. He's even slowly accepted again by Claire when he offers her the vaccine he finds on the airdropped palette in the jungle.❖ Eko's mentoring of Charlie lasts until "Three Minutes" when Eko moves into the hatch to take over Locke's position entering the code. While Charlie is past his drug addiction, he's still not past the immature responses, and Charlie feels abandoned by Eko. He continues working on the church on his own, when Walt's dog Vincent finds Charlie's remaining hidden Virgin Mary statues and brings one to him. Charlie had all but forgotten about them: "Are you kidding me?" He realizes he truly doesn't need the heroin anymore and throws the statues into the ocean. The symbolic mixing of religion and opiates, and the image of tossing both away, is not accidental; Charlie is at turns enslaved by each, and may have had to get rid of both to be truly free.†

The hatch is a problem for Charlie; the two people he confided in – Locke and Eko – have each forsaken him for the hatch. In the second season finale "Live Together, Die Alone," the day after Charlie tosses his religion and dope away, the hatch's former attendant Desmond returns. Desmond eventually helps Locke seal Eko out of the hatch to let the count run down, and the first person Eko turns to for help is Charlie, who finally gets

⊠Charlie's gun is like Chekov's gun; he ends up giving it to Sayid in "The Whole Truth," and Sayid hasn't used it yet, but we know it's there, and will most likely be used.

❖This is the palette of food and supplies dropped on the island during the lockdown in, well, "Lockdown."

† An obvious statement, but the image is also a literal manifestation of Karl Marx's claim that religion was the opiate of the masses.

past his hurt feelings when he's made to feel useful. Charlie leads Eko to the dynamite used to blow open the hatch, and they use it on the blast doors, but the explosion only succeeds in injuring Eko. Charlie manages to bring Eko back to consciousness and tries to get him out of the hatch as the Swan station's system fails and the machinery begins swimming around the room in a wash of electromagnetism. Charlie manages to escape and is warmly greeted by Claire, but he lost part of his hearing in the blast.

Claire Littleton is an Australian new-ager who was on her way to Los Angeles to give up her unborn baby for adoption. Aside from the Tailie flight attendant Cindy Chandler (who was either taken or killed by the Others), Claire is so far the only known Aussie on the island. She had few prospects when she got pregnant, and then her boyfriend Thomas (a struggling artist like Michael) left her. Claire visited a psychic to seek advice on what to do with her unborn baby. The psychic; Richard Malkin, was quite disturbed by what he sensed in Claire, and told her that she must raise the child herself: "It can't be another. You mustn't allow another to raise your baby" (or possibly "You mustn't allow *an Other* to raise your baby"). (Season One, "Raised by Another.") Malkin continued to warn Claire, calling her often and fearfully telling her how important it was that she raised the baby. However, one day Malkin changed his tune, abruptly informing Claire he had found a family in L.A. that would like to adopt the baby: "And they're not strangers, Claire, they're good people," (a phrase which echoes the Others' distinction of "good" and "bad" people). Claire took Malkin's offer, and boarded Oceanic 815.

On the island, Claire becomes an immediate focus of concern and care due to her advanced pregnancy. She is one of the first people Jack and Hurley help after the crash, as the shock

of the situation causes her to begin having contractions. These opening scenes mark Claire and her baby, as well as Jack and Hurley, as figures of significance. Hurley gives Claire extra airline meals, and Boone brings her fresh water. The day after the crash, Claire confesses to Shannon that she hasn't felt the baby move since the accident, making her fear the worst. But as she is writing in her diary later that day, Jin approaches her (and everyone else) with sea urchin he formally prepared. Claire politely eats a piece, and immediately feels her baby kick. In her excitement she forces the very traditional Jin to feel her tummy; Jin is at first mortified until he feels the baby and shares Claire's moment.

Claire's pregnancy makes her feel useless compared to other survivors, so she takes it upon herself to find a way to contribute. In the episode "Walkabout," Claire is sorting through the luggage from the plane's wreckage when she discovers Sayid's envelope with Nadia's photograph and returns it to him. Her magnanimous action even spurs Sawyer to hand over a stack of wallets he'd scavenged from the bodies. After going through so many dead people's belongings, she asks Jack to lead some sort of commemorative service, but when he refuses, she takes it upon herself to lead the service; this is her first act of communal spirituality, which opens a narrative avenue the show might follow in the future.

As Claire's pregnancy advances, she lacks fresh water and begins to faint. When Jack discovers the caves and an endless supply of fresh water, Charlie tries to convince Claire to move there, but she won't leave the beach. Charlie finally makes a deal with her: if he can get her some peanut butter (the only food she craves), she will move to the caves. Charlie manages to charm her by presenting an empty jar of peanut butter – "it's extra-smooth" – and coaxes Claire to the caves.

Once in the caves, in the episode "Raised by Another," Claire begins having nightmares that someone is trying to get to the baby inside her. In her first dream, she sees Locke as he lays out tarot cards and scolds, "He was your responsibility but you gave him away, Claire. Everyone pays the price now." When Locke looks up at Claire in the dream, he has one completely black eyeball and one completely white. Claire awakens to find herself wandering in the jungle, screaming, so shaken by the nightmare that she dug her fingernails into her palms until they bled. In another dream, someone tries to push a needle into her stomach. Jack chalks it up to stress and offers Claire a sedative after the second nightmare. But the dreams weren't entirely imaginary; Claire refuses Jack's offer and returns to the beach with Charlie, and along the way they are abducted by Ethan Rom, an Other posing as an Oceanic 815 survivor. Determined to fix his error, Jack leads a search party into the jungle, but he is soon caught by Ethan, who beats Jack and tells him, "If you do not stop following me, I will kill one of them." (Season One, "All the Best Cowboys Have Daddy Issues.") Of course Jack keeps going, and when he catches up to Charlie, he finds him hung by the neck from a vine.

It wasn't until a second season flashback in "Maternity Leave" that we found what happened to Claire. Ethan took her to the Staff station, a medical post across the island. He kept her drugged, gave the unborn baby vaccinations, and convinced Claire that giving up her baby was the best thing to do because they (the Others) were a "good family." But as they prepared to operate and remove her baby, one of the Others knocked Claire out, dragged her from the Staff station, and left her unconscious in the jungle.☆ Claire is eventually found wandering outside the Lostaways' camp in the first season episode "Special," but she has no memory of anything since the crash, and she doesn't even recognize Charlie. Ethan isn't done with Claire; he returns to their camp the next day, attacks Jin and Charlie in the jungle and demands that Charlie return Claire to him, or he'll kill the other survivors every day until he gets Claire. (Season One, "Homecoming.") Claire willingly agrees to pose as bait to catch Ethan, which leads to Ethan's death at Charlie's hands.

Claire's baby is born in the first season episode "Do No Harm" (the same night Boone dies), and she eventually names him Aaron. Claire starts to settle into mother mode, but she also realizes that Charlie is not completely stable, constantly keeping a Virgin Mary statue with him and insisting that Aaron be baptized. (Season Two, "The 23rd Psalm.") Mr. Eko reveals the truth

---

☆We learn that Claire's liberator was Alex, Rousseau's daughter who herself had been taken by the others as a newborn.

of the statue's (heroin) contents to Claire; she knows Charlie is a recovering addict, and fearing for her baby's safety, demands that Charlie leave her and Aaron alone. But Claire does not lack for caregivers, and she turns to Locke for protection. Charlie does not give up on his mission to baptize Aaron, and sets a fire as a distraction to grab the baby and baptize him in the ocean. As a result, Locke beats the hell out of Charlie, leading to the Charlie/Locke rift. (Season Two, "Fire + Water.")

At first Aaron appears healthy, but when he comes down with a rash and a fever in the second season episode "Maternity Leave," Rousseau shows up at the camp to ask about the baby, and Claire begins recalling more flashes of memory from her abduction; from the first season finale, she already recalled scratching Rousseau's arm, and more memories start to emerge, such as the vaccinations Ethan gave her.□ Her fear piqued, Claire asks Libby, a Tailie with training as a psychologist, to help her recover her memory. With Libby's help, Claire comes to believe that the vaccine Ethan gave her will keep Aaron safe from some unknown infection, and she sets off in search of the Staff station with Kate and Libby; they are joined by Rousseau, who originally found Claire when she was released from the Staff station, and knows the general direction. When they find the station, it's abandoned, nearly empty, and without vaccine. Claire demands that Rousseau tell them where the vaccine is, mistakenly believing Rousseau helped abduct her. In fact, when Alex released Claire, Claire began calling for Ethan, putting herself back in danger. Rousseau heard Claire in the jungle and tried to quiet her until Claire scratched her arm, leaving the marks which would eventually trigger the (mistaken) memory.

□Which also means Rousseau was hanging on the outskirts of the Lostaways' camp, keeping an eye on the baby. She's creepily protective.

Rousseau then knocked Claire out – a blow which may have caused her memory loss – and carried her back to the Lostaways' camp. Rousseau was out to protect Claire and her baby, not hurt them.

After the women return from the Staff, Aaron's rash clears and fever breaks, and things get a bit better. Drugs, the reason for the rift between her and Charlie, provide a catalyst for reunion when Charlie presents Claire with some of the vaccine found on the air-dropped palette. Claire seems to show a sincere desire to trust Charlie again, but makes him earn it. Just as Claire is given a second chance to be a mother, she gives Charlie a new opportunity to be part of their life.

Jin-Soo Kwon is a Korean businessperson from a working class background who married Sun Paik, the wealthy daughter of a rather shady but powerful Korean businessman. Jin and Sun were traveling through Sydney on Oceanic 815 on a mission to deliver Rolex watches to Mr. Paik's associates in Los Angeles. Jin gained his father-in-law's approval by being a mafia-like heavy for his business, a job that turned the once-gentle Jin into someone his wife barely recognized. Jin came a long way from his humble beginnings; much of his ambition was fueled by his desire to ask Mr. Paik for Sun's hand in marriage; along the way, he grew rich, but also grew distant, cold, angry, and tough, and estranged from his fisherman father. Jin didn't know Sun was planning to leave him (and her father) the day of Oceanic flight 815; a car waited for her outside the airport in Sydney, ready to take her away from Jin forever.

But while Jin was unaware of Sun's intentions, Mr. Paik was not so oblivious; in the airport bathroom, one of Mr. Paik's associates confronted Jin,☝ warning him that Mr. Paik was having

Jin and his wife followed to make sure they didn't use the trip to try to escape. (It's unclear whether Mr. Paik was just referring to Sun's escape, or if Jin was planning his own departure as well.) Sun didn't know she was being watched, but when her chance came to escape, she debated with herself over what to do. When she saw Jin holding a single white flower for her, she was reminded of the Jin she had fallen in love with; the small gesture was enough to make Sun reconsider her escape and give Jin a second chance. (Season One, "House of the Rising Sun.") Jin can be harsh, but he also shows flashes of gentleness that contradict her expectations of violent reactions. When Sun spills coffee on Jin's lap in the airport, she anticipates anger, but Jin is forgiving. (Season One, "Exodus, pt. 1.")▲ It is clear that Jin still loves Sun, and in our first glimpse of Jin on the island following the crash, he is shouting her name.

In the first days on the island, Jin's inability to speak English, as well as his strict adherence to conservative traditions and honor, keep him (and Sun) isolated from the other survivors. (At times, the audience hears the other survivors speak through Jin's ears as gibberish looped backwards.) Jin's separateness sows discord between him and the other survivors; they literally can't understand where Jin is coming from. Jin makes some attempts to connect with the other survivors in the pilot episode, preparing sea urchin for them to eat, but he is frustrated when most of them refuse the foreign

❂A white tourist who spoke Korean to him, taking Jin off-guard and suggesting that Mr. Paik had spies of all sorts around.

▲It's tricky to determine if Jin gave Sun the flower before she spilled the coffee on his lap or after, and it's important; if he did it *before*, that would mean they had already started repairing their relationship and Sun had already chosen to stay with Jin. If he did it *after*, that would mean that the flower was like an "it's alright" gift after she burned him with the coffee. The fact that this scene is split between two episodes that occur 22 episodes apart doesn't help. But there is a quick shot showing the flower on the table on which Sun spills the coffee, which means they were most likely already repairing their relationship when it happened.

food. In "Walkabout," Sun encourages him to make more of an effort to communicate with the other survivors, but Jin will hear none of it: "We'll be fine. We don't need anyone else. I'll tell you what to do." Jin's reactions are often unreasonable given the difficult circumstances, and his relationship with Sun appears strained and strange to those around them, especially to Michael, who has several early encounters with the couple. When Jin sees his father-in-law's watch on Michael's wrist, he brutally attacks him, believing Michael is a thief. Because his attack is so ferocious and seemingly random, the other survivors use the marshal's handcuffs to pin him to some of the plane's wreckage. Michael eventually frees Jin by cutting the cuff chain with an axe, but not before putting a scare into him; Jin wears the wrist cuff, a constant reminder of his transgression, for weeks until Locke hacks the cuff off. Jin's relationship with Michael eventually grows into a trusted friendship.

When Jin learns Sun can speak English, he feels betrayed and ashamed, and refuses to speak with her. As a result, Jin decides to help Michael build his raft and accompany him on his voyage to find help off the island. Sun continues to reach out to Jin, and presents him with a small Korean-English glossary of sailing terms to help him on his way. By the time the raft sails in the first season finale, Jin has forgiven Sun, and is leaving to save her rather than avoid her. But their attempt to escape the island is unsuccessful: the Others attack the raft, kidnapping Walt and blowing the raft apart before they make it even one day at sea. Jin eventually washes ashore on the other side of the island with Sawyer and Michael, only to be taken prisoner by the Tailies.

With the Tailies, Jin again proves his loyalty to his friends. He runs to the beach warning them of the people he sees in the jungle, believing they're Others. He helps both Michael and the injured Sawyer, and when Michael goes into the jungle looking for Walt, Jin follows to help him. When Mr. Eko tries to stop him, Jin attacks Eko and gets thumped in return. Eko recognizes Jin's devotion to Michael, and against Tailie leader Ana-Lucia's demands, gives Jin a weapon and joins him in his search for Michael. (Season Two, "...And Found.")

Jin's protectiveness of his wife verges on obsessive, yet he is working toward changing his hyper-controlling ways. When Michael goes into the jungle looking for Walt, Jin tries to go after him until Sun stops him, telling him she won't let him leave again. Jin later quietly tells her he doesn't like being told what to do, and Sun rejoins, "Being told what to do was my life for four years. I didn't like it much either." Jin simply puts his arm around her in a gesture of understanding. (Season Two, "The Hunting Party.") When Sun is attacked in her garden, Jin wants her to abandon the area; when Sun won't leave, he destroys the garden so she has no reason to stay. But after he learns of Sun's pregnancy, he shows his humility again by helping her replant the garden. At that point, Jin finally breaks: "I need you. I hate being this way, fighting. And I can't... I can't talk to anyone. I can't understand them. I need you, Sun." (Season Two, "The Whole Truth.") Sun responds to Jin's confession with one of her own, telling Jin that she wasn't infertile, but he was sterile, and their fertility doctor in South Korea had lied to them because he feared a violent reaction from Jin and Mr. Paik. Jin, in his joy, simply accepts the pregnancy it as a miracle, and realizes why Sawyer had earlier called him "Daddy-O."❑

❑Sun had to get the pregnancy test from Sawyer, who of course had scavenged such things from the plane. Incidentally, when Sawyer gives Jin the nickname "Chewie," it sets up a kind of Han Solo/Chewbacca dynamic that makes Jin's Korean seem more intelligible to those who can't understand Korean (and know *Star Wars*).

After Jin allows his English-speaking wife be the communication conduit between him and the other survivors, their relationship enters a more mutually-respectful phase. Sun accompanies Jin and Sayid on Desmond's sailboat when Michael leads Jack, Kate, Hurley and Sawyer to the Others' camp. From this, we learn that both Jin and Sun can sail, and they are on the sailboat when the electromagnetic pulse courses across the island in the second season finale. But in the third season episode "The Glass Ballerina," we learn that Jin knew Sun has betrayed him in the past. Jin loves Sun and wants to protect her, but he also understands he needs to trust, but verify.

Sun Kwon is the daughter of the wealthy Korean businessperson, and was on Oceanic 815 accompanying her husband Jin on a business trip to deliver Rolex watches to her father's business partners in America. Her marriage to Jin began as a princess-and-pauper type story, but became cold and distant as Jin began working for her father. Jin's work for Sun's father made him so hard and violent that Sun planned to escape from him. Part of her plan was to learn English on the sly from Jae, a man her mother once introduced her to as a potential husband. When he met Sun, Jae was already in love with an American woman he met in college, but by the third season, it becomes clear through flashbacks that he and Sun in fact had an affair – which, when Sun's father found out, led to Jae's death.* (Season Three, "The Glass Ballerina.")

---

*Mr. Paik caught Sun with Jae, and sent Jin to "deliver a message," but didn't tell Jin that Sun cheated on him. Jin beat the hell out of Jae in his hotel room, but rather than kill him as instructed, he told Jae to leave the country and never return. As Jin got into his car after delivering his message, Jae fell from the sky onto his car; he either jumped after Jin delivered his message, or was thrown from the building. If he was thrown, it means Jin was being followed, which is a strong possibility after he was met in the Sydney airport restroom by the stranger hired by Mr. Paik to tail him.

Sun carefully planned her escape: She would create a distraction in the Sydney airport, meet a car waiting outside, and be spirited to freedom. But at the last minute, when Jin showed the gentle and more humble side she fell in love with, Sun changed her mind and chose not to leave her husband. If it weren't for this change of heart, Sun would not have been on Oceanic 815.

While Sun may despair that Jin is no longer the man she married, she has also changed drastically. In flashbacks from the time she met and fell in love with Jin, we see a wealthy, beautiful, confident young woman; on the island, we see a defeated, scared, and dominated shell of her former self. She is strictly subordinate to Jin, consciously choosing to remain in the silent, traditional role, when she could assert herself by speaking English and gaining a measure of power. Her ability to communicate with the other survivors eventually evens out the marital balance – once Jin's shock and shame wears off. Sun then helps Jin learn some English, and gives him a Korean-English glossary of sailing terms before he leaves on Michael's raft. But Sun also may be staying close to her husband out of guilt for her marital transgression with Jae. In the flashback from "The Glass Ballerina," we see that Sun broke a decorative glass ballerina as a child, but blamed it on the maid. Her father knew and warned her that if she didn't confess, he would have to fire the maid, yet Sun wouldn't confess. This introduces an element of duplicity to Sun's character, and throws her promise to Jin that she'd not been with another man into question (and of course she was with Jae). Jin lets on that he knows more than she suspects when he tells Sun and Sayid that he understands more English than they think, and that he knows she betrayed him.

Sun, Jin and Michael share an interesting relationship. Sun

watches Walt for Michael soon after the crash in the pilot episode, and Michael is the first person on the island to hear Sun speak English when she explains why Jin attacked him. In speaking English with Michael in these early episodes, Sun creates an intimacy between the two of them; Michael now knows something about Sun her own husband doesn't know. But when Jin scolds Sun for wearing a bikini on the beach in the first season episode "...In Translation" and Michael steps in to stop him, Sun slaps Michael before anything can happen. She later finds Michael and explains that she was actually trying to protect him from Jin, again sharing something with Michael without her husband's knowledge. Back in the caves, Jin asks Sun if something is going on between her and Michael, foreshadowing that he had reason not to trust Sun.

The animosity between Jin and Michael (with Sun caught in between) leads the Lostaways to assume Jin is responsible when Michael's raft is destroyed (when it was actually Walt, his own son, who set the fire). Michael attacks Jin, and this time no one intervenes: As Sayid says, "This is between them." Jin takes a beating from Michael and refuses to defend himself until Sun cries – in English – "Stop it," finally revealing her ability to communicate with the other survivors. Publicly embarrassed, ashamed and angry, Jin leaves Sun to join Michael in rebuilding the raft. The three are later re-connected when Sun tries to keep Jin from leaving on Michael's raft in "Born to Run." Sun conspires with Kate to spike Jin's water bottle with an herb that will make him violently ill and unable to sail, thereby keeping Jin on the island while creating a spot on the raft for Kate, but instead Michael drinks from Jin's bottle and becomes ill. Sun's accidental poisoning of Michael has a huge unforeseen domino effect: If Sun hadn't poisoned Michael, Walt would not have gone to Locke to tell him he wasn't responsible, Locke would not have touched Walt's arm to comfort him, and Walt wouldn't have realized that Locke was about to do something dangerous (opening the hatch). That realization spurs Walt to convince Michael that they need to get off the island, which of course leads to the raft launch and Walt's abduction by the Others. Eventually Michael becomes a good friend to both Sun and Jin. The three are again connected when Sun and Jin sail with Sayid around the island to follow Michael in the second season finale. Their relationship presents a counter to the model that Michael hinted at when Jin first attacked him, that "Korean people don't like black people." (Season One, "House of the Rising Sun.")

In Sun's effort to contribute to the group, she establishes a garden of medicinal herbs. She gives Sawyer herbs to help his headaches, teaches Walt to brush his teeth with a plant, and is able to help Shannon's asthma attacks with eucalyptus she harvests. If Jack is the medicine man, she is the medicine woman, and is there to help Jack when Boone is injured in the Nigerian plane accident. She helps Jack work a sea urchin spine into a needle, and keeps Jack from uselessly transfusing too much of his own blood into Boone. But Sun's garden is also a dangerous place; its isolated location makes her an easy target for Charlie to stage an attack.

After Jin returned from the other side of the island, where he was captured by the Tailies, Sun learns she is pregnant. Conception was supposed to be impossible for the couple; their doctor in Korea had confirmed that they could not have children, and explained to the couple that it was because Sun was barren, but in private told Sun that Jin was sterile (which they hid from Jin out of fear, for their own protection). As with Locke's paralysis and Rose's cancer, the island seems to be able to heal *some* physical ailments (but it didn't do much for Shannon's asthma, Boone's leg, or Sawyer's need for reading glasses), so perhaps it has healed Jin. But the flashback in the third season episode "The Glass Ballerina" proves that Sun was unfaithful to Jin; what isn't clear by this episode is how long ago her transgression took place. If it was long ago (and from Jin's haircut in the flashback, it looks like it was), then Sun wasn't already preggers when she got on Oceanic 815. But whether the baby is a miracle or not, the impending presence of another child on the island will most likely attract the attention of the Others.

In the same third season episode, we learn something else of Sun; not only is she capable of adultery, but she's also capable of shooting another person point-blank. She remains on the sailboat as she, Jin and Sayid wait for Jack and the other survivors to come back from the Others' side of the island. When the Others steal onto the boat in order to take it, Sun fires a pistol into an Other named Colleen, killing her.

Rose Nadler is a newlywed cancer patient who thought she was going to Australia for her honeymoon. In fact, her husband Bernard chose Australia so they could visit a healer in the Outback, Isaac of Uluru; Bernard didn't tell Rose this was his reason for choosing Australia. But Isaac told Rose he couldn't heal her: "It's not that you can't be healed. Like I said, there's different energies. This is not the right place for you." (Season Two, "S.O.S.") The scene where Isaac tried to perform his mojo on Rose is reminicent of the scene where Richard Malkin tried to read Claire's future; both seers were startled, pulled up short, and told their clients they couldn't help them. Rose decided not to tell Bernard that her cancer wasn't healed; if Bernard knew Isaac had been unsuccessful, he would have kept trying to find a way to heal her rather than just being with her.

Bernard was in the tail section – visiting the bathroom – when the plane began to tear apart. Despite having no hard evidence that anyone from the tail section survived, Rose repeatedly affirms that Bernard is still alive and will return to her. When she and Hurley find the Apollo candy bars in the hatch, she saves one for Bernard because he has "a mouth full of sweet teeth," a funny condition for a dentist. (Season Two, "Everybody Hates Hugo.") And indeed, Rose was right: Bernard did survive with the Tailies, and the couple is reunited when the Tailies join the Lostaways.

Rose has a double-connection with the healing power of the island. When at the Sydney airport waiting for Oceanic 815, Rose dropped her medication. The meds were picked up and returned by Locke – making Rose the one person who knows that Locke was wheelchair-bound before the crash. Once on the island, Rose feels her cancer subsiding, and believes the change is because of the island – it seems the island is the place for Rose that Isaac of Uluru mentioned. Rose's belief in the power of the island – and the necessity of her remaining there – causes tension between her and Bernard when he tries to create a giant rescue sign. Bernard is irritated and frustrated by what he perceives as his wife's lack of support. Rose finally explains that she had lied to Bernard in Australia, that Isaac didn't heal her, the island did. Since Bernard's overriding desire is to help Rose, he gives up his quest for rescue, and agrees to a new life on the island with his wife. (Season Two, "S.O.S.") Rose's connection with Locke allows her to comfort him as no one else could when his leg is broken by the hatch's blast door. Immobility is especially frustrating for someone who had been in a wheelchair, and Locke is having trouble accepting Jack's prediction of at least four weeks before he could get around on his injured leg. Rose simply looks at Locke and says, "But honey, you and I both know it's not going to take that long." Rose is right: Locke is up and about in no time.

Boone Carlyle was the son of a millionaire Martha Stewart-type wedding maven, and before the crash he accepted a job managing the family business. He was on the flight home after going to Sydney to rescue his stepsister Shannon when he boarded Oceanic 815.

Boone's over-eager sense of helpfulness and justice sometimes makes him an easy mark, and also leads him to act impulsively. After the crash, he misapplies his lifeguard training by improperly performing mouth to mouth resuscitation on Rose. Jack catches Boone's mistake and takes over helping Rose, while Boone suggests they try the "hole thing... where you stick the pen in the throat."✛ Jack's sarcastic response is lost on Boone, who begins tirelessly searching for pens. Jack and Boone square off again when a fellow survivor calls for help as she struggles in the surf. Boone goes in first, but begins to flounder.❖ Jack catches up to Boone, and drags Boone in before he goes after the woman Boone was trying to save; the woman drowns. (Season One, "White Rabbit.") Boone's sense of justice is revealed early on when he accuses Hurley of setting up his "own little Patriot Act" as Hurley take a census of the survivors. Shannon explains that Boone is "a Libertarian." (Season One, "Raised by Another").△

Boone's relationship with his stepsister dominates his life before and after arriving on the island. Boone constantly chides

✛A tracheotomy.
❖So much for being a licensed lifeguard.
△Shannon's remark serves as a reminder that these characters are living in the same world as the audience.

Shannon, yet he always takes care of her, and in fact had a not-so-secret crush on her. Shannon took advantage of Boone's affection, convincing him to come to Sydney to save her from an abusive boyfriend, all in an attempt to extort money from Boone. Shannon's manipulation reached new heights the night before the Oceanic 815 flight left Sydney; when her boyfriend double-crossed her and left with Boone's money, Shannon went to Boone's hotel room in Sydney and slept with him. This more than anything may have led to Boone's being extra-protective of Shannon on the island.

It wasn't until Boone fell in with Locke that he was able to get past his hang-ups over Shannon. Boone became one of Locke's apprentices, and the two eventually come upon the lid of the wan hatch on the jungle floor. They spend weeks uncovering the hatch and working out how to get in, all the while telling the other survivors they were hunting for boar. When Shannon becomes suspicious of their excursions in the first season episode "Hearts and Minds," Boone tells Locke he wants to tell Shannon about the hatch, so Locke knocks Boone out with the butt of his hunting knife. He then ties Boone up and spreads a paste with a hallucinogen in it over Boone's wound, drops the knife in front of Boone, and leaves him. After Locke leaves, Boone hears Shannon screaming in the jungle. He strains for Locke's knife, frees himself to go after Shannon, and finds her in time to see her being killed by the smoke monster in the jungle. Boone didn't realize he was hallucinating and encountering his own subconscious anxiety, not Shannon herself (although Shannon *was* that anxiety). Going through the experience of watching his anxiety die helped Boone be free of the hold Shannon always had on him.

In the first season episode "Deus ex Machina," Boone and

Locke are work on opening the hatch when they come across the treed Nigerian Beechcraft 18. For some unexplained reason, Locke's legs are giving out, which understandably scares him; it is left to Boone alone to crawl up into the plane and check it out. Once inside, Boone finds a radio, and is able to briefly make contact with someone (Bernard with the Tailies, as it turns out, who was operating a two-way radio from the Arrow station). But Boone's weight shifts the plane, tilting it out of the trees and crashing it to the ground with him inside. Boone's body is broken by the fall. Locke regains strength in his legs after the accident and brings Boone to the caves for medical attention; however, he lies to Jack about the cause of Boone's injuries in order to protect the discovery of the hatch and the Nigerian plane.✿ In the subsequent episode "Do No Harm," Jack accepts Locke's explanation that Boone fell from a cliff, but because Jack doesn't understand the nature of the accident, he isn't able to properly treat Boone. Jack transfuses his own blood into Boone and is about to amputate Boone's shattered leg when Boone asks Jack to just let him go. Boone dies that night as a result of this second plane crash.

Strangely enough, Boone and Shannon's fate had roots in Jack's medical career. In a flashback, we learn that Boone's stepfather (Shannon's father) Adam Rutherford was in the car wreck that damaged the spinal cord of Jack's future wife, Sarah; when Sarah and Adam were brought into the ER, Jack had to choose which patient to save. Despite the bad odds (or perhaps because of the challenge), Jack chose to attend to Sarah,

---

✿Locke, like Rose, is in no hurry to get off the island now that his legs work again. He guards any information he comes across that could get them off the island, like the plane and its radio.

effectively leaving Adam to die. (Season Two, "Man of Science, Man of Faith.") Were it not for her father's death, Shannon would not have been cut off financially by her stepmother, and would not have had to ask Boone for money; Boone would not have been in Australia helping Shannon, and neither of them would have been on Oceanic 815. So in a sense, Jack's choice to save the more damaged patient repercussed across two generations and an ocean.

Shannon Rutherford is a spoiled rich girl and aspiring ballet dancer who was in Australia, trying to scam her family out of money she felt she was owed. She had recently lost her father, Adam Rutherford, the other victim of the car wreck with Jack's wife-to-be Sarah. After Adam died, Shannon learned that her father had made no will, leaving all his money in a living trust that went to his wife (her stepmother), Sabrina Carlyle. Sabrina refused to support Shannon, which Shannon responded to by becoming a con artist (creating a parallel with Sawyer). Shannon was in Australia after pulling a con on her stepbrother Boone. They were returning to the U.S. together on Oceanic 815 when it went down.

On the island, Shannon at first comes off as irritatingly precious, self-involved and reluctant to help; she spent her days on activities like tanning on the beach while the other survivors built camp and looked for food. Boone captured Shannon's character best when he said to her, "We've all been through a trauma. The only difference is since the crash you've actually given yourself a pedicure." (Season One, "Pilot.") In a flashback, we learn that Shannon threw a fit at the Sydney airport when she and Boone couldn't get into first class; if she had received the upgrade, she would not been seated in the middle section of the plane, and may not have survived the crash with the Lostaways. However, she eventually found some purpose on the island – or had purpose thrust upon her – when Sayid needed her limited French skills and enlisted her as a translator.

Early in the first season we learn that Shannon suffers from asthma, and ran out of medicine shortly after the crash. The island's healing powers weren't working on Shannon, but Sun's eucalyptus leaves soothed her breathing after her medication was gone. Her asthma, coupled with her pampered lifestyle before the crash, makes Shannon feel useless; Boone adds to her frustration at one point by calling her "worthless." Partly as a way to irritate Boone, Shannon joins a group of survivors on a hike in search of a radio signal; the group is able to tune in a French language transmission on the plane's transceiver, and Shannon is enlisted to use her limited French to help translate the transmission – but she has to be convinced by both Boone and Sayid that she can actually do it, which suggests her self-confidence is much lower than she outwardly presents.☆

When Sayid returns from Rousseau's camp with maps of the island, he again asks Shannon for help translating Rousseau's French notes. Shannon still feels she isn't up to the task, and Sayid once again has to convince her she can do it. In a strange twist, Sayid is actually able to use his ability to coerce someone in a positive way, and their time together eventually leads to Sayid and Shannon developing a romantic relationship. But Sayid might have been too quick to fall; he was flying Oceanic 815 to L.A. to meet his past love Nadia, and may have been a bit vulnerable given his history with Nadia. Shannon was a convenient but dangerous surrogate. When Boone died in the service of Locke, Shannon takes advantage of Sayid's vulnerability and tries to get

---

☆This insecurity may be why Shannon found it easier to con than work to make money; perhaps she didn't have the confidence that she could actually be useful in the workplace.

him to kill Locke in the episode "The Greater Good." When this fails, she attempts to kill Locke herself, and Sayid has to stop her. Their relationship took some time to mend after this, but they eventually came together; for Shannon, this may have been one of the few times she became involved with someone she wasn't trying to scam.

Just before Walt left on Michael's raft, he entrusted his dog Vincent to Shannon, in part as a way to help her heal after her brother Boone's death: "Vincent took care of me when my mom died and nobody would talk to me. They pretended like nothing happened. So I had to talk to Vincent. He's a good listener. You could talk to him about Boone if you want." (Season One, "Exodus.") This gesture brings out a little latent responsibility in Shannon, and she faithfully cares for the dog. But after the raft sets sail (and before anyone on the island knew Walt had been kidnapped by the Others), Shannon begins seeing Walt in the jungle, each time warning her in a silent, backwards voice, "Push the button, don't push the button, bad," and, "They are coming and they are close." (Season Two, "Abandoned.") Shannon finally becomes determined to find Walt, and takes Vincent with her into the jungle to begin searching. Sayid believed Shannon was just stressed and imagining things (much as Jack didn't believe Claire's dreams were anything to worry about), and he chases after Shannon and Vincent. Shannon saw Walt in the jungle yet again, but this time Sayid was there to witness the vision; Walt stood before them, dripping wet, saying "Sssshhh...." Shannon and Sayid had no idea that the Tailies were close by, armed, and working their way through the jungle with Michael, Jin and Sawyer. When Shannon ran after Walt through the jungle, the noise she makes surprises the Tailies, and Ana-Lucia shoots and kills her.

The Tailies: Back Section of Oceanic Flight 815; landed on the Other Side of the Island; Lived in the Abandoned Station "the Arrow"

Ana-Lucia Cortez was an ex-Los Angeles cop who left the force after killing the man who shot her, and was in Australia working as a personal bodyguard (for Jack's father Christian, no less). Like all of the survivors, Ana-Lucia carried a lot of personal baggage onto Flight 815, but hers was more traumatic than most. She had been shot point-blank in the line of duty; although she wore protective armor, she was pregnant at the time and miscarried. Soon after, Ana-Lucia's boyfriend left her; this negatively parallels her narrative to Claire's, where both boyfriends leave because of incidents surrounding a pregnancy. Ana-Lucia returned to duty against the wishes of her chief of police (and mother), Teresa Cortez, and soon hatched a plan to assassinate the man who shot her. When her shooter was found, Ana-Lucia wouldn't identify him at the police station. She later followed him to a bar; when he left the bar, Ana-Lucia confronted him in the parking lot and shot him repeatedly. Teresa knew Ana-Lucia was the main suspect in that shooting, which led to Ana-Lucia's leaving the force – a situation which negatively parallels her narrative with Jack's, who worked for his father and whose father left the job.

After leaving the force, Ana-Lucia took a security job at LAX; it was in this capacity that she met Jack's father, Christian Shephard, on his way to Australia for his death-bender. Christian invited Ana-Lucia to be his bodyguard, and she took the opportunity for a new start. After they arrived, Christian took Ana-Lucia with him when he drunkenly confronted his former mistress Lindsey and tried to see their daughter (which also means Jack has a half-sister he doesn't know about). Shaken by the incident, Ana-Lucia left Christian at a remote bar and set herself to return to the U.S.*Later, at the Sydney airport, she overheard Jack pleading with an Oceanic check-in agent about getting his father's remains home; Ana reacted by calling her mother and asking to come home. She later shared a drink with Jack in the airport bar, which created a familiarity that helped them relate to each other when the Tailies eventually met the middle section survivors. And it was important for Ana to have Jack as an ally, since she entered the Lostaways' camp by killing one of their own, Shannon. Ana never knew that the man she went to Sydney with was Jack's father, and Jack never knew Ana had helped Christian.

Ana-Lucia was the self-appointed leader of the Tailies, a position of authority she seized through fear and intimidation, rather than being chosen for her innate ability (as Jack had been by the Lostaways). Ana-Lucia claimed the role after the Tailies were first attacked by the Others; it seemed to fit well with her previous life as a protector.■ But she soon went from trying to be a protector to a dictator, which contrasts her leadership style with Jack's.

Ana-Lucia could never quite shake the stress of her recent experiences, and acted and reacted on the island as much out of fear and anger as she did out of a sense of survival and respon-

---

*Christian met Sawyer at this bar, and told Sawyer that Jack is "a good man, maybe a great one." (Season Two, "Outlaws.")

■ It's interesting to consider what might have happened had Mr. Eko not taken his vow of silence after killing two of the Others the first night (see Eko's section). Given his past as a warlord, he could easily have assumed the leadership role, but of course things didn't work out that way.

sibility. Her guiding instinct in protecting the Tailies was to re-unite the children with their parents, reflecting the issues in her own life; after all, she had just lost her own baby, and was in the process of re-connecting with her mother. But while her motives were laudable, her methods became brutal. Early on, in the second season episode "The Other 48 Days," she suspects two members of their group, Nathan and Goodwin, of being threats, and throws Nathan in a pit to torture him for information. Although Nathan's true identity was never made clear, Goodwin – a confirmed Other – freed Nathan from the pit, only to promptly break his neck and dispose of his body. Ana later confronted Goodwin and told him she knew he was an Other, and in the ensuing fight she ran him through with a sharp stick, killing him instantly.

After their raft was ambushed by the Others, Michael, Sawyer and Jin washed up on the shore near the Tailies' camp. After being caught by the Tailies in the second season episode "Orientation," Eko beats them and tosses them into the prison pit. Ana-Lucia didn't trust them; with the tension amped because of the attacks by the Others, she convinces Eko to punch her in the face (so she looked sincerely beaten), and then dump her in the pit so she could pose as another prisoner. Ana then tries to determine if their story was legit, but when Sawyer shows her his gun, her mistrust is confirmed, and she takes the weapon and leaves. Michael eventually convinces her that they were in fact all survivors of Oceanic flight 815, and she releases the prisoners, but despite his injured shoulder (and because of his wise-ass comments) Sawyer, continues to take the brunt of her brutality

In the second season episode "...And Found," the Tailies take Michael, Sawyer and Jin back to their camp at the Arrow station.

But when Michael learns the direction the Others came from, he takes off into the jungle to find Walt. Mr. Eko and Jin follow and retrieve Michael, but in the process they hear the Others in the jungle, and know they can no longer stay at their camp. Ana-Lucia decides they'll have to make their way to the Lostaways' side of the island by traveling around the island's perimeter. But Sawyer's bullet wound worsens and becomes septic, and Eko decides to take Sawyer straight through the jungle against Ana's wishes in order to get him to Jack as quickly as possible. As they work their way through the jungle, Sawyer's condition deteriorates. They make a stretcher for Sawyer, after which yet another Tailie (Cindy) is taken by the Others.□ The Tailies hear the Others' whispers, and Ana tells everyone to run; as they enter the Lostaways' area of the jungle, they're surprised by Shannon looking for Walt. Thinking Shannon was an Other, Ana-Lucia shoots Shannon in the stomach, killing her. In "Collision," the enraged Sayid tries to kill Ana in response (he was with Shannon in the jungle), but is stopped by Eko. Ana keeps Sayid hostage in the jungle as Eko takes Sawyer to Jack for medical care, and when alone, Ana and Sayid find some common ground – they had both seen enough tragedy to feel dead inside.

Both Jack and Locke found Ana-Lucia's police background useful: In "The Hunting Party," Jack asks her to help him form an army in response to threats from the Others, and in "The Whole Truth" Locke asks her to interrogate Ben (who was posing as "Henry Gale"). Ana got Ben to draw a map of where he claimed his balloon had gone down, and with Sayid and Charlie's help in the episode "Lockdown," she found the wreckage, along with the grave Ben claimed contained his wife. They dug it up

□Or rather, she disappears as they make their way up a cliff. But Cindy's status is in question.

and found the real Henry Gale, proving Ben was an imposter. By working together to investigate Ben, Sayid and Ana also bridge the rift caused by Shannon's death.

While guarding Ben in the episode "Two for the Road," Ana-Lucia tells him that she'd been around a lot of killers as a cop, and they all liked to talk, "but you're different, Henry, hmm? Quiet." Ben whispers something back to Ana, and as she leans in close to hear him, he attacks her: "You killed two of us – good people who were leaving you alone! You're the killer, Ana-Lucia!" Locke helps Ana by knocking Ben out with a crutch, but her rage was sparked. Since Sawyer stole all the guns, she goes to him for one, and when he won't give her a gun, she first attacks him, and then has sex with him, distracting him long enough to grab his gun. But when she returns to kill Ben, he tells her, "Goodwin thought you were worthy, and he could change you. But he was wrong, and it cost him his life." Something trips in her when she learns that someone else had seen good in her, and she doesn't shoot Ben. However this moment was short-lived, and when Michael returned from the Others' camp, he convinces Ana to give him her gun and let him kill Ben for her. After Michael opens the armory, he turns on Ana and kills her. Ana's time on the island thus began and ended in brutal violence.★

Mr. Eko was a Nigerian gangster-warlord who was posing as a priest in Australia. He was on his way to Los Angeles with a new

---

★It was rumored that Ana-Lucia's character was killed off because of actor Michelle Rodriguez's run-ins with the law (three speeding tickets and a drunk-driving citation while on probation). She was picked up for drunk driving the same night Cynthia Watros, the actor who who plays Libby, was picked up for the same thing. Both characters died in "Two for the Road," and all have gone on record that this was the plan in their contracts from the beginning, not a consequence of the citations. But the title of the episode is an intriguing double-entrendre.

forged passport when he boarded Flight 815.

In the second season episode "The 23rd Psalm," we learn that when Eko was a boy his village in Nigeria was attacked by guerilla soldiers. The men ordered his brother Yemi to kill a man, but Eko stepped in and killed the man in Yemi's place. Yemi was much smaller than Eko and from their behavior in this scene, it seemed Eko often protected his brother.✦ But this act led to their initial separation; the soldiers took Eko with them when they left the village, leading Eko into a violent world and leaving Yemi behind. Eko grew up to become a thug and crime lord, while Yemi became a priest. Eko's criminal activities consisted mainly of illegal exports, and his reunion with his brother came after Eko killed two Moroccan drug dealers who were looking to move a stash of heroin out of Nigeria. Eko appealed to Yemi for papers confirming himself and his associates as priest missionaries so they could secret their supply out of the country hidden inside statues of the Virgin Mary. He offered Yemi a good price for the statues, money which Yemi could use to help his people, and when Yemi refused, Eko's associates threatened to burn the church if Yemi didn't take the deal. The plan was to leave Nigeria in priests' clothing on a Beechcraft 18 plane, but they were met by Nigerian military on the runway. Yemi had turned them in, and arrived just ahead of them to try to save his brother from the bust (similar to the way Sayid gave Essam the chance to escape in Sydney). But Yemi was shot in the ensuing fracas and dragged aboard the plane, and the man who dragged Yemi aboard kicked Eko out the door.

✦In unstable regions worldwide, militias abducting children to be used as fighters is not uncommon; in a February 15, 2005 report, the BBC's Will Ross related that the Ugandan Lord's Resistance Army had recruited over 20,000 children in 19 years of fighting, and like Yemi, were given the choice of kill or be killed.

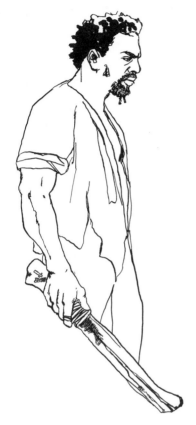

Eko posed as a priest in order to escape the military, and spent his next years living as a real priest, perhaps to honor Yemi's memory. As seen in the flashbacks from the second season episode "?," Eko was working in a parish in Australia when his monsignor sent him to investigate the claim of a miracle resurrection of a girl named Charlotte Malkin. (Richard Malkin, Charlotte's father, was the psychic who told Claire that she "mustn't allow another to raise your baby.") This investigation upset Eko's schedule; he had just secured a passport and was trying to make his way to the U.S., but had to postpone his plans to complete the assignment. If it weren't for Charlotte and Richard Malkin, Mr. Eko would not have been on Oceanic 815.□ Charlotte appeared to have drowned in a mountain stream and was declared dead, but she miraculously coughed back to life while on the autopsy table. Malkin appealed to Eko to call off the Church's investigation, explaining his wife's claims of a miracle were

□That's two people Richard Malkin is partially responsible for getting on Oceanic Flight 815 - Eko and Claire (three if you count Claire's baby, Aaron).

simply an attempt to discredit him because he was a fraud psychic. It's unclear whether Richard Malkin's admission was true or just a ruse to get Eko to stop investigating, but Eko ceased the investigation. Charlotte Malkin, however, followed Eko to the Sydney airport and told him she met Yemi while between worlds, a claim which deeply disturbed Eko.

In the second season episode "The Other 48 Days," we learn that after the crash Eko first helps the children, and then retrieves the dead bodies from the water, a sign of his respect for human dignity. Eko is one of the first people the Others attempt to abduct, possibly due to his imposing size and strength, but in the skirmish he kills two of the Others with a rock and escapes. After the attack, Eko refuses to talk for 40 days. He fashions a large stick into a club that he etches with biblical passages (an act which symbolically marks him as both a shepherd and a warrior), and as his beard grows, he ties two twisted tufts of hair off his chin, one for each victim.▲ Later, in the episode "Maternity Leave," Eko confesses his murders to the imprisoned Ben in the hatch, cuts the tufts off and presents them to him.

After the Tailies find the Lostaways and Ana-Lucia kills Shannon in "Collision," Eko presses on, carrying Sawyer to Jack. Ana begs Eko not to leave, implying that if the tables were turned Sawyer would certainly let him die, but Eko replies, "I'm not doing it for him. I'm doing it for me." This response, coupled with his self-imposed penance for killing the two Others, establishes a complex moral center for his character. Eko brings Sawyer to Jack,

▲Eko's carving of bible passages into his club also recalls Cormac McCarthy's character Judge Holden from his western novel *Blood Meridian*; the Judge had the Latin phrase "Et in Arcadia Ego" - I am also in Arcadia - engraved in his rifle. Arcadia was a Greek province and counterpart to the biblical paradise, and the phrase was often used as a memento mori in early modern art.

but refuses to say anything more when Jack demands to know where Michael, Jin and Sayid are. When the rest arrive without Sayid (who is being held hostage by Ana-Lucia), he becomes angry and goes for the armory guns. At that point Eko presents another moral stance, one that resonates beyond the bounds of the narrative: "Stop! Please, what do you want? Peace? Revenge? Justice? And you are going out with all these guns? What do you want?" Eko stands with his palms facing upwards, his tone, posture and words suggesting retaliation will not gain them nything. When Jack says he just wants his people back safely, Eko responds, "Ana-Lucia made a mistake," and Jack realizes he knows who killed Shannon.* This time Eko established a kind of moral compass by asking Jack to think through what violent retaliation would actually accomplish after a tragedy. Such words tend to carry more weight when they come from a subject who has lived inside violence and revenge.

Eko soon establishes himself as a kind of Christian counterpart to Locke's position as the island shaman. In "What Kate Did," after Eko learns a bit about the hatch, he tells Locke a biblical tale of Josiah trying to rebuild the temple with the ancient book of law. When he's done, he gives Locke the bible he got from the Arrow station, telling him, "I believe what's inside there will be of great value to you." Inside the book was a roll of film containing the scenes excised from the Swan's orientation film. But although Eko and Locke start on reasonably good footing, they go in decisively different directions after they find the Pearl station and Locke loses faith in the hatch. Eko then takes over Locke's role in the Swan station (not unlike the way he took over

*He shared a drink with her in the airport bar before departing on Oceanic 815.

his brother's role as priest).

Cindy Chandler was a flight attendant on Oceanic 815 who was short-lived on the island, and really only appears in the second season episode "The Other 48 Days" (so far). In some flashbacks, she is seen on the flight briefly speaking with Jack, and she chased Charlie into the bathroom. Cindy is with the Tailies when they decide to leave the Arrow station and join the Lostaways on the other side of the island. After they fix the injured Sawyer to a stretcher and haul him up a cliff, Cindy disappears, and the rest of the Tailies hear the whispers of the Others out in the jungle.

What's most notable about Cindy is that the *Bad Twin* manuscript found by Sawyer is dedicated to her; she was Gary Troup's "high flying angel."* This suggests she may have also read the manuscript, and therefore would have had some knowledge of the Hanso Foundation, mentioned in the book as a mysterious but powerful organization, a kind of Bilderberg or Carlyle Group with New York offices. This is the same foundation that supports the Dharma Initiative. But ultimately we did not see what happened to Cindy, so we have no idea at this point if she was killed by the Others, taken by them, or may have been some other kind of infiltrator.

Bernard Nadler, a dentist, is Rose's husband. After thecrash, Rose continually affirmed her belief that Bernard was alive and

---

*Quick run-down of *Bad Twin*. It's a kind of existential detective novel where the protagonist is hired by a wealthy industrialist to find his ne'er-do-well twin. The family is the American branch of the Scottish Widmore family, and the detective Paul Artisan ends up tracking the twin Zander to Australia. A number of key features from *Lost* make their way into the narrative, such as the Widmores, The Hanso Foundation, Thomas Mittelwerk, a hidden place off Australia, some general themes, and of course Cindy. The book is… it's not Thomas Pynchon or Paul Auster. In fact some comments on the online forums discussing *Lost* wondered if the book was purposely written in a way that dares you to keep reading. The text seems to be pointing to something beyond itself and toward the greater narrative of *Lost*, but it doesn't yield much, and could be seen as a blind alley of a lead.

well, despite having no evidence whatsoever. Bernard is indeed alive; his seat landed in a tree after the crash, and Goodwin, an Other posing as a fellow survivor, called Tailie Ana-Lucia into to the jungle to help Bernard to safety.

As seen in flashbacks from the episode "S.O.S.," Bernard was a confirmed bachelor for over 50 years until he met Rose and proposed after a few months' courtship. Rose almost didn't accept his proposal of marriage because of her terminal cancer, but Bernard was willing to accept her situation – almost. He arranged for a honeymoon trip to Australia, but secretly intended to bring Rose to Isaac, a famous healer at Uluru (Ayer's Rock), a location sacred to the local Aboriginal people and thought by some to have anomalous magnetic and even healing qualities. Prior to her arrival at the healer's, Rose believed that Bernard had accepted her terminal condition.

Bernard donated $10,000 to Isaac in the hope that he could cure Rose. Isaac told Rose that some places have healing qualities, possibly due to geomagnetism, and that Uluru is one of those places; his gift was channeling that energy to the infirm in order to heal them. However he soon stopped his session with Rose and told her that Uluru was not the right place for her: "It's not that you can't be healed. Like I said, there's different energies." Rose chose not to tell Bernard that Isaac couldn't heal her, and told Isaac to keep Bernard's donation. (Season Two, "S.O.S.")

On the island, when the Tailies were still separated from the Lostaways, Bernard manned the radio they found in the Arrow station, and momentarily communicated with Boone when he called for help on the radio in the drug runner's plane. (Season Two, "The Other 48 Days.") For a while Bernard showed a distinct incapacity to sit still and constantly wanted to do something to get off the island. In the episode "S.O.S." he attempts to organize the construction of a large S.O.S. sign on the beach, but his abrasive nature aggravates too many of his helpers, and he eventually ends up working alone. Rose tries to talk him out of building the sign; like Locke, she is in no hurry to leave the island since it seems somehow to have healed her. Bernard's persistence finally forces Rose to tell him that it wasn't Isaac that healed her, it was the island. With that Bernard gives up the S.O.S. sign and settles in for a tropical life with his new wife. Bernard and Rose are still somewhat unknown quantities – we don't even know their last names – and even though they seem to be resolved, there are a few things that could use explanation. For instance, how many people in the medical profession pass off $10,000 to a faith healer? And what were Bernard and Rose up to during the 50-some years before they met?

Libby (last name unknown) was a psychologist with some medical training who crashed with the Tailies. She provided the best medical care the Tailies had, and helped counsel some of her fellow survivors through difficult emotional situations, especially Hurley.

Libby had an unusual connection with the island from long before the September 22, 2004 crash. In 2000, a month after Libby's husband died, she met Desmond Hume in a café; Desmond had recently been released from a military prison in the UK. Libby learned that Desmond was about to embark on a solo open-water sailboat race around the world to regain his honor and his great love, Penelope Widmore. Penelope's father Charles is the sponsor of the race that Desmond planned to enter, but Desmond did not yet have the boat he needed for the race. As it turned out, Libby's late husband David had a sailboat (named after her, the "Elizabeth"), and after hearing Desmond's story she offered him the boat for the race – perhaps a little too readily for having just met Desmond. If it weren't for Libby's boat, though, Desmond may not have embarked on the race and would not have landed on the island.

After the Tailies meet the Lostaways, Libby puts her psychological training to work. In "Maternity Leave," she helps Claire recover memories of her abduction by Ethan. This information helps Kate and Claire (and later Rousseau) find the Staff station, where they discover that the Others had been wearing disguises and were not the primitives they pretended to be. In the episode "Dave," Libby also helps Hurley come to grips with his overeating and get past thoughts that Dave, his imaginary friend from the mental institute, had returned. Hurley had come to believe that Dave's presence meant that he had created the entire island in his imagination.○ Early on in the second season, Libby also takes a strong interest in Hurley; she may have honestly felt for him, or this may have been misdirection to keep Hurley from discovering something she was trying to hide, as Hurley keeps noting how familiar she looks. But Libby and Hurley's relationship eventually grows from friendship to romance, and in "Two for the Road" they plan a picnic. When Libby discovers Hurley had not brought blankets, she heads back to the hatch to fetch some. When she enters the hatch, she surprises Michael after he just shot Ana-Lucia and freed Ben. Michael shoots Libby twice in the stomach – a slow and painful way to die (as Jack explained when Mars was injured after the crash).

Just before she dies in "?," Libby moans Michael's name

○Is it a coincidence that Hurley's imaginary friend and Libby's deceased husband were both named Dave?

while Hurley and Jack attend to her, but Jack believed Libby was simply concerned for Michael's welfare and failed to recognize that Libby was identifying her killer. Meanwhile, Michael kept watch over Libby much as Kate had as Mars lay dying; he didn't want her letting his secret out. Just days after she died (in fact, during her funeral), Desmond returned to the island in the very boat Libby offered him years earlier for his race.

Libby's comforting personality masked a mysterious past. We don't know her last name, we don't know why she was in Australia or on Oceanic 815, and Hurley swore he recognized her from someplace. When Hurley asks her in "Fire + Water" if he knew her from somewhere, she says Hurley stepped on her foot when he got on the plane; yet Libby was in the tail section and Hurley sat in the middle and was the last one on the plane, so its unclear how he managed to stretch his foot all the way to Libby's seat in the plane's tail section. However, in a flashback from "Dave," we learn that Libby was in fact Hurley's fellow inpatient at the Santa Rosa Mental Institute, where she watched him closely. (Season Two, "Dave.")

Those Already On the Island (Who Aren't the Others)

Danielle Rousseau was already on the island for about 16 years by the time Flight 815 showed up, and is sort of the Ben Gunn figure of the island.△ According to Rousseau, she was part of a science expedition on a ship that crashed into the island, and was pregnant at the time of her arrival. After arriving on the island, something happened to the rest of her expedition; Rousseau

△Ben Gunn is the crazed, marooned sailor that Jim Hawkins meets on the island in Robert Louis Stevenson's *Treasure Island.*

claimed her colleagues caught an as-yet unidentified sickness (which may be what the Others' vaccine is for); they either died from the sickness, or were possibly killed by Rousseau. She used her expedition's equipment to create a looped distress signal that has been broadcasting over the years, a signal that was picked up by Sayid and translated by Shannon. In this signal she states (in French), "Please help me. Please come get me. I'm alone now, on the island alone. Please someone come. The others, they're, they're dead. It killed them. It killed them all." (Season One, "Pilot.")

Rousseau was first encountered by Sayid. Sayid was in a self-imposed exile after torturing Sawyer in the first season episode "Solitary." He came upon a cable leading from the ocean into the jungle, and followed it to Rousseau's camp. When he approached her camp, Rousseau attacked him, strung him up on a wire bedspring frame, and electrocuted him for information about her missing daughter Alex. After her daughter was born on the island, the Others kidnapped the baby, just as they would later take Walt and try to take Aaron. Like Rose's faith that Bernard was still alive, Rousseau continues to search for Alex, even though Rousseau has little evidence Alex is still alive. And like Michael, she is obsessed with getting her child back from the Others. We don't know if she's ever seen Alex since she was taken; we do know she has never seen the Others, she only hears them whispering in the jungle. She initially assumed Sayid was an Other who knew where Alex was, and reacted accordingly.

Rousseau's years of solitude and desperate search have left her mentally unbalanced, yet savvy in the jungle; she lays traps and snares all around her part of the island to protect herself from the Others and the polar bears, and as a result she can move about the island relatively freely (and undetected). The fact that

Rousseau notes the presence of polar bears is important, because it indicates they were there before Walt arrived, and therefore not solely the manifestation of Walt's consciousness – which seemed to be a possibility, given Walt's history.

In the first season, Rousseau knows that Claire is about to have a baby, and takes it upon herself to try to protect the child (she just doesn't communicate her intention very well). In the first season episode "Raised by Another," Claire has nightmares that she and her unborn baby were being attacked, and she believes the dreams to be real, or at least prophetic. When Rousseau shows up to warn the Lostaways that the Others were coming in the first season finale "Exodus," Claire spots scratch marks on Rousseau's arm. The marks prompt her to recall scratching her attacker as she was kidnapped, and lead her to think Rousseau was the one trying to steal her baby, perhaps to trade for Alex. But in fact Claire's attacker was Ethan, and Rousseau was scratched trying to protect Claire from him. Later, Rousseau returned to the Lostaways after seeing the Others' smoke signal in the first season finale; she believed the Others were coming to attack the survivors and steal Aaron. Rousseau took Aaron with her into the jungle, and it was left to Sayid to retrieve the infant. Rousseau learns that Aaron broke out in a rash in the second season episode "Maternity Leave," and helps Claire and Kate find the Staff station in search of vaccine for the baby. Her obsession with Claire's baby is disturbing, but protectively magnanimous.

Despite having made a map of the island (with French notations mixed in with song lyrics from the Disney cartoon *Finding Nemo*), Rousseau had not yet come across the Dharma Initiative stations, or if she had, she doesn't tell the survivors. She did, however, find the 19th century slave ship the Black Rock, which somehow was beached deep inside the jungle, and scavenged dynamite and materials from the ship to help make her traps in the jungle.⊗ It's unclear whether Rousseau knew of the other people on the island who weren't Others and weren't survivors of Oceanic 815.

Desmond Hume is a former Scottish soldier in the British Army who ended up on the island when he went off-course during a solo open-water sailboat race around the world. He hardly appears in the narrative until just after Michael released Ben from the hatch. But just as he was always there under the ground in the hatch for the first 48 days, his narrative underlines just about every other story on the island.

About five years earlier, Desmond was released from a military prison, having been dishonorably discharged from the Royal Scots Borderers regiment of the British Army. Through the second season, it's unclear exactly why he was in prison; the soldier who discharged him at the prison said it was because of his failure to follow orders, but it may have more to do with his love, Penelope Widmore, and her father Charles Widmore's disapproval of their relationship. Charles Widmore is noted as a wealthy industrialist and philanthropist, and shares the same name as the wealthy family under investigation in the manuscript of *Bad Twin* that Sawyer finds in the wreckage.

In a flashback from the second season finale "Live Together, Die Alone," Charles waits for Desmond outside the prison on the

---

⊗Incidentally, the word 'nemo' is Latin for 'no one'; *Finding Nemo* might be read as *Finding No One*, which may have some resonance with Rousseau's search for her daughter. Nemo is also the name of Jules Verne's captain in *20,000 Leagues Under the Sea*, and is what Odysseus tells the Cyclops Polyphemus his name is after putting out the monster's eye.

day he's released and offers him two boxes; one all the letters he'd written to Penelope while in prison (which Widmore kept from his daughter), and one full of money to stay away from her. This aspect of Desmond's narrative parallels Michael's, as Walt's mother kept Michael's letters from Walt; it also parallels Shannon's narrative, whose scam was to get Boone to pay her boyfriend to leave her alone. Widmore tells

Desmond that Penelope believes he had forsaken her because she never received any of his letters, and that she'd become engaged to another man. This affront sparks Desmond to enter Widmore's world-wide open-water sailboat race; Desmond became determined to win Widmore's race and regain his honor (and Penelope).

After being released from prison, Desmond goes to the United States to train for the race. Upon arrival, he meets Libby in a coffee shop and Libby soon offers Desmond her late husband David's sailboat for the race. One might be justifiably suspicious at Libby's readiness to part with the boat, but Desmond accepts her offer. (Season Two, "Live Together, Die Alone.") Just before the race, as seen in a flashback from "Man of Science, Man of Faith," Desmond meets a despondent Jack as they each run the steps at a stadium. Jack twists his ankle, and Desmond stops to help him, telling Jack he was once almost a doctor and to "lift it up." Desmond was telling Jack to lift his ankle up, but the line echoes writing seen on the hidden map on the Swan station blast wall from "Lockdown," *sursum corda* ("lift up your hearts").

When Desmond was in the race, he believed he was about a week outside of Fiji when he ran aground on the island in the midst of a storm. He was found on the beach by Kelvin Inman, the former Defense Intelligence Agency (DIA) officer who operated the Swan station for the Dharma Initiative. (Season Two, "Live Together, Die Alone.") Desmond worked in the Swan station with Kelvin for almost three years, faithfully entering the code every 108 minutes, reading, exercising, listening to the Swan's classic record collection, and taking the vaccinations as Kelvin instructed. Kelvin also explains to him that the station was all about the geologically unique electromagnetism on the island, and there had been some kind of incident: "So now the charge builds up, and every time we push the button... it discharges it ... before it gets too big." This all suggests that the Swan held a mechanism to harness that unique electromagnetism; to what use the energy was being put is unknown, but obviously something is powering the hatches on the island.

Kelvin takes regular walks around the island in his HAZMAT suit, instructing Desmond to remain inside the station. One day Kelvin says, "Goodbye, Desmond," for the first and only time before he goes for his walk, which draws Desmond's attention. Des then notices a hole in Kelvin's protective suit; if the suit was torn, Kelvin either wasn't safe, or had been lying to Desmond about the infectious disease on the island. Desmond covers his mouth with a cloth and follows Kelvin out into the island, and soon sees Kelvin take off his mask. He then finds that Kelvin had been repairing Desmond's sailboat, apparently to make his own escape. In a rage, Desmond confronts and attacks Kelvin; as they struggle, Kelvin smacks his head hard against the rocks, and appears to die, but Desmond has no time to confirm Kelvin's condition because he is late entering the code, so he just rips Kelvin's failsafe key from his neck and runs back to the Swan. As Desmond enters the hatch, metal objects begin to fly across the room and the whole structure begins to shake. This was September 22, 2004, the very day Oceanic 815 went down. (Season Two, "Live Together, Die Alone.")

When Locke encountered Desmond, about 45 days into the Lostaways' time on the island (but again seen by the audience in a "Live Together, Die Alone" flashback), Des was preparing to read Charles Dickens's last novel, *Our Mutual Friend*. When he left prison, Desmond told the guard *Our Mutual Friend* would be the last book he read before he died. Believing he had killed Kelvin, he was stuck on the island, he'd failed in the race and wouldn't see Penelope again, Desmond hit the depths of his own despair. He opens *Our Mutual Friend* and prepares to kill himself, but then he hears Locke pounding on the hatch from above. Locke's arrival at the hatch gave Desmond hope that he wasn't alone. Locke finally makes it into the Swan station with Kate and in "Adrift" they encounter Desmond, who asks the same question Kelvin asked Desmond: "Are you him?" Desmond soon realizes Locke isn't "him," and he has Locke tie Kate up in the hatch pantry; but Locke also slips her a knife that she uses to free herself.[⑳] Kate then works her way through the air ducts, finding the armory and a shotgun.

---

⑳Locke is never without a knife.

Locke has his first experience with the code when Desmond forces him enter it into the computer. Desmond then hears Jack calling after Kate and Locke. Jack had gone down the hatch to find Kate and Locke, and is surprised to find Locke held at gunpoint by Desmond, who says to Jack, "Lower your gun or I'll blow his head off, brother." Jack picks up on the colloquial use of *brother*, and he and Desmond vaguely recognize each other from their meeting at the L.A. stadium. But this stand-off soon comes to an end when Kate sneaks up behind Desmond and whacks him with the butt of the shotgun. The shock makes Desmond fire his pistol erratically, and he accidentally shoots the computer, then breaks down: "What did you do? What did you do? We're all going to die! We're all going to die!" When he finds he can't repair the computer, he takes off, knowing his sailboat was still hidden on another part of the island. (Season Two, "Orientation.")

After nearly a month at sea, Desmond ends up landing back on the island in the season two episode "Three Minutes"; if indeed there is a strong electromagnetic force on the island, it could mess with compass instruments, making North always point in the direction of the island. His spirits sunk, Desmond spends the next few days soused on Dharma Initiative booze. By the time Desmond returns, Locke and Eko are at odds about the function of the hatch computer; Locke had lost faith in it and thought nothing would happen if the code wasn't entered (the same thing Jack believed when they first encountered the hatch), while Eko's faith grew and he believed he had to enter the code. Locke tells Desmond about the Pearl station revelation, and gets him to help seal Eko out of the hatch with Kelvin's blast-door-trip trick so they can let the timer run down.

Once back in the Swan, Locke shows Desmond the Pearl's

printout logs, which show the repeating "system failure" that Desmond encountered on September 22, 2004. He then realizes that the last time the code wasn't correctly entered, the day he followed Kelvin outside the hatch and killed him, was the same day Oceanic 815 went down. Desmond tells Locke that he believes he crashed the plane, and immediately tries to enter the code, but Locke smashes the computer against the ground. Soon the timer runs down, the "system failure" alarm sounds, and metal objects begin flying around the hatch. Locke soon understands he made a mistake, and simply says, "I was wrong." Desmond retrieves the failsafe key that he kept inside his copy of *Our Mutual Friend,* trips the failsafe, and a crazy wave of light and a loud hum wash over the island.❋

Kelvin Joe Inman was the lone inhabitant of the Swan station on the island when Desmond arrived. He joined the Dharma Initiative some time after the first Gulf War, where he worked in military intelligence (the Defense Intelligence Agency, it seems). In the flashback from "Live Together, Die Alone," he tells Desmond that he left the military and joined the Dharma Initiative "because men followed my orders."

Many of Kelvin's statements are questionable. From the flashback in "One of Them," we learn that Kelvin worked with Sergeant Major Sam Austen (Kate's stepfather) while in the first Gulf War, and together they convinced captured Republic Guard Sayid Jarrah to torture his own commanding officer for information. Kelvin claims they needed someone who spoke the language to do the interrogation, but when Kelvin later frees Sayid, he speaks to him in Arabic; the truth was that they needed

---

❋If the leak was an electromagnetic charge, the crazy light would make some sense, because electromagnetic radiation is just that - the full spectrum of light.

someone not connected with the U.S. military to perform the torture.★ And after Kelvin finds Desmond, he lies to him about the condition of his boat. The one thing Kelvin seems straight-up about is entering the code in the hatch and pushing the button. He even keeps a failsafe key around his neck.

On the island Kelvin tells Desmond about his previous partner, a man named Radzinsky who had a photographic memory and was making a map of the island on the blast door. That went on until, according to Kelvin, Radzinsky went stir crazy and blew his head off with a shotgun in the hatch; all that's left of Radzinsky is a brown stain on the hatch ceiling by the bunk beds. Kelvin and Radzinsky had figured out a way to trip the mechanism that drops the blast doors during the air drops of food and supplies, and paint the map on the door with Dharma detergent; dried detergent does not show up in regular light, but glows under a black light, and when the blast doors drop the regular lights cut and black lights turn on. Kelvin took over the map after Radzinsky killed himself, but it isn't clear how much of this map is Radzinsky's and how much is Kelvin's; in fact we have no proof that Radzinsky did indeed kill himself, or if Kelvin helped him, or if Radzinsky even existed. But whoever designed the map filled it with cryptic phrases and notations in both English and Latin.

Kelvin convinces Desmond it isn't safe for him to go outside without a HAZMAT suit because of some island infection, and there is only one HAZMAT suit and Kelvin wasn't sharing: "Sorry,

---

★This is a micro-version of what's become known as "extraordinary rendition," where battlefield prisoners (either POWs or enemy combatants) are sent to places with more flexible human rights laws in order to have them tortured without technically committing a war crime.

Des, you stay here. You push the button. That's an order." (Season Two, "Live Together, Die Alone.") And if the infection didn't get him, the "hostiles" would. But Kelvin's scouting missions are actually ruses to work on Desmond's sailboat, the Elizabeth, for his own escape. Desmond eventually follows Kelvin out of the hatch when he sees the tear in the HAZMAT suit and finds out what Kelvin was really doing all this time. Desmond attacks Kelvin, cracking the back of Kelvin's head against the rocky ground. This seems to kill Kelvin, but in about 65 days on the island, Kelvin's body has not been found, nor has Kelvin appeared to the survivors of Oceanic 815, and it doesn't seem that Desmond has gone back looking for Kelvin's body.

The Others

The Others were on the island long before the survivors landed there, before Kelvin and Desmond arrived, and before Rousseau's expedition team crashed there. They live on a different side of the island in round huts made of lattice-work frames and covered in canvas, like Mongolian gers. They at first appear shoeless, rather dirty, smart, quiet, and quite possibly very strong. What's more, the way they act and talk suggests they're from modern North America, complete with American accents (and they often claim to be Canadian), yet they're remotely sequestered someplace in the South Pacific.

The Others' presence is initially marked by whispers in the jungle; the survivors may hear them, but they rarely see the Others until it's too late to escape. Rousseau claims never to have seen them, only to hear them. The Others kidnapped several of the Tailies immediately after the crash of Flight 815, including all of the children, and seem to be dividing people they're interested in between "good" and "bad"; they even have lists of names and descriptions of the survivors – why, we don't at first know, nor do we know what they're doing with the people they take or what they mean by "good" (morally good? physically? good for spare parts?). They are particularly interested in children: they have taken Walt, Alex, and the two children from the tail section, Zack and Emma; they tried to take Aaron before he was even born. While they are adept at living on and moving about the island, they are not super-human; several of the Others have been killed since Oceanic 815 landed. At the end of the second season, one of the Others' leaders, Ben, told the Lostaways that they didn't get it: they, the Others, "are the good guys." But after about three months on the island, from both the survivors' standpoint and ours as an audience, the Others have seemed to pose nothing but a threat to the survivors and the other inhabitants of the island. The beginnings of the third season just present more enigmas, where we see that they actually live in a very pleasant, hidden village on the island reminiscent of the village from the 1960's series *The Prisoner*. When in their village, they appear very civilized (the third season opener, "A Tale of Two Cities," shows the Others holding a book group), but when they see Oceanic 815 crash, Ben immediately sends out two of the Others to infiltrate the groups of survivors, and the rest occasionally go out on guerilla-type missions dressed as rough savages to find out more about the survivors. What follows is just a cursory look at some of the individual Others that have been seen so far.

Ethan Rom was the first of the Others to be introduced. He infiltrated the Lostaways' camp, coming out of the jungle after the crash and helping with the wreckage and injured. As noted above,

Ethan's name is also an anagram for "Other Man," and like Nathan, he claimed to be from Canada.* Ethan seemed benign and even helpful at first, but later kidnapped Charlie and Claire (and her unborn child), kicked Jack around in the jungle when he went after them, and strung Charlie up by the neck with a vine, proving he was one hard man.

Ethan first makes his presence felt after about a week on the island in the first season episode "Raised by Another," when Jack convinces some of the survivors (including the pregnant Claire) to move to the caves he discovered. Ethan wants to get to Claire's baby, and uses the secluded area to attack Claire at night, attacks which were dismissed by Jack as night terrors. After Claire refuses Jack's sedative and leaves the caves for the beach, Charlie in tow, she begins having contractions, and the first person they see is Ethan, who kidnaps Claire and Charlie. When H Wurley later compares his census of survivors against the flight manifest, he realizes Ethan's name is nowhere on the list.

In the subsequent episode "All the Best Cowboys Have Daddy Issues," Jack organizes a quick search party to follow Claire and Charlie's trail of broken twigs, drag marks, and fragments of Charlie's bandages on the ground.◻ However, Ethan finds Jack before anyone finds Ethan, beats him into the jungle mud and warns him, "If you do not stop following me, I will kill one of them." When Jack and Kate continue despite Ethan's warning, they find Charlie hung by his neck with a vine, and Jack is barely

---

*An old American backpacker abroad trick is to claim you're actually Canadian. Not every country approves of U.S. foreign policy, and given the U.S. is nominally a democracy, they tend to hold U.S. voters/citizens responsible.

◻*A la* Merry leaving a trail for Aragorn when he and Pippin were abducted by orcs in *The Lord of the Rings*, the actor Dominic Monaghan, who played Merry, now plays Charlie in *Lost*.

able to resuscitate him. From this, it's clear that Ethan is at least exceptionally physically strong.

As seen in the flashback from "Maternity Leave," Ethan takes Claire to a medical station across the island, the Staff station. There, the Others keep her drugged, and Ethan administers vaccinations for the unborn child – the shots seemed to be the same vaccination that Kelvin instructed Desmond to give himself, and there are hints of a possible quarantine situation on the island that the survivors are unaware of. While at the station, Ethan tells Claire that they, the Others, were "good people" and a "good family," two more of the many "good" (and "bad") references made by the Others. When Claire is released from the Staff by another Other named Alex (Rousseau's abducted daughter), Ethan returns to the survivors' camp and demands her return. In the episode "Homecoming," Ethan first finds Charlie and Jin in the jungle, knocks Jin out with a rock and sling, and then picks Charlie up by the throat and coolly says, "You bring her here. If you don't, I'm going to kill one of them. And then if you don't bring her back before sundown tomorrow, I'll kill another, and another, and another, one every day. And Charlie, I'll kill you last."

The next day, despite the tripwire warning systems set up around the camp perimeter at the beach, Ethan manages to kill a survivor named Scott by emerging from the water. He breaks Scott's neck, arms and more, again showing just how damaging he can be. Jack then decides to reveal to the group they had found four 9mm pistols from Mars's briefcase. The Lostaways then set a trap for Ethan, using Claire as bait. But before they could interrogate him, Charlie takes one of the guns and shoots Ethan six times, point-blank.

Goodwin was another of the Others who, like Ethan, infiltrated the survivors' camp; but while Ethan targeted the Lostaways, Goodwin joined the Tailies. Also like Ethan, he identifies himself as being from Canada. He first emerges from the jungle after the crash in "The Other 48 Days" to alert someone that Bernard was stuck up in a tree, and Ana-Lucia is the first person to go to Bernard's aid (marking her as a possible "good person"). Soon the Others begin attacking the Tailies, killing some and taking others. Ana-Lucia manages to kill one of the Others and finds an old army knife and a list of nine survivors on the attacker's body.

As their numbers became decimated from attacks and abductions, Ana-Lucia becomes suspicious of a Tailie named Nathan because he keeps leaving for extended bathroom breaks and no one remembers him from the plane. Nathan is eventually thrown into their prison pit, and Ana hints to Goodwin that she plans to torture Nathan for answers. Goodwin releases Nathan from the pit that night, only to break his neck and hide the body. For the Tailies, Nathan's disappearance seems to confirm that Nathan was an Other. It's possible that Nathan was an Other, and that Goodwin killed him simply to keep Nathan from betraying their presence, but it's just as possible that Nathan was an innocent by-stander with a bad digestive system.

Later on, the Tailies decide to move their camp into the Arrow station, a Dharma bunker they discover. Goodwin and Ana-Lucia hike to higher ground to get a better view of their new surroundings, and on the way Ana confronts Goodwin. The tail section had landed in the water, ut when Goodwin first came out of the jungle after the crash yelling for help for Bernard, his clothes were dry – Ana correctly concluded Goodwin couldn't have come from the plane. Goodwin confirms he is an Other and that he had murdered Nathan to protect his own cover: "If you had cut off his finger and he still told you he was on the plane, I think maybe you would have started to believe you had the wrong guy." (Season Two, "The Other 48 Days.") When Ana asks him if he killed Nathan, Goodwin just says, "Nathan was not a good person. That's why he wasn't on the list," a statement which implies that Nathan was not one of Goodwin's people (but that may have been a ruse). Ana-Lucia attacks him, and in the struggle they fall down a hill and she skewers Goodwin through with a stick.

Tom (a.k.a. Mr. Friendly) is one of the supposed leaders of the Others who is first seen abducting Walt from Michael's raft as they tried to escape the island in the first season finale. He was most often seen wearing a beard and an old stocking cap, but in a flashback at the Staff station, he is seen clean-shaven and casually dressed, and his costume and beard are found in a locker, clearly props for his disguise. (Season Two, "Maternity Leave.")

Around the 50th day on the island, Michael goes into the jungle to get Walt back from the Others. Jack, Sawyer and Locke go after Michael, but they didn't know Kate was following behind. On the trail they hear gunfire, which turns out to be Tom and the Others capturing Michael.* Later that night, they're surprised by Tom who walks out of the jungle and casually joins their conversation, as if he'd always been a part of it; he first addresses Jack and Locke by name, and when Sawyer moves forward, a warning bullet from somewhere in the jungle grazes his ear. (The Others are apparently sharpshooters on top of everything else.) Tom asks them to make a fire and to have a talk with him, and he says it all in a jovial, neighbor-with-a-six-pack tone. (Season Two, "The Hunting Party.")

---

*A fact that's not revealed until a flashback from "Three Minutes," ten episodes later.

What Tom says reveals quite a bit. He asks the Lostaways if they make themselves at home when they enter a man's house for the first time, and says, "You know, somebody a whole lot smarter than anybody here once said, 'Since the dawn of our species, man's been blessed with curiosity.' You know the other one about curiosity, don't you, Jack?" and "This is not your island. This is our island. And the only reason you're living on it is because we *let* you live on it." His quote from the somebody a whole lot smarter than anyone there was from Alvar Hanso, the financier of the Dharma Initiative, and that same quote appears in the Hanso Foundation commercials from the alternate reality game bridging season two with season three.

When Tom then asks the search party to hand over their guns and go home, Jack says he thinks Tom only has one shooter in the jungle and doesn't have any real strength. Tom called Jack's bluff: "That's an interesting theory. LIGHT 'EM UP!" At that, a number of torches lit up in the jungle to show survivors that they were surrounded, and that the Others were serious, quiet, and armed. "We got a misunderstanding, Jack – your people, my people – so listen carefully: Right here, there's a line. You cross that line, and we go from misunderstanding to something else." He then asked Alex to bring Kate forward; they caught Kate in the jungle around the same time they caught Michael, and Tom holds her at gunpoint until Jack and the rest hand over their guns, and then release Kate. His threat worked. (Season Two, "The Hunting Party.") Tom and the Others then march Michael for four days, day and night, across the island to the Others' compound. This suggests a few things: either the island is large enough to take days to cross, or the Others were just marching Michael in disorienting circles (perhaps both), and the Others are strong enough to keep on the move day and night.

Tom at first seems to be a leader of the Others, but Claire's flashbacks from the Staff indicate he was not the final authority. When he admonishes Ethan for not making a list of survivors before abducting Claire, he warns Ethan about "what He's going to do when he finds out." (Season Two, "Maternity Leave.") Although Tom holds some authority, the leader seems to be Ben, but even Ben seems to answer to Him.

Tom didn't appear again until around the 65th day on the island in the second season finale, "Live Together, Die Alone." Michael agreed to lead Jack, Sawyer, Hurley and Kate into a trap in the jungle in exchange for Walt and a boat to leave the island. On the way, the Others ambushed them with poisoned darts, gagged them and bagged their heads, and brought them to the Pala Ferry, a dock along a beach on the island. As they're held captive on the dock, Kate muffles through her gag that she knows Tom's beard was fake. Tom couldn't understand her, until Ms. Klugh clarifies, "She said she knows your beard's fake, Tom." He takes off the beard, thanks Kate for pointing that out (because it itched), and says to Ms. Klugh, "And thanks for telling her my *name*, Bea." When Ben arrived at the dock, he asks Tom in an irritated way what happened to his beard, and from their interaction it becomes clear that Ben has a measure of authority over Tom.

Alex Rousseau, Danielle Rousseau's daughter, was abducted by the Others as a baby about 16 years before the crash of Oceanic 815. Alex is first mentioned by Tom at the jungle clearing in "The Hunting Party" (and in a flashback in "Three Minutes"). While Tom talks with Jack, Locke and Sawyer, she guards Kate and questions her about Claire's baby – had she given birth yet? Was it a boy or a girl? Was it okay?❖ Alex appears again in Claire's flashbacks of the Staff station in "Maternity Leave," and it becomes clear that she is the one who freed Claire before her baby could be cut out of her body. Alex is also part of the group that captures Jack, Sawyer, Kate and Hurley in Michael's double-cross in "Live Together, Die Alone." We know little of Alex at this point, except that her freeing of Claire compromised the Others' plans. She may have done this because she was abducted like Claire's baby was about to be and she felt for Claire, or perhaps she is actually attempting to subvert the Others in some way. Then again, perhaps she was ordered to free Claire. Alex, however, did not ask about her mother; she may not even know she still has a mother.

Pickett is one of the Others who has so far made only short appearances, but seems to have an important function. He is a larger man who Michael finds peeing in the jungle in "Three Minutes" when he searches for Walt. But Pickett was only there as a ruse; when Michael puts his gun to Pickett, Tom comes up from behind and takes Michael. At the Others' compound, Pickett takes blood from Michael with a syringe, which suggested he has some sort of medical training. He was also part of the group that took Sawyer, Jack, Kate and Hurley in the second season finale.

Early on in the third season, Pickett keeps Sawyer in a bear cage, and puts Sawyer and Kate to work breaking and hauling rocks. (Season Three, "The Glass Ballerina.") He guards them with a tazer gun, and warns them that if they talk, or do anything other than what he tells them to do, they'll get shocked.

❖This gets a bit tricky, as the same scene is repeated ten episodes apart, but from different perspectives. In "The Hunting Party," we see the front side of the scene, as Tom talks with Jack, Locke and Sawyer. In "Three Minutes," we see the back side of the scene, with Alex and Pickett guarding Kate and Michael back in the jungle while Tom holds forth.

When Kate refuses to work until she sees Jack, Pickett immediately walks up to Sawyer and shocks him to the ground. He later gets Sawyer's fist in his jaw when Sawyer stops working and kisses Kate in order to see how much fight the Others actually had in them.

Pickett appears to be involved with another Other named Colleen, who was shot by Sun when the Others took the sailboat. When Colleen dies from her wound, Pickett takes his rage out on Sawyer.

Ms. Klugh is the first of the Others to talk with Michael about Walt in "Three Minutes." After Michael is captured in the jungle and brought to their compound, she asks him some interesting questions about Walt: How old was he when he started talking? Did Walt ever get headaches or fainting spells? Did he ever appear someplace he wasn't supposed to be? She allows Michael to see Walt for three minutes, but as soon as Walt says that the Others make him take tests and were "pretending," Klugh has Walt taken away. She was next seen at the Pala Ferry dock in the second season finale, where Tom called her "Bea." At the dock she tells Hurley that his job is to return to the other survivors and tell them that they were never to come to that side of the island.

Ben Linus (or "Fenry," the Fake Henry Gale) first appears about 55 days after the crash when he is caught in one of Rousseau's nets in "One of Them." Rousseau finds Sayid and they free Ben from the net, but when Ben tries to run, Rousseau shoots him through the shoulder with a crossbow. Ben seems to be the most significant of the Others, and becomes a chief focus of the days preceding Michael's betrayal.

Rousseau and Sayid are immediately suspicious of Ben, and Sayid locks him in the hatch armory for interrogation and medical treatment. As Jack removes the bolt from Ben's shoulder, Ben claims his name is Henry Gale, that he's from Minnesota, and that he and his wife were crossing the Pacific in a hot air balloon when it crashed on the island four months earlier. He also tells them his wife had since died from some illness, which again raises the specter of an island infection.

At first, only Sayid, Locke and Jack know about the prisoner, but his presence is disruptive. When Sayid interrogates him in "One of Them," he shows an in-depth knowledge of the hot air balloon the real Henry Gale flew, which suggests the Others do their homework. He manages to turn Sayid's interrogation around mid-question, rightly sensing that Sayid had lost someone (both Nadia and Shannon). Ben played on this weakness, and Sayid battered Ben for it.✸ When Jack hears the beating and the yelling coming from the locked armory, he tries get in, but Locke had changed the combination on the armory door and wouldn't let Jack in until Jack kept Locke from entering the computer's code.

Jack, Locke and Sayid tried to keep Ben's presence a secret for as long as they could, but somehow Mr. Eko figures it out and asks to meet Ben. Eko tells Ben of the two men who dragged Eko into the jungle his first night on the island, that he smashed both their heads in with a stone, and that he "needed to tell someone." Ben looks on, unsure what to make of this, as Eko then pulls out a large knife, cuts off the two twisted tufts of hair he had tied out of his beard (one for each man he killed), and drops them at Ben's feet.

Ben eventually takes advantage of his imprisonment to sow increasing discord between Locke and Jack. In "Maternity Leave,"

✸If the Others are exceptionally strong like Ethan, this strength may have helped Ben withstand the beating.

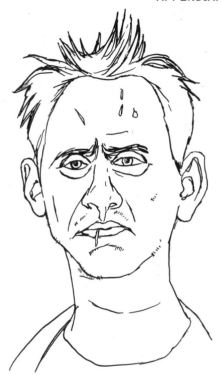

he plays on Locke's pride, intelligence, and tension with Jack when he asks, "Are you the genius, or are you the guy who always feels like he's living in the shadow of the genius?" and "I just don't understand why you let the doctor call the shots." Locke leaves Ben in the armory and in frustration sweeps some plates off the kitchen counter; as he does so, the scene cuts from Locke to Ben as he slowly looks up, aware that he's planted a seed.

Locke appeals to Ana-Lucia and her police background to get information from Ben in "The Whole Truth." But he doesn't discuss the idea with Jack first, and in doing so, breaks an agreement with Jack and does just what Ben wants. Ana talks Ben into drawing a map to the hot air balloon and his wife's grave, a map which she doesn't tell Locke or Jack about because "Jack and Locke are a little too busy worrying about Locke and Jack." Ben later tells Locke and Jack about the map he gave Ana, and plays on their fears by implying it's a trap

Ben seems to show a kind of faithfulness in the episode "Lockdown." As Locke is attending to the hatch, he hears a staticky voice announcing a countdown over the hatch's speakers. When the count reaches zero, blast doors drop down and seal the different rooms of the hatch shut. Ben takes full advantage of the lockdown incident, which shows that he keeps his presence of mind even when in desperate circumstances. Locke makes a deal with Ben that he won't let anyone hurt him if he helps Locke open the door, and together they manage to pry up the door enough to shove a toolbox under it. Locke then tries to slide under the door, but the door crushes the toolbox and pins him down, breaking his right leg.

Locke's concern quickly shifts to making sure the code is entered into the computer. Locke tells Ben what needs to be done, and Ben climbs through an air vent to reach the computer just as the warning sirens go off. Ben manages to reset the timer, and the blast doors recede, freeing Locke. Ben helps Locke over to a couch just as Jack returns with Sayid, Ana-Lucia and Charlie. They had found Henry Gale's balloon and his wife's grave, it was all where Ben said it would be, but Sayid didn't believe Ben's alibi and dug up the grave. Instead of a woman, Sayid found a man with a broken neck and a driver's license identifying "Henry Gale" as a black man from Wayzata, Minnesota, not the white man in the armory. When they confirm that Ben is at least a liar, Locke's faith takes another hit. Sayid interrogates Ben again in the subsequent episode "Dave," stringing him up by his wrists and demanding more information: What did he do to the real Henry Gale? Where were the Others? How many were there? Ben refuses to give straight answers, saying Henry's neck was already broken when they found the basket. Sayid finally produces the note the real Henry wrote on a $20 bill that describes his crash, and asks Ben how Henry managed to write the letter on the island if he arrived with a neck already broken. Ben balks, Sayid pulls his gun, and Ben yells, "You can't do this! I am not a bad person!" Sayid would have killed Ben had Ana-Lucia not blocked his shot.

But if Ben is a liar, did he really enter the code during the lockdown? After learning Ben is an Other, Locke confronts him in "Two for the Road" and asks if he got caught on purpose to get to the hatch: "You and your people have been here for God knows how long, and you got caught in a net?..." Ben cuts Locke off, exclaiming that God doesn't know how long they'd been there, that God couldn't see that island better than any of the rest of the world, and as for the hatch, "This place? This place is a joke, John." Ben then explains that not only did he not enter the code, but when he watched the timer count down, he saw the hieroglyphs, heard a clunk and a humming "like a magnet, a big magnet, it was really very frightening," and then the timer just reset on its own. At this point, neither Locke nor the audience has any idea if Ben is telling the truth or was manipulating Locke yet again. Ben's presence at the Swan was all a play, a kind of con that even Sawyer couldn't pull off.

Ben eventually starts refusing food and water. When Ana-Lucia tries to talk to him in "Two for the Road," he attacks and chokes her because, as he says, she killed two "good people who were leaving you alone." Locke keeps Ben from killing Ana by knocking him out, and later asks Ben why he didn't just kill him when he was pinned under the blast door. Ben responds that none of it mattered because he failed in his mission and his people were going to kill him if they found him. When Locke asks about this mission, Ben states that he went to the survivors' camp to recruit Locke, "Because you're one of the good ones, John. I was coming for you."

But Ben's attack kicks up Ana-Lucia's anger, and she decides to kill him, a pre-meditated murder like the one she committed in L.A. After getting Sawyer's gun, she gives Ben a knife to free himself so the murder looks like self-defense. Ben then manipulates Ana like he did Locke, telling her that Goodwin claimed she *could* be a good person. In less-is-more fashion, we don't see Ana not kill Ben; we only find out she hadn't after Michael awakens in the hatch and Ana tells him one of the Others is locked in the armory.

Of course Michael had already been compromised by the Others by this point, and was sent back to the survivors' camp to free Ben in exchange for Walt. He offers to kill Ben for Ana-Lucia, gets the armory combination, and then shoots Ana. When Libby unexpectedly enters the hatch and surprises Michael, she gets shot too. Michael then shoots himself in the arm to make it look like a struggle, and Ben goes free, leaving no trail.

When Michael successfully completes his mission for the Others, they return Walt and give Michael a boat. Ben tells him to follow a bearing of 325 degrees to find rescue. "Once you leave, you'll never be able to get back here. And my hunch is you won't say a word to anybody. Because if you do, people will find out what you did to get your son back." Michael finally asks Ben who the Others were, and Ben simply said "We're the good guys, Michael." Like the smoke monster, the polar bears, and the numbers, Ben proves to be inscrutable and almost impossible to pin down. When Desmond tripped the failsafe in the hatch and the electromagnetic charge set off, everyone on the island covered their heads and ducked, while Ben just covered his ears and looked up to the sky, out-staring the light.

Early into the third season, Ben presents a very different person from the haggard self the survivors knew. After capture

Jack, Kate and Sawyer, he reveals himself to be well dressed and very civilized. He offers Kate a dress and a nice breakfast because "the next two weeks are going to be very unpleasant." (Season Three, "A Tale of Two Cities.") In "The Glass Ballerina," he also formally introduces himself to Jack as Ben Linus, claims he's been on the island all his life, and situates Jack (and the audience) within the timeline of the narrative: "Your flight crashed on September 22nd, 2004. Today is November 29th. That means you've been on our island for 69 days." As Jack looks on incredulously, Ben continues: "Yes, we do have contact with the outside world, Jack. That's how we know that during those 69 days your fellow Americans re-elected George W. Bush; Christopher Reeve has passed away; the Boston Red Sox won the World Series."

Juliet is an unnervingly calm and steady person who deals with Jack after the Others abduct him and lock him in the underwater station, the Hydra. She has some medical background, and runs a book group for the Others (and is a big Stephen King fan, like writer/producer Damon Lindelof). In the season three opener "A Tale of Two Cities," she repeatedly questions Jack about his history, but then reveals that she knows pretty much his entire biography, which they have collected in a fat file. How or why they have this information, she's not saying. In "The Glass Ballerina," it becomes clear she's also a little irritable; when Colleen walks in on her and Ben to tell them about the boat, Colleen asks if she's interrupting something, and Juliet responds, "Would it really matter if you were?" Juliet also holds Kate at gunpoint when Sawyer creates a ruckus to determine how strong the Others were; she asks Sawyer to put the gun that he grabs down as calmly as if she were asking a child to make the bed. Sawyer later tells Kate that "she would have shot you – no problem." Juliet has some medical training, but not enough to save Colleen after she is shot by Sun, not even with Jack's assistance.

Colleen is Pickett's love interest and the one who discovers that Sayid, Jin and Sun followed Michael and the rest by sailboat around the edge of the island. When she reports the Lostaway's sailboat to Ben in "The Glass Ballerina," he immediately sends her out to get the boat. Colleen leads an ambush from the water, not unlike Ethan emerging from the water and killing Scott in the first season. However, when she finds Sun on the boat, Sun puts a gun to her and threatens to kill her: "No you won't, Sun. I know you, Sun-Hwa Kwon. And I know you're not a killer. But despite what you may think, I'm not the enemy. We are not the enemy. But if you shoot me, that's exactly what we'll become." Sun does shoot Colleen, mortally wounding her.

Karl seems to be another prisoner like Sawyer, and is in the opposite bear cage when Sawyer regains consciousness after his abduction. As Sawyer tries to figure out the cage's food mechanism in "A Tale of Two Cities," he keeps hitting the cage's big red button until Karl warns him not to. Sawyer continues, and gets knocked on his ass by a jolt of electricity. Later, Karl appears at Sawyer's cage and releases him, telling him to run in the opposite direction. They're both captured, and Karl is later shoved up against Sawyer's cage by Tom, his face well-beaten, and forced to apologize: "I'm sorry, sorry I involved you in my break-out attempt." In the October 17, 2006 Official *Lost* Podcast, writer/producer Damon Lindelof admitted that Karl was indeed one of the Others, but his attempt to escape suggests there may be more than one faction of Others.

He, whoever he is, is a seemingly important, intelligent, and powerful man. He's only mentioned a few times by Tom and Ben, and seems to hold rank over both of them. In "Maternity Leave," when Tom finds out that Ethan took Claire without first making a list, he admonishes Ethan, saying, "Well what am I supposed to tell him? You know what he's going to do when he finds out... Dammit, Ethan..." Later, when Ben was being interrogated by Sayid about the Others in "Dave," Ben says, "If I told you about them you have no idea what he'll do"; Ana-Lucia asks if he meant their leader, the guy with the beard (Tom), and Ben says, "Him? He's no one!" Finally, when Locke tries to find out why Ben spared Locke but tried to kill Ana-Lucia in "Two for the Road," Ben says none of it mattered because if his people found where he was they would kill him anyway, "Because the man in charge, he's a great man, John, a brilliant man, but he's not a forgiving man. He'll kill me because I failed, John. I failed my mission." "He" could possibly be the financier behind the Dharma Initiative, Alvar Hanso, or possibly its founder, Gerald DeGroot. Or Ben's claims could have been another ruse to throw the survivors off the truth.

Those Off the Island

Penelope Widmore is Desmond's lost love interest – or rather, Desmond is her lost love interest. They were together until Desmond was sent to military prison. Before he went in, Penny slipped a love letter into his coy of *Our Mutual Friend*, the book Desmond is saving for the last book he'll read. Penny never heard from Desmond while he was in prison, and ended up getting engaged to another man. However she never stopped caring for him, and before Desmond embarks on his round-the-world race, she tries to get him to stay with her. What Des doesn't know is that Penelope has been searching for something ever since, employing her fortune in the endeavor, and when the electromagnetic pulse surges across the island in "Live Together, Die Alone," she is alerted to it by two people she employs at an arctic listening station.

Charles Widmore is Penelope's father, an industrialist and the head of the Widmore Corporation. He also has something against Desmond. He may have engineered Desmond's incarceration, and while imprisoned, Charles intercepts all Desmond's letters to Penelope and hides them from her. He offers Desmond a large sum of cash when he's released if Desmond will leave his daughter alone, but Des turns the offer down. Charles Widmore sponsored the race Desmond entered, which led to Desmond's arrival on the island. If one watches closely, many items on the show (such as Sun's pregnancy test) are made by the Widmore Corporation.

Mathias and Henrik are two Portuguese-speaking hands hired by Penelope Widmore to work the arctic listening station. They first note the electromagnetic pulse on their instruments and alert Penny that they think they "found it," whatever it is. Their introduction was important because it proved that the outside world still existed.

Leonard Simms and Sam Toomey worked a different listening station, a Navy station, in the late 1980's. Leonard and Sam came across the numbers while working the station; like Hurley, Sam used the numbers to win money, but then had nothing but bad luck befall those around him, and ended up committing suicide. Leonard, on the other hand, lost his mind and ended up in the Santa Rosa Mental Institute, where he played games of Connect Four with Hurley and constantly repeated the numbers to himself. Hurley first learned about the numbers from Leonard.

The Lost Experience

The Lost Experience is the alternate reality game set up by the producers of the show to help develop the narrative's mythology and bridge the summer gap between the second and third seasons. The game began as a series of Hanso Foundation commercials for that were presented as regular, average television commercials. Much of the game occurred over the Internet, and it introduced a number of fringe characters who play tangential parts in the overall narrative.

Gary Troup was a writer who was on Oceanic 815 heading to L.A. with his latest manuscript when the flight went down. His book, *Bad Twin*, is a detective novel that was found by Sawyer on the island, and was actually published by Hyperion Press in the summer of 2006. Troup dedicated his book to the Australian flight attendant who was with the Tailies, Cindy Chandler, his "highest flying angel." Some in the *Lost* online community believe Troup was the man who was sucked into the jet engine in the pilot episode. As noted above, his name is also an anagram for "purgatory."

Bad Twin begins as a kind of self-reflexive, existential detective novel, and at the very middle of the book, questions what happens at the half-way point of solving a mystery when one realizes all assumptions were wrong. The mystery in question here is the whereabouts of Zander Widmore, the mirror twin of the scion of the Widmore family and fortune, Cliff Widmore. The text is full of allusions to peripheral figures from the *Lost* narrative (the Widmores, Alvar Hanso, Thomas Mittelwerk, Paik Heavy Industries, Cindy Chandler), and offers some perspectives on recurring themes from *Lost*, such as twinning, deception and pretense, and escaping one's past. However, after that half-way point, the narrative begins to move in the direction of traditional pot-boiler detective fiction, and does not necessarily reveal all that much about the *Lost* mythology. It was published *as if* Gary Troup was a real individual, and many *Lost* fans read it looking for clues; but perhaps the real clue was the warning at the half-way point, and the assumption there would be clues in that text to *Lost* were wrong. When one of the theories being kicked around was that the Lostaways were in purgatory, the anagram of Gary Troup's name seemed to confirm the suspicion, until Damon Lindelof firmly denied the purgatory idea in a *New York Times* interview. Much of *Bad Twin* leads down similar blind alleys, as far as the mythology of *Lost* goes, but at any rate, it was red meat to hungry fans.

Troup also wrote a book about the Italian mathematician Enzo Valenzetti, whose Valenzetti Equation forms the central mystery of *Lost* (4, 8, 15, 16, 23, 42). The book is listed by publisher Hyperion Press as "out of print." In some online video interviews that appeared on the web in conjunction with *Bad Twin*, Troup claims Alvar Hanso bought up all the existing copies of the book, and the rights to reprint the book.

Rachel Blake (a.k.a. Persephone) appeared online across the summer of 2006 in a number of cryptic video posts and websites that revealed information about The Hanso Foundation. Her back-story is nearly as mysterious as some of the people she investigates, as she refuses to reveal anything about her motivations or purpose beyond trying to bring down the foundation. What is known is she's a young woman in her mid-twenties, shares the same name as Tom Brennan's wife (Kate's former (and now dead) boyfriend), is technologically savvy, once worked for the Widmore Corporation, and is tracking The Hanso Foundation around the world.

Her basic claim is that the foundation is not "reaching out for a better tomorrow," but in fact has been taken over by a cabal that has replaced Alvar Hanso and the other founding members; it is now run by an Austrian man named Thomas Mittelwerk. She first hacked The Hanso Foundation's website, and then created a blog and other sites that were part of a Hanso Foundation counter-information campaign (with names like www.hansoexposed.com). She released a number of online videos detailing her investigations from different sites around the world (Denmark, Iceland, Italy, France, Sri Lanka). Rachel also appeared at the 2006 San Diego Comic Con *Lost* panel, where she accused writers Damon Lindelof and Carlton Cuse of being front men covering for The Hanso Foundation and Mittelwerk.□

Her videos and blog posts include cryptic clues that were similar in nature to the strange clues dropped in the regular *Lost* narrative. She revealed the existence of The Hanso Group, which may be the corporate side of the philanthropic Hanso Foundation. One of her videos from Iceland features her interviewing a turncoat named Dr. Armand Zander from the Vik Institute, a mental research facility run by The Hanso Foundation. The video suggests that the institute is not dealing with mental patients, but actually keeps a herd of autistic mathematical savants to work on an equation that uses the same hieroglyphic symbols that appear on the Swan hatch timer when it reaches zero.

Much of Rachel Blake's summer was spent collecting fragments of the "Sri Lanka Video," another orientation film featuring a young Alvar Hanso explaining just what the Dharma Initiative is about. At the end of the video, we see that Rachel was

---

□Although clever, this mixing of fiction and reality seemed a bit too contrived, especially when security had to be called to drag her away.

actually filming a screening of the orientation film from a hiding spot; Thomas Mittelwerk was presenting the video to new foundation workers, caught a glint from Rachel's camera, and the end of her video is a jumble of images as she's seized by the Hanso people.

Rachel released a final video just before the start of the third season, where she finally finds and talks with Alvar Hanso. However, it's likely this video isn't to be trusted; Hanso claims, *a la* Darth Vader, to be Rachel's father; this was one of the theories kicked around by the online community over the summer of 2006 as they tried to puzzle out who Hanso and Rachel were, and given the writers and producers penchant for paying attention to and playing with the online communities theories, this may be a misdirection play – it's silly enough to be.

DJ Dan is a paranoid conspiracy theorist who hosted a podcast dealing with the typical conspiracy topics: Bigfoot, UFOs, the New World Order, the moon landing as a hoax, as well as exposing The Hanso Foundation. His website first appeared hidden in the source code of The Hanso Foundation website.[64] His podcasts appeared on his site, as well as numerous other sites scattered across the web that are part of the alternate reality game. His show was fast-moving and slick, more like commercial radio than home-brewed podcasts, and Rachel has appeared on his show.

☆It's elements like this hidden Easter egg that play directly into the strengths of the tech savvy fans, who have carried on *The Lost Experience* across the summer of 2006 by forming their own community of clue-finders and problem-solvers. The producers of the narrative have watched how the community developed and responded, and have added elements in ways that challenge and utilize that community's abilities. But it should also be noted that many of these clues are tied in to commercial endeavors that want to capitalize on *Lost*'s name recognition and advertise through the game. Although it's unclear whether the game could have gone forward without such ad-supported revenue, it does present a new model of advertising in entertainment where the venue of the advertising is more directly determined by the audience.

Much of his information, however, is just vague enough, and save for the few live broadcasts, the programs short enough, to keep people guessing (which is part of the point of the game). This is in contrast to other conspiracy theory podcasts, which go on for large chunks of time and try their damndest to give answers to their audience. Rachel and DJ Dan planned a September 24, 2006 podcast that would reveal everything about The Hanso Foundation, but this date was moved three times.

Alvar Hanso is the Danish industrialist whose venture (The Hanso Foundation) funded the Dharma Initiative on the island. Hanso was an industrialist who made his fortune manufacturing munitions for resistance movements in WWII, and then provided armaments to NATO. The Sri Lanka video Rachel Blake helps assemble reveals much of what Hanso was up to in his post-war years. After the Cuban Missile Crisis, the UN Security Council hired Italian mathematician Enzo Valenzetti to develop a theorem that predicted through core environmental and human factors how much time was left before human life extinguished itself. Those factors were represented numerically in the sequence 4, 8, 15, 16, 23 and 42; Alvar Hanso initiated the Dharma Initiative to find ways of manipulating those values in the hopes of altering or avoiding the theorem's prediction.

The video also explains that besides the traditional Buddhist meaning of "the one true way," *Dharma* is also an acronym for Department of Heuristics and Research on Material Applications. Hanso claims that Valenzetti equation had been consistently predicting humanity's slide to destruction through disease, environmental degradation, war, and so forth. The numerical values each represent a major human or environmental factor of the equation, and the only way to change the equation's outcome is to alter the values by scientifically manipulating the very environmental and human factors that determine the equation's outcome. But those values are not easily manipulated; according to the equation, the human race is heading inevitably into its predictions. The Dharma Initiative was begun as a research syndicate charged with discovering ways to alter those values, and thereby alter the future of human history.*

Hanso was reclusive. Little is known of him except that he is the grandson of 19th century sea merchant Magnus Hanso, who captained a ship called the Black Rock (which happens to be in the middle of the island). Much of what is known of Hanso comes from what Rachel Blake assembled across the summer of 2006. His Hanso Foundation is the philanthropic arm of The Hanso Group, which has interests in large industrial concerns like Paik Heavy Industries and The Widmore Corporation; indeed, Hanso sat on the Widmore Corporation board. The Hanso Foundation was established to develop projects exploring the betterment and extension of human life through science, including: The Life Extension Project,◻ Mental Health Appeal, Electromagnetic Research Initiative, Mathematical Forecasting Initiative, Institute for Genomic Advancement, and Worldwide Wellness and Prevention Development Program. Hanso's words were echoed by Tom when he met Jack, Sawyer and Locke in the jungle: "You know, somebody a whole lot smarter than anybody

---

*It sounds more complicated than it is. Think of it like this: Farmers in grassland areas who over-farm and don't use renewable practices will turn their fertile lands into dustbowls, which will drive the farmers into poverty, shrink the food supply, shift populations as people move to find food and work, and upset the ecology of those lands. Valenzetti basically indexed a number of the most import such factors and their possible consequences were represented mathematically.

◻DJ Dan claims Hanso is 112 years old, but DJ Dan claims a lot of things.

here once said: 'Since the dawn of our species, man's been blessed with curiosity.' " (Season Two, "The Hunting Party.") A similar phrase appears at the beginning of The Hanso Foundation commercials: "Since the dawn of time, man has been curious, imagining all that is possible."

Hanso disappeared in 2002, and since then his position at The Hanso Foundation has been taken over (or possibly usurped) by Thomas Mittelwerk, a man who claims Hanso hand-picked him to work at the foundation.

Enzo Valenzetti was a reclusive Italian mathematician who developed the very Valenzetti Equation that the Dharma Initiative set out to manipulate. Valenzetti, a math prodigy, was born in Sardinia in the 1920s and apparently attended the Fibonacci State Institute of Advanced Sciences in Trento, Italy (although no record of his being at any institute exists). He also apparently hung out with the likes of Albert Einstein, John Nash, and Kurt Gödel, and is another enigmatic scientific genius cut from similar cloth as J.J. Abrams's renaissance genius Milo Rimbaldi from the show *Alias*. He is rumored to be the first mathematician to solve Fermat's last theorem,▲ but after doing so, he destroyed his proof. He was commissioned by the UN Security Council to develop an algorithm predicting the extinction of the human race, and this, the Valenzetti Equation, is what pushed Alvar Hanso to start the Dharma Initiative. The equation was developed some time between the end of the Cuban Missile Crisis and 1975, when Hanso began the Dharma Initiative. The values he gave to the environmental and human factors influencing the algorithm are familiar by now – 4, 8, 15, 16, 23, and 42. But

▲If an integer n is greater than 2, then $a^n + b^n = c^n$ has no solutions in non-zero integers a, b, and c.

he also employed symbols in his equation in the form of hieroglyphs. Valenzetti died in a plane crash along with the only copy of the equation.

Thomas Mittelwerk is supposedly an Austrian-born scientist who is the current president and chief technologist of The Hanso Foundation. According to Rachel Blake, no record of the man having attended any institution of higher learning exists, although his story is he was hand-picked by Alvar Hanso while still studying at Cal Tech.

Mittelwerk's scientific interests revolve primarily around biology and genetics. This interest began when his mother died from a genetic disorder when he was still young, and he set out to become a foremost expert on genetics. Little is known of him, except that he is running The Hanso Foundation's projects. Rachel managed to get audio of him discussing a special ship being built for him by Paik Heavy Industries (Mr. Paik is Sun's father, and Jin's boss), which he plans on taking to a place near the equator in order to initiate something called the "Spider Protocol."

Mittelwerk is mentioned in the Gary Troup book *Bad Twin* as Alvar Hanso's replacement on the Widmore Corporation board, and he isn't trusted by anyone on the board except Cliff. This suggests that Hanso was involved with the Widmore Corporation, and indeed the Widmore Corporation and Paik Heavy Industries may operate under the corporate leadership of The Hanso Group.

Just before Mittelwerk spots Rachel hiding and filming him, he makes this revelation to the group of people whom he showed Alvar Hanso's orientation film:

We all know what happened. The Dharma Initiative failed. And in spite of every effort of the foundation, we are gripped in the tyranny of those six numbers. We have tried to change those values by manipulating the environment in many, many ways. We have done our level best, and yet this inscrutable equation keeps bringing us back to the numbers. So now we have to take radical action, and I just want to tell all of you that I trust you to do what is best. The villages of Filan and Vetul-Milani❧ have allowed us to test our vaccine on them. They think they are infected by a virus carried by local macaques, and they believe we are bringing them the cure. So when you go in, you *have* to keep up the story. You know it by heart; don't waver. When the deaths begin you must comfort everyone with compassion and empathy. Then the bodies of the dead must be brought to the station immediately for full genetic work-up. We must make absolutely certain we are hitting precise genetic targets we have engineered into the virus. The optimal mortality rate is 30 percent. Our operatives at the Vik Institute have verified this figure. If more or less people succumb, we have failed. We need not take any more lives than is absolutely necessary.

❧It's a grainy video with poor sound; Filan and Vetul-Milani may not be the names.

When Mittelwerk is asked by someone in the group if the deaths were necessary, he responds:

> If you knew, with mathematical certainty, that you could end all famine, war, and poverty, what would you do? ... Exactly. You'd find the best way to get it done – precisely, surgically, without allowing for any more suffering than is absolutely necessary. It is not fair that innocents have to die so that we can perfect this virus, but I promise you, someone is going to hell.

The future story of Mittelwerk will reveal much about the purpose of the island, the Others, and the reasons behind the computer in the Swan hatch and the vaccine on the island.